£30.00

BRITISH AND AMERICAN PLAYWRIGHTS
1750–1920

General editors: Martin Banham and Peter Thomson

Dion Boucicault

OTHER VOLUMES IN THIS SERIES

Already published

TOM ROBERTSON edited by William Tydeman
W. S. GILBERT edited by George Rowell
HENRY ARTHUR JONES edited by Russell Jackson
DAVID GARRICK AND GEORGE COLMAN THE ELDER
   edited by E. R. Wood
WILLIAM GILLETTE edited by Rosemary Cullen and Don Wilmeth
GEORGE COLMAN THE YOUNGER AND THOMAS
   MORTON edited by Barry Sutcliffe
ARTHUR MURPHY AND SAMUEL FOOTE edited by George
   Taylor
H. J. BYRON edited by J. T. L. Davis
AUGUSTIN DALY edited by Don Wilmeth and Rosemary Cullen

Further volumes will include:

J. R. PLANCHÉ edited by Don Roy
A. W. PINERO edited by George Rowell
CHARLES READE edited by M. Hammet
TOM TAYLOR edited by Martin Banham

Plays by

Dion Boucicault

USED UP

OLD HEADS AND YOUNG HEARTS

JESSIE BROWN

THE OCTOROON

THE SHAUGHRAUN

Edited with an introduction and notes by
Peter Thomson

The right of the
University of Cambridge
to print and sell
all manner of books
was granted by
Henry VIII in 1534.
The University has printed
and published continuously
since 1584.

CAMBRIDGE UNIVERSITY PRESS

Cambridge

London   New York   New Rochelle

Melbourne   Sydney

Published by the Press Syndicate of the University of Cambridge
The Pitt Building, Trumpington Street, Cambridge CB2 1RP
32 East 57th Street, New York, NY 10022, USA
296 Beaconsfield Parade, Middle Park, Melbourne 3206, Australia

First published 1984

Printed in Great Britain at the
University Press, Cambridge

Library of Congress catalogue card number: 83-20897

British Library Cataloguing in Publication Data
Boucicault, Dion
Plays. – (British and American playwrights (1750–1920))
I. Title   II. Thomson, Peter   III. Series
822'.   PR4161.B2
ISBN 0 521 23997 4 hard covers
ISBN 0 521 28395 7 paperback

BB

GENERAL EDITORS' PREFACE

It is the primary aim of this series to make available to the British and American theatre plays which were effective in their own time, and which are good enough to be effective still.

Each volume assembles a number of plays, normally by a single author, scrupulously edited but sparingly annotated. Textual variations are recorded where individual editors have found them either essential or interesting. Introductions give an account of the theatrical context, and locate playwrights and plays within it. Biographical and chronological tables, brief bibliographies, and the complete listing of known plays provide information useful in itself, and which also offers guidance and incentive to further exploration.

Many of the plays published in this series have appeared in modern anthologies. Such representation is scarcely distinguishable from anonymity. We have relished the tendency of individual editors to make claims for the dramatists of whom they write. These are not plays best forgotten. They are plays best remembered. If the series is a contribution to theatre history, that is well and good. If it is a contribution to the continuing life of the theatre, that is well and better.

We have been lucky. The Cambridge University Press has supported the venture beyond our legitimate expectations. Acknowledgement is not, in this case, perfunctory. Sarah Stanton's contribution to the series has been substantial, and it has enhanced our work.

Martin Banham
Peter Thomson

TO FOUR REMARKABLE PEOPLE
James, Kate, Stephen, Anne

CONTENTS

ILLUSTRATIONS

ACKNOWLEDGEMENTS

My chief debts are to Richard Fawkes, Boucicault's biographer, and to Christopher Calthrop, Boucicault's great-grandson. They are generous men. I have had help, way beyond the call of duty, from Paul Eugen Camp, curator of the Boucicault Collection at the University of South Florida, and Stephen Holland, librarian at the University of Kent at Canterbury. Jane O'Sullivan and Tom Brown advised me on the songs in *Jessie Brown*; Richard Skerrett, gentlest of polyglots, deciphered some of Boucicault's hopeful forays into foreign languages, and my colleague Professor Shaban helped me with others. To Martin Banham, friend and fellow-editor, and to Sarah Stanton, this book, like the whole series, owes its appearance.

INTRODUCTION

It was more likely vanity than confusion that led Boucicault to claim 1822 as the year of his birth. He was, in fact, born into the family of Samuel Boursiquot, a Dublin wine-merchant, in December 1820. His growing up was done in an atmosphere of sexual equivocation. Samuel's wife, Anne, was twenty-six years her husband's junior. Her stronger romantic attachment was to the talented and glib Dionysius Lardner, at that time a lecturer at Trinity College, Dublin. We must assume that Samuel tolerated his wife's adultery, since the decision to christen their fifth child Dionysius Lardner Boursiquot would otherwise have been a grotesque mockery. It was Lardner who supervised and paid for the education of young Dionysius, and who planned for him a career as a civil engineer. Lardner's own considerable achievements – the 134 volumes of *The Cabinet Cyclopedia* made him, literally, a household name – were coated with chicanery. Thackeray recreated him as Dr Dionysius Diddler, perceiving that, though Lardner was talented enough not to need to cheat his way to celebrity, he was prepared to. It was a preparedness that Boucicault inherited. Both men possessed vast energy and application, but when energy and application failed, both resorted to deviousness. Boucicault's career was spattered with charges of plagiarism (he certainly filched the sensation scene of *After Dark* from Augustin Daly's *Under the Gaslight*, and that was only the most shameless of his thefts) and sharp practice. The drive to succeed in public trapped him, as it trapped Lardner, in an inglorious privacy. Boucicault's life combined brave ambitions and squalid compromises in almost equal measure, and he was afflicted with a vanity that treated him as ruthlessly as it led him to treat others. For fifty years, and on both sides of the Atlantic, he won and lost battles many of which he did not need to fight. He made and squandered two or three fortunes. If it was, in part, a trick of taste that elevated him to greater heights than he deserved or could cope with, it was also a trick of taste that relegated him to an unmerited posthumous obscurity, from which he is only now emerging. A just estimate would recognise in him one of history's most skilful shapers of stories for the theatre. Even at his most hurried or casual, he is rarely dull. What he lacks altogether is the high seriousness that characterises much of the best writing of the Victorian age; but that high seriousness did not flourish in the theatres of the period. He had neither the wit nor the will profoundly to challenge the taste of his audience. He preferred to take advantage of it.

Boucicault began his theatrical career in 1838, under the protection of a pseudonym, Lee Moreton. He seems to have had ambitions as a playwright from the start, but it was his acting that first excited controversy. The favourable reviews of his provincial performances are couched in familiar language, and could have been

applied to almost any novice. What is more surprising is the antagonism he sometimes provoked. The more splenetic outbursts of the provincial critics indicate a
precocious self-confidence that amounted to cockiness. They give early evidence of
Boucicault's persistent ability to draw attention to himself. He was never a great
actor, though there are many testimonials to his quality as an instructor of actors.
He became, however, an effective portrayer of heavy 'character' parts. The extravagant theatricality that served him so well in the invention of sensation scenes
became his strongest asset as a performer. It is a quality that can best be defined
negatively – a 'not being abashed'. Sir Donald Wolfit, among twentieth-century
actors, had it in abundance. During the years in America, Boucicault's own acting
skills were generally eclipsed by those of his wife, Agnes Robertson. Sensing this,
he looked to cast himself in parts in which peculiarities of voice and appearance
could make a direct appeal to the audience: parts such as Nana Sahib in *Jessie
Brown*, Wahnotee in *The Octoroon* (for the play's English performances he could
risk himself as Salem Scudder, since the voyage across the Atlantic turned that into
a 'character' role), and, supremely, as the lovable Irish scoundrels Myles-na-
Coppaleen in *The Colleen Bawn*, Shaun the Post in *Arrah-na-Pogue*, and Conn in
The Shaughraun. It is always possible for a small actor to disguise himself as a big
one in characters so much larger than life, but it is arguable that in the creation of
these energetic Irish layabouts Boucicault, in the latter half of his career, approached
greatness.

Too much has sometimes been made of the ideas on acting formulated in, for
example, the essay on 'The Art of Acting', or of the advice Boucicault is known to
have given to the player of the telegraph operator in *The Long Strike* (1866) – that
he should go to a telegraph office to learn how the machine worked.[1] Such attention to detail might have been revolutionary at the beginning of the nineteenth century, but it was no longer so by the end. Only in the flimsiest sense does Boucicault
anticipate Stanislavsky, though his professionalism certainly contributed to a climate
of reform. Surviving evidence suggests that his own acting was recognisably in the
barnstorming tradition, but his best plays call for something if not subtle, certainly
more sophisticated. They are concerned with the totality of the stage picture rather
than with the star actor's cadenza. Boucicault's is almost as much a pictorial as a
verbal art, and the actor, carefully costumed and vigorously transformed by stage
make-up, is a component part of the picture.

Boucicault was lucky to fall among good actors at the outset of his career as a
dramatist. He had had two or three plays professionally staged in the provinces –
and buried there – when Charles Mathews was prevailed upon to risk producing the
unknown author's five-act comedy *London Assurance.* Mathews and his astonish-
ingly enterprising wife, Madame Vestris, had held the lease of Covent Garden
Theatre since 1839. It was a theatre in which fortunes had been more often lost
than made, particularly since the minor theatres had begun to mount their successful challenge against the might of the Patent Houses. The exclusive right of Drury
Lane and Covent Garden to produce legitimate drama in London was, by now, an

anachronism; it would be abolished by act of parliament in 1843. The managers of the Patent Theatres were quite as much slaves as beneficiaries of privilege. They had a vast establishment to maintain, including separate companies of musicians, singers, dancers, comic and tragic actors, as well as a multitude of staff, backstage and front-of-house. The Vestris management of the smaller Olympic Theatre from 1830 to 1839 had been innovative and successful, and her partnership with Charles Mathews was a popular one; but their Covent Garden career was badly in need of a success at the beginning of 1841. Madame Vestris had owed her early success to her legs, her singing voice, and the drawing power of salacious rumour. She was in her mid-forties in 1841, and her health was failing, but there is no questioning her pedigree. Her Olympic seasons had introduced to the English theatre the notion of ensemble acting (not highly developed, but certainly adumbrated), and had raised to a new level the art of scene design. Her husband, Charles Mathews – they had married as recently as 1838 – was six years younger, and at the height of his career. He was the son of a famous 'low' comedian, but his own line was 'gentlemanly'. Contemporaries considered him the most 'natural' of English actors, and were captivated by his ability to import into the theatre the relaxed charm of the drawing-room habitué. Boucicault had a lot to learn from both of them (she played Grace Harkaway and he played Dazzle), as well as from old William Farren, who created Sir Harcourt Courtly. *London Assurance* was retitled and extensively re-written during rehearsal – flattered by its success, Boucicault would never be so compliant again. The scenery, designed and built by the Grieves, with 'Decorations and Appointments' specially provided by Bradwell, made its own considerable contribution. It moved the English theatre a significant step away from the tradi-tional wings and shutters towards the box set. *London Assurance*, when it was first performed on 4 March 1841, looked well and was acted well. Its durability was tested by the 1970 production of the Royal Shakespeare Company, which proved, more than anything else, how well Boucicault had assimilated the techniques of manners comedy from the previous century. Donald Sinden, another modern master of unabashed acting, relished the opportunities provided by Sir Harcourt Courtly. 'Boucicault', he has since written, 'wrote for actors and his writing is, above all, theatrical. He knew how to use words and he knew the possibilities of a scene . . . A play like *London Assurance* . . . is great fun to do.'[2] That is a fair ver-dict on a play that is scarcely more a period piece now than it was when it was first performed.

London Assurance brought Boucicault into sudden prominence. Not surprisingly, it went to his already giddy head. He spent several months living a debtor's parody of the life of gilded youth, and it was almost a year before he completed his next play for the Vestris–Mathews management. *The Irish Heiress* looked back once again to Restoration comedy, still through the filter of Goldsmith and the eight-eenth century, cutting several corners and all the cuckolds. There is not much sub-stance in a Restoration comedy plot, once seduction has been replaced by flirtation and appetite by attraction. Boucicault could plump out the eccentricities of his characters with a liveliness of dialogue rarely encountered in the nineteenth century, but he had nothing serious to say. The contemporary setting of *The Irish Heiress* is as much a disguise as that of *London Assurance*. The mode of living is remote from that of England's hungry forties. At their best, Boucicault's comedies have a life in the theatre, but even at their best they have no discernible reference to life outside it. *The Irish Heiress* suffered the critical fate of many second plays. Always prone to exonerate himself, Boucicault blamed Mathews and Vestris for its failure, and shifted his custom to Benjamin Webster at the Haymarket. It was not until 1844 that he had his next real success - ironically in association with Charles Mathews.

Used Up is a two-act comedy in praise of the simple life, something about which Boucicault knew little and Mathews less. The Vestris–Mathews management of Covent Garden had ended in financial disarray in 1842, and Mathews, a notorious spendthrift, was due to appear before the bankruptcy commissioners on 8 February, two days after the scheduled opening of *Used Up* at the Haymarket. The associated gossip did no harm to the play's prospects. The public was quick to relate the feckless Mathews and the dispirited Sir Charles Coldstream, whom he was to impersonate. Boucicault had still the sense to benefit from Mathews's suggestions for improvement, and the collaboration was mutually beneficial. The part of Sir Charles Coldstream remained in Mathews's repertoire for upwards of thirty years; and Boucicault, in the more relaxed atmosphere of the Haymarket, took the opportunity of observing Mathews at work. Mathews enjoyed the detail of stage business but could not orate. He wanted lines that could be spoken. We can never know the extent of the Boucicault–Mathews collaboration on the text of *Used Up*, though Mathews later went so far as to dispute Boucicault's claim to authorship in the Court of Chancery. The title was probably his - Boucicault seems to have proposed the more literal *Bored to Death* - and many of the lines allotted to Sir Charles Coldstream were changed to his order. What is finally more significant is the subtler effect of Mathews's acting style on Boucicault's writing. Never averse to the pleasing phrase or witty inversion, Boucicault could learn from Mathews how to place them - how, for example, to give to Captain Molineux in *The Shaughraun* a relaxed charm quite unexpected in an English officer among Fenian patriots. It was as Sir Charles Coldstream that Boucicault made his acting debut on the New York stage in 1854, a decision which, with hindsight, looks more like homage to Mathews than an intelligent estimation of his own range as an actor.

Used Up is an effectively anglicised version of a French play. It was written as an afterpiece for a theatre that preserved the taste for long, mixed programmes. The Shilling Dramatic Library edition advertises seventy minutes as the playing time, implying an unrushed performance but not a slow one. It leans away from comedy towards the more honest nineteenth-century mode of farce, and the experience of its central character - his discovery that life may be worth living if its artificial embellishments can be shed - often rises above the level of cliché. Much nineteenth-century writing expresses a nostalgia for rural values - unsurprisingly, in the wake of the Industrial Revolution – and Boucicault is obviously less at ease when he gets to the country (in Act II) than when he is plotting to get there. It was the incongruity of Charles Mathews in a ploughman's smock rather than the effectiveness of his disguise that delighted the play's original audience. But *Used Up* is not a solo piece. Everyone, from cameo butler to typical lawyer, has something to do.

The collaboration of Mathews and Boucicault ended less happily with *Old Heads and Young Hearts*, also staged at the Haymarket in 1844. This is an ambitious comedy in five acts, with a character written for Mathews and another for Madame Vestris. Boucicault felt surer of himself by now, and rehearsals were sometimes stormy. Once, 'after the gross impertinence of Mr. Bourcicault [sic]', Mathews returned his script to Webster, together with that of his wife, explaining in his accompanying letter:

> His last words were these: 'I want no one's opinions but my own as to the *consistency* of the characters I draw – *your* business is to utter what *I* create.' As I differ in toto from this inflated view of the relative positions of actor and dramatist I at once decline subscribing to it.[3]

The letter tells us much about the playwright's status in the nineteenth century, a status which Boucicault worked to raise, but Mathews was not, on this occasion, the winner. Webster persuaded him to remain, and the play opened as scheduled, with Mathews as Littleton Coke and Madame Vestris as Lady Alice Hawthorn. Webster himself played Tom Coke – it was one of those 'solid' parts in which he excelled – and William Farren, whose memory was growing unreliable, had a further opportunity to endear himself to his admirers in the attractive role of Jesse Rural. From a purist point of view, too much of the play's plotting depends on Rural's confusion. He is a well-conceived minor character, but an inadequate pivot. Boucicault's models – Congreve's *The Double Dealer* was certainly in his mind, as well, perhaps, as Goldsmith's *The Good Natured Man* – are careful to leave the central complications to those who are competent to resolve them. Happy on the fringes of the play, Jesse Rural is uncomfortable at its centre. It is a blemish in a piece that generally develops its complications with inventiveness. It remains a pity, though, that Boucicault has so little to say about his own age. *Old Heads and Young Hearts* is speckled with references to London life in the 1840s, but its heart is in the Regency world of idleness and jolly scandal. It deals with the equitable distribution of love and money according to rules established not in the city of London, but in its theatres. Sealed off from serious social comment by censorship, prejudice, and the demand for easy entertainment, the nineteenth-century theatre produced few comedies better than *Old Heads and Young Hearts*, and few dramatists more adept than Boucicault in the redeployment of second-hand material. *Love in a Maze*, staged by Charles Kean at the Princess's in 1851, is a franker five-act comedy, though less lively than its predecessors. It is set in the seventeenth century, where, with minor alterations, it could be joined by *London Assurance* and *Old Heads and Young Hearts.*

It was a working dramatist's need to earn his keep that led Boucicault to take the next decisive step in his career. Urged on by Benjamin Webster, he travelled to France in search of plays to translate and adapt for the English stage. Paris was the acknowledged market-place of the popular drama, and Boucicault had the advantage of fluency in French. His Parisian experience, together with the need to make money faster, changed the direction of his work. He may not have known that he had not the talent to write great literary comedies, but he knew that he had not the time. France led the way in farce and melodrama, and Boucicault followed. John Lynaugh's view that Boucicault was 'more a comic playwright who wrote melodramas, than a melodramatist who wrote comedies'[4] is usefully provocative, but at the same time misleading. Our understanding of melodrama has been blurred by literary snobbery. It is not an inferior nineteenth-century form merely because it was a popular one. On the contrary, it supplied an essential (and acceptable) antidote to the drabber aspects of Victorian respectability. What we find least impressive – the specious motivation and inevitable overthrow of villainy, the pallor and sanctimoniousness of the threatened heroine – represented something much stronger then. Melodrama was at once family entertainment and soft pornography. It was not the pious protestations of the heroine that interested the audience, but the threat to her virtue. The smothered libido of the late nineteenth century escaped into melodrama. Lynaugh is right to emphasise the continuity of comedy and melodrama in Boucicault's work, but he confuses his priorities. It is as the best melodramatist of the third quarter of the nineteenth century that Boucicault most deserves to be remembered.

The most successful immediate outcome of the trip to France was the version of *The Corsican Brothers* staged by Charles Kean at the Princess's in 1852. Kean had employed Boucicault as a house dramatist in 1850, perhaps to remind his detractors that he had an interest in modern as well as ancient plays. It was a significant elevation for Boucicault, but fraught with danger. The relationship of the determinedly respectable Kean and the raffish young playwright was unlikely to be easy, and it was not long before Kean began to question the wisdom of conducting the fight for the greater dignity of the theatre with Boucicault as one of his generals. In retrospect, Kean could be grateful to Boucicault for providing him with one of his greatest successes in what came to be known as 'gentlemanly melodrama', *The Corsican Brothers*, and one of his oddest, *Louis XI*. Boucicault, on his side of the bargain, won himself kudos and a wife.

It was his entanglement with Agnes Robertson that terminated Boucicault's association with Kean. She was Kean's ward, as well as a member of his company, and Boucicault was just the kind of man he was anxious to protect her from. He may have known no more about Boucicault's first marriage than we do, but the mystery would not have increased his confidence. When the secret meetings of the lovers were discovered, Agnes chose to defy her guardian by moving in with Boucicault. Assuming for the first time the mantle of an entrepreneur, Boucicault arranged for Agnes an engagement at Burton's Theatre in New York. By the end of October 1853 they were together, and probably married,[5] in New York.

Boucicault's place in the history of the American theatre is distinct from his English one. He had not yet staked his claim for the further distinction of a place in Irish theatre history. His reputation had preceded him, but it was Agnes whom the American audiences took to their hearts. It was as her manager even more than as a playwright or an actor that Boucicault established his American footholds. The first 'American' plays were vehicles for her, and it was not until December 1857 that Boucicault struck gold in his own right. *The Poor of New York* was an opportunistic adaptation from the French, in which Boucicault was the chief of three collaborators. It is not remarkable, unless the ability to write such *typical* melodrama is seen as remarkable, but it is important in two respects. The sensational fire scene, ingeniously staged, set a precedent for all subsequent 'sensation scenes'; and the idea of building into the play references to the recent financial panic in New York opened Boucicault's eyes to the potential attractiveness of contemporaneity. He followed it up at once with two more 'contemporaneous melodramas',[6] *Jessie Brown; or, The Relief of Lucknow* and *Brigham Young; or, The Revolt of the Harem.* Both were staged at Wallack's Theatre in the first half of 1858. *Brigham Young* left little impression, but *Jessie Brown* is included in this collection as an outstanding example of formula writing.

Information about the siege and relief of Lucknow was sparse – we have to take account of the slow passage of news from India to America, and of the fact that rehearsals began less than four months after Sir Colin Campbell's entry into the Lucknow Residency. Boucicault based his play on a single press report,[7] filling it out with scraps of ill-tested rumour. There is nothing historical about the piece. On the contrary, it is a kind of soap opera, with melodramatic highlights and a gallery of stereotypical characters. Add to that a vision of Indians as serpents and savages, and we have what sounds like a very bad play indeed. And yet *Jessie Brown* is a wonderfully vivid illustration of the strengths of melodrama. The stage is kept constantly busy with scenes that are necessary to the conduct of the story, and the characters, without bursting the bonds of stereotype, stretch them to the limit. It would be difficult, in the modern theatre, to stage the final tableau without a smirk, and not easy to find a modern theatre well enough equipped to make the most of Achmet's magnificent death; but the effort is worth making. The political propaganda is too naive to be offensive. The world of *Jessie Brown* amalgamates *Black Eyed Susan* and *The Master of Ballantrae.* The New York audience of 1858 loved it. The critics were less impressed. One of them called it 'bunkum'. He may be right; but if there is such a thing as good bunkum, *Jessie Brown* is that thing. The title role remained in Agnes Robertson's repertoire for many years, and it is not hard to see why. While the men fight, Jessie carries the burden of the siege. There is no break in the pathos. A Dorothy Parker would have said of Agnes Robertson in *Jessie Brown* what she said of Katharine Hepburn in *The Lake*: 'She runs the gamut of emotions all the way from A to B'; but being embarrassed by the pathetic is a twentieth-century problem. The heroine of melodrama demands pathetic acting. Boucicault may well have relished the opposite task of playing the villain, though according to Richard

Fawkes it was as much a matter of necessity as of choice.[8] Nobody else would risk the audience's wrath in the part of Nana Sahib, the reviled instigator of the massacre at Cawnpore.[9]

Just before the opening of *Jessie Brown*, Boucicault had tried a second term as manager of an American theatre. The first had been in New Orleans in 1855-56; it lasted three months. The second, in Washington, was over inside a month. Nothing daunted, he tried again in September 1859, and once again in partnership with William Stuart, with whom he had quarrelled in Washington. The theatre this time was the vast Metropolitan in New York, renamed the Winter Garden by the partners. The opening production was *Dot*, a sentimental fantasy based on Dickens's *The Cricket on the Hearth.* Agnes played Dot, and the Caleb Plummer was a young actor with a growing reputation as a comedian, Joseph Jefferson. Jefferson was intelligent enough to shift from the comic to the pathetic, but Boucicault's faith in him helped. His appreciation survived the blows that Boucicault seems to have given to all his friends at some time or another. *Smike*, another exercise in Dickensian pathos, was hastily written to capitalise on the success of *Dot*. Boucicault was approaching forty, confident and industrious. While performing the part of Mantolini in *Smike*, he found time to complete and rehearse *The Octoroon* for its opening at the Winter Garden on 6 December. Less than four months later, and with two further adaptations under his belt as well, he was playing Myles-na-Coppaleen on the first night of *The Colleen Bawn.* The years from 1857 to 1860 were his best in the American theatre.

For a playwright to write a play about slavery in America in 1859 was necessarily to take a risk. For a manager to stage such a play was riskier. Boucicault, simultaneously writer and manager, enjoyed the risk, but took care to to exaggerate it. Jefferson, who created the part of Salem Scudder, considered *The Octoroon* 'noncommittal', and it may seem almost risibly so when it is remembered that it opened four days after the execution of John Brown. Certainly, Boucicault takes little account of the passionate polarities that would soon express themselves in the Civil War. As Jefferson recorded in his *Autobiography*, 'The dialogue and characters of the play made one feel for the South, but the action proclaimed against slavery, and called loudly for its abolition.'[10] There is, clearly, some equivocation. Mayne Reid's *The Quadroon*, the play's major source, issues a clear challenge to prevalent American views of racial purity by having its hero marry the quadroon of the title. Zoe's death, in Boucicault's original five-act version, denies George Peyton the opportunity of repeating the challenge. He would have been breaking state laws against miscegenation if he had, and Boucicault was probably too nervous to advocate law-breaking. Even so, it would be a disservice to him to understate the abolitionist impulses behind the play. He had something serious and pertinent to say to his adopted country. It was, for once, the theme of *The Octoroon* as much as the sensational fire-on-a-river-steamer scene and the ingenious use of the (recently invented) camera as detective that commanded the audience's attention. Boucicault never wrote a more consistently serious play. It is doubtful that he could have done.

Sadly, his behaviour during the rehearsals and the run of the play was less high-minded. His reputation was unusually at risk, and that may have caused tension. If so, the ungrateful role of Wahnotee would not have helped to release it. But the real problem, as so often with Boucicault, seems to have been money. When, a week into the run, Stuart declined to raise his and Agnes's salary, Boucicault broke off the partnership and left the cast, taking Agnes with him. Stuart found replacements for his lost Zoe and Wahnotee at once, and the run continued, despite Boucicault's application for an injunction. The application was rejected partly because the public was still clamouring to see the play, and partly because the rapidity of Boucicault's employment by Laura Keene at her nearby theatre led to suspicions that the arrangement had pre-dated his departure from the Winter Garden. Self-interest shading into sharp practice was not outlawed by Boucicault's flexible morality. On the subject of *The Octoroon*, though, he remained unusually firm. When the London public objected to Zoe's dying, he resisted the demand for a rewriting of the last act for as long as he dared. It was, in his view, a story that could not accommodate a happy ending. That confrontation did not come until 1861, the year in which the American Civil War began, and British righteousness ran high. To understand why Boucicault was back in London, we need to consider *The Colleen Bawn.*

Less than a month after leaving the Winter Garden, Agnes and Boucicault opened at Laura Keene's Theatre in *Jeanie Deans*, a dramatisation by Boucicault of Effie's trial and its context from Scott's *Heart of Midlothian.* Like Madame Vestris, who had died in 1856, Laura Keene was an actress of charm and talent, and the first of her countrywomen to undertake the management of a theatre. She called the theatre after herself, and invested her pride as well as her money in it. To get the Boucicaults at all was a triumph; but to get *The Colleen Bawn* as well was too good to be true. It would probably not have come about if *Vanity Fair* (from the French, not from Thackeray), the second of the plays Boucicault brought to her, had been as successful as *Jeanie Deans.* Its failure to attract called for a hasty response. *The Colleen Bawn*, one of Boucicault's best plays, was probably written and rehearsed in little more than a fortnight. Given the importance of the sensation scene – Boucicault as Myles diving off a rock to rescue Agnes as Eily O'Connor after Danny Mann, the hunchback, has tried to drown her – considerable praise is due to Laura Keene's stage-carpenters. But it was the acting that the audience talked about. Agnes was pathetic, as usual, and Laura Keene charming in the sprightlier role of Anne Chute, but Boucicault's Myles, of the dancing brogue and the acrobatic leap, was the main attraction. *The Colleen Bawn* opened on 29 March 1860, and played to capacity houses until the season ended on 12 May. It is an accomplished play, and for several reasons a landmark in the history of the theatre. It has its place in the Irish dramatic movement, by virtue of both flattering imitation and indignant counteraction. Despite the grimness of its subject – it was based on Gerald Griffin's novel *The Collegians*, a moralising fiction built on the factual murder, in 1819, of a sixteen-year-old Irish peasant girl – it brought the spirit of comedy further into melodrama than it had ever been. It became a model for the single-story play, in which the complications of subsidiary plotting are either removed or formally related to the central narrative. And it was instrumental in improving the financial prospects of playwrights. That final point requires further explanation.

We do not know the nature of the financial arrangement between Laura Keene and Boucicault. What we do know is that *The Colleen Bawn*'s success enabled him to buy two houses in New York, and to furnish at least one of them with lavish ostentation. It seems certain that he had negotiated with his new employer a profit-sharing system of the kind he would have hoped to benefit by if he had remained in partnership with Stuart. Glorying in his new prosperity, he decided to return to London. He had no clear plans, but he carried with him copies of *Jessie Brown*, *The Octoroon*, and *The Colleen Bawn*. It was his old mentor Benjamin Webster, now at the Adelphi, who signed him up, but the terms were Boucicault's. In return for playing *The Colleen Bawn*, he and Agnes would be paid a weekly fee as actors, in addition to which he as author would receive, according to his own choice, either £50 per week or a share of any takings in excess of £600 per week. The play ran to full houses at the Adelphi for an unprecedented 230 performances, a success which hastened the establishment in London of the long-run system, and brought suffi-cient wealth to Boucicault to encourage other playwrights to think twice before selling their plays to managers for a flat fee. By any reckoning, the staging of *The Colleen Bawn* contributed significantly to the betterment of the playwright's status, and, given the greater stability of the long run, the actor's too.

Whenever there was money in his pocket, Boucicault spent it. With earnings of £23,000 during their first year in England, Agnes and he bought the capacious Hereford House in the Brompton Road, and entertained conspicuous people con-spicuously. *The Colleen Bawn* was a gold-mine, and Boucicault had the tempera-ment of a prospector. As the clamour for licences to produce the play in provincial theatres grew, it occurred to him that he might, with profit, send the applicants a production instead of a licence. He had learned a lot about touring during his American years. Early in 1861, he began rehearsing two companies in *The Colleen Bawn*. By mid-February, one was playing in Sunderland and the other in Brighton. The first year of operation brought him £10,000. It had long been common practice for London stars to tour the provinces, but rarely since Shakespeare's days had a whole 'London' production toured. For the provincial stock companies, it was the beginning of the end. Not until the growth of the repertory movement would local theatres begin to recover a full pride in their own identities.

Sitting so unexpectedly pretty, Boucicault prolonged his residence in England. An arrangement with Webster in 1861 brought him into joint management and complete artistic control of the Adelphi. It was from this vantage-point that he con-ducted his fight with the British public over the ending of *The Octoroon* – and lost. He held out for three weeks, but the fourth week playbills carried this announce-ment:

Mr. Boucicault begs to acknowledge the hourly receipt of many letters, entreating that the termination of the 'Octoroon' should be modified, and the Slave Heroine saved from an unhappy end. He cannot resist the kind feeling expressed throughout this correspondence, nor refuse compliance with a request so easily granted. A New Last Act of the Drama, composed by the Public, and edited by the Author, will be represented on Monday night. He trusts the Audience will accept it as a very grateful tribute to their judgment and taste, which he should be the last to dispute.

The ill-disguised irony protected Boucicault in defeat, but his partnership with Webster did not long survive the *Octoroon* affair. His next speculation has the desperation of defiance. At the end of 1862, having acquired the lease of Astley's Amphitheatre in Lambeth, he undertook its costly conversion into a conventional theatre. He was in pursuit of a fashionable audience, and it was a disadvantage that Astley's was situated on the unfashionable Surrey side of the River Thames. Boucicault, in a mood to take on anyone or anything, decided to rename Astley's the New Theatre Royal, *Westminster.* Lambeth and the Thames were not so easily beaten, and the venture got off to a slow start. The publicity given to Boucicault's affair with an actress called Emily Jordan made matters worse. English society, including Boucicault's financial backers, expected adultery to be conducted under the decent disguise of effective hypocrisy. By July 1863, he was bankrupt, his declared debts amounting to £31,000. Hereford House was sold, and the Boucicaults went north, to Liverpool.

For Agnes, there was a sour familiarity about the turn of events. After the birth of their first child in 1855, she had been back on the stage within a month. Now she had four, the youngest a year old. She would have two more before the marriage finally broke down. But however depressed, Boucicault remained buoyant. *The Poor of New York* had made money, at least partly on the strength of its title. It would be less likely to succeed in Liverpool, unless . . . Boucicault had an idea. He described the outcome in a notorious letter to Edward Stirling:

> I have tried the bold step of producing – originally in the provinces – a sensation drama, without aid or assistance of any kind. The experiment has succeeded. I introduced *The Poor of Liverpool*, a bob-tail piece, with local scenery, and Mr Cowper in the principal part. I share after thirty pounds a night, and I am making a hundred pounds a week on the damned thing. I localize it for each town, and hit the public between the eyes; so they see nothing but fire. Eh voila! I can spin out these rough-and-tumble dramas as a hen lays eggs. It's a degrading occupation, but more money has been made out of guano than out of poetry.

The cynicism tells a truth about Boucicault's career as a dramatist, but not the whole truth. He was prepared to call his hack-work hack-work, but he did not confine himself to it. *The Poor of Liverpool* (or Leeds, or Dublin, or anywhere) was cobbled together in February 1864, but it was also in 1864 that he wrote *Arrah-na-Pogue*, and supervised its sentimental opening in Dublin. *Arrah-na-Pogue* never quite lives up to the promise of its magnificent opening scene. It is the most flawed of the three major Irish plays – but it was written for more than money. Boucicault's Irish patriotism was not deeply thought, but it was not trumped-up either. When he wrote about Ireland, he wrote better. *The Colleen Bawn, Arrah-na-Pogue*, and particularly *The Shaughraun* are excellent comedy-melodramas, written with respect for the melodramatic mode, and without any patronising of the audience. They are not without mechanical villainy, but they are not dependent on it. The sugar-and-spice heroines are there, to be married by heroes with mouths full of fine sentiments, but their ponderousness is buoyed up by the life around them. They are not critical of inert social values, as even *The Octoroon* is, but neither are they complacent. Above all, they remain superbly playable by theatre companies bold enough to take them seriously. Half-inclined to swallow his words, O'Casey has put on record the bold view that 'Shakespeare's good in bits, but for colour and stir give me Boucicault.'[11]

The ten years that separate *Arrah-na-Pogue* from *The Shaughraun* were not Boucicault's best. The success of *The Poor of Liverpool* in its various guises enabled him to claw his way back to solvency, but his relationship with Agnes was persistently soured by his philandering, while the critics came increasingly to assess him as a playwright whose achievement was behind him. His skill as a doctor of sick plays was triumphantly displayed in the version of *Rip Van Winkle* he pieced together for Joseph Jefferson at the Adelphi in 1865. The sheer profusion of *Flying Scud* (1866) and *After Dark* (1868) is oddly impressive. *Formosa* (1869) scandalised enough respectable people to bring a twinkle to Boucicault's eye and the crowds to Drury Lane. But by 1870, he was feeling displaced and depressed. The wildly extravagant *Babil and Bijou* (1872), a Covent Garden spectacular in eighteen tableaux purporting to tell the story of Man, brought his twelve years in England to an end. He returned to New York, and to the reward of American citizenship.

The writing of *The Shaughraun*, and his performance, at the age of nearly fifty-five, brought Boucicault to the final peak of both his careers. Conn combines the unprincipled charm of Autolycus with the loyal bravery of Mutch, the miller's son, who risked all for Robin Hood. His wake in Act III, scene 2 is one of the great set-pieces of the 'English' drama. It is not simply that Conn is a wonderful dramatic 'character', but that his placing in the unfolding story is so exact. It was not unusual, in nineteenth-century melodrama, for the comic man to usurp the hero's right to heroism. What is unusual in *The Shaughraun* is that the usurpation is so appropriate. There are costs involved. Robert Ffolliott is a fairly limp rag of a hero, and Kinchela's toughs are not much more than pantomime bailiffs. But it was a wise decision to pair the virtuous heroine, Arte O'Neal, with Robert Ffolliott's sprightly sister, Claire. It is such a pairing that lifts Tom Robertson's *Caste*. Both dramatists are indebted to Thackeray's recognition that Amelia Sedley is made more tolerable by the lively contrast of Becky Sharp. The relationship of Claire Ffolliott and Captain Molineux is exquisitely contrived to enhance both of them. It is in such contrivance that Boucicault exhibits the true extent of his craftsmanship. *The Shaughraun* opened at Wallack's Theatre, New York on 14 November 1874, and earned Boucicault another fortune. As always, wealth made him silly. Having bought himself a steam yacht, he thought of crossing the Atlantic in it, sailing up the Solent, and hoisting the rebel Irish flag. His *Shaughraun* companies were transported round the United States in special railway carriages, with Boucicault's name painted on them. Photographs of him in full, bizarre costume as Conn 'mysteriously' found their way into shops wherever he toured. Increasingly, his antics displayed his anxiety. Try as he might – and he never gave up – he could not repeat the sucess of *The Shaughraun.* He wrangled over divorce proceedings with Agnes for years. Eventually, and bigamously, he married the twenty-one-year-old American actress Louise Thorndyke. He was sixty-four, and touring Australia with a company of six. Perhaps he hoped that a wedding in Sydney would not matter. 'Poor Agnes Robertson,' Sir William Howard Russell noted in his diary; 'But she was queer too . . .'[12] Queer or not, Agnes was probably right in her view that, all in all, Boucicault got off too lightly. His financial struggles continued to the end. So, however unsuccessfully, did his writing. When, in 1888, he was asked by Albert Palmer to run the drama school he was about to found at the Madison Square Theatre, Boucicault accepted. It was too late, perhaps, to expect much more than the quiet respect he earned from his pupils. Theatrical taste in America, as well as in England, had changed more than he was able to recognise. The English-speaking theatre was beginning to confront Ibsen. It would soon have to take account of Shaw.

In an active career of over fifty years, Boucicault achieved many things. His energetic pursuit of his own financial interests led, indirectly but surely, to the improvement of other playwrights' prospects, too. One of the effects was to encourage men and women of superior talent to write plays. To that extent at least, Shaw and Synge were indebted to him, as they were for his determined contribution to the improved framing and observation of copyright laws on both sides of the Atlantic. His sensation scenes demonstrated his unusual sensitivity to the stage as a practical space, and advanced the art of stage design. His advocacy accelerated the adoption of fireproofed scenery in the American theatre. There was an accidental benefit to actors in the impetus given by *The Colleen Bawn* to long runs, and that had its effect on writing, too. It reduced the demand for a constant successsion of made-to-measure plays. Above all, though, it is by his best plays that Boucicault deserves to be remembered. He can be fairly credited with having written two of the best comedies and three of the best melodramas of the nineteenth century. They were popular when the theatre was popular, and that, in days of dwindling audiences and governmentally accredited philistinism, is worth recalling.

That Boucicault was out of touch with developments can be easily recognised by reference to the year 1887. It was the year in which Strindberg wrote *The Father*; Ibsen, having just completed *Rosmersholm*, was working on *The Lady from the Sea*; and in Paris, Antoine founded the Théâtre Libre as a home for naturalism.

Boucicault's only contribution that year was a new play with the tell-tale title *Phryne; or, The Romance of a Young Wife.* It opened in San Francisco, and survived two weeks. Had he lived a few years longer, he would have been more at home in the new cinema than in the new theatre.

NOTES

I have relied, for most of the biographical material, on Richard Fawkes's *Dion Boucicault* (London, 1979).

1 See, for example, J. B. Lynaugh, *The Forgotten Contributions and Comedies of Dion Boucicault*, unpublished Ph.D. thesis, University of Wisconsin, 1974 (University Microfilms 74-24, 734, 1980), pp. 68-78.

2 Sinden, Foreword to Fawkes's biography, p. xiv.

3 Quoted in Fawkes, p. 57.

4 Lynaugh, p. 6.

5 To the very end of their divorce proceedings in 1880-83, Boucicault was to claim that his New York 'marriage' to Agnes was not legal, but it should be noted that he made no such claim until it became convenient to do so. Agnes had public opinion on her side in wishing to establish the legitimacy of their six children.

6 It was a New York critic who coined the description 'contemporaneous melodrama'. See Lynaugh, p. 44.

7 See Appendix A.

8 Fawkes, p. 99.

9 The extent of Nana Sahib's responsibility for the Cawnpore massacre is a matter of dispute now, but it was not doubted in 1858. His press coverage in England and America was of the kind that Hitler might expect in modern Israel.

10 *The Autobiography of Joseph Jefferson* (New York, 1890), p. 214.

11 Sean O'Casey, *Pictures in the Hallway* (London, 1942), p. 26.

12 Quoted in Fawkes, p. 227.

BIOGRAPHICAL RECORD

27 December 1820	The likeliest of the many dates suggested – by himself as well as by others – for the birth of Dionysius Lardner Boursiquot in Dublin. His mother, Anne, was the sister of the poet and critic George Darley. His father was more probably Anne's lodger, the encyclopaedist Dionysius Lardner, than her elderly husband, Samuel Boursiquot, a wine-merchant.
1827	Samuel Boursiquot's wine business fails, and he tries a fresh start as a general merchant.
1828	Lardner appointed to chair of Natural Philosophy and Astronomy at University College, London. Anne Boursiquot takes Dion and three of her other four children to London.
1828-1834	At various schools in and around London. Lonely, reading greedily, and learning French.
1834-1835	At University College School, where he began his friendship with the dramatist, Charles Kenney.
1836	At Brentford Collegiate School. Plays Rolla in Sheridan's *Pizarro*, and writes his first play, *Napoleon's Old Guard*.
1837	Completes his schooling in Dublin, then is sent back to London as apprentice civil engineer to Lardner.
1838	Taking the stage name Lee Moreton, DB risks a career as an actor. Makes his debut at Cheltenham (probably on 2 April), then accompanies the manager, Charles Hill, to Brighton. Begins to cultivate the style of a dandy.
1839	Acting at Bristol and at Hull.
18 February	*Lodgings to Let* staged at Bristol.
26 December	*Jack Sheppard* staged at Hull.
1840	Shares London lodgings with the Irish actor John Brougham, who may have helped DB to the attention of Charles Mathews and Madame Vestris, managers of Covent Garden.
4 March 1841	Success of *London Assurance* at Covent Garden. DB settles in London, trying to live beyond his means.
1842	DB's financial problems eased by an arrangement with Benjamin Webster, manager of the Haymarket. Recognising his skill, Webster is prepared to advance him money on unwritten plays. Webster remains a 'banker' until about 1851.
6 February 1844	Charles Mathews makes an outstanding success of the part of Sir Charles Coldstream in *Used Up*.
18 November	*Old Heads and Young Hearts* opens at the Haymarket, after

	much tension between the stars, Mathews and Vestris, and DB over the relative status of actor and playwright. It is a *succès d'estime.*
December	DB goes to Paris in search of French plays.
9 July 1845	DB marries Anne Guiot, a French widow, tolerably wealthy and some years older than himself. In Paris, DB is prepared to call himself Vicomte de Boucicault.
1846	Five plays on the London stage. Anne Guiot may have died in September, or some time in 1847, or even as late as 1848. DB's silence on her death allowed some lurid gossip to develop. 'Boucicault went up the Alps with a wife, and came down with a black hatband,' wrote one obituarist in 1890. Did she fall, or . . . ? Agnes Robertson says she died, after a long illness, in March 1848. DB probably enjoyed the mystery. The death did not disturb him for long.
November 1848	DB declared bankrupt. Acted successfully in his own *The Knight of Arva* as Connor the Rash, an Irish soldier of fortune. Much concerned with money, DB proposes to Dramatic Authors' Society a shift from lump-sum payment for plays to the French system of 10% of the box office takings: the proposal is overruled.
1850	Appointed as house dramatist by Charles Kean at the Princess's, but continues his work for and with Webster into 1851.
6 March 1851	*Love in a Maze*, his first full play for Kean, at the Princess's. Queen Victoria admired it – 'full of wit – with an excellent moral, particularly for young ladies'.
24 February 1852	*The Corsican Brothers*, in DB's clever version, establishes Charles Kean's reputation in 'gentlemanly melodrama'.
Summer	DB and Agnes Robertson, Charles Kean's ward and an actress with the company, become lovers. Kean is outraged, and the pair leave the Princess's, though not before both have had acting triumphs, he in *The Vampire*, and she in *The Prima Donna.*
1853	DB arranges a New York season for Agnes, and buys passage by selling Webster plays, not all written.
18 September	Arrives in New York where he hears of Agnes's triumphant season in Montreal. They marry, according to New York law, by simple formal declaration.
1853–1855	Agnes is hugely successful in tours of plays by DB across the USA. Somewhat irked, DB tries his hand as a lecturer, with limited success.

10 November 1854	Makes his New York debut as Sir Charles Coldstream in *Used Up*.
13 January 1855	Swallowing his anger, Charles Kean stages *Louis XI* at the Princess's.
10 May 1855	Birth of first child, Dion William. Within a month, Agnes is back on stage.
December 1855	Hoping to settle, DB leases theatre in New Orleans, renaming it the Gaiety. The plan is to star himself and Agnes in his own plays.
March 1856	After the comparative failure of the New Orleans venture, DB and Agnes return to the road prior to an extended season at Wallack's Theatre, New York.
18 August 1856	DB instrumental in the passing of an amendment to the copyright law in Congress. In November, DB is the first author to make use of it, when he has a Boston theatre manager arrested.
15 August 1857	DB arranges what may have been the first matinee performance in the American theatre, at the New York Academy of Music.
10 October 1857	Birth of second child, Eve.
8 December 1857	*The Poor of New York* begins a successful run at Wallack's.
January 1858	DB makes a second unsuccessful venture into theatre management, this time in Washington.
22 February 1858	*Jessie Brown* begins a triumphant run at Wallack's, with DB as Nana Sahib.
23 May 1859	Birth of third child, Darley George (Dot).
September 1859	Third, short-lived venture into management – at the Winter Garden, New York.
6 December 1859	*The Octoroon* opens at the Winter Garden, with DB as Wahnotee and Agnes as Zoe. After a quarrel with joint manager, William Stuart, they walk out, and are annoyed that the play's successful run continues.
1860	The success of *The Colleen Bawn* at Laura Keene's Theatre, with DB as Myles and Agnes as Eily, restores finances. They sail to England in July, and open *The Colleen Bawn* at the Adelphi, where it runs for 230 performances, DB having negotiated a very favourable financial deal with Benjamin Webster.
1861	Having earned £23,000 during their year in England, DB and Agnes buy Hereford House in the Brompton Road, and begin to bargain hard with Webster. The resulting agreement, signed in July, gave DB artistic control of the Adelphi, and a

	royalty payment of £1 per act each night of a play's performance. Meanwhile DB was organising provincial tours of *The Colleen Bawn*.
1862	DB's relationship with Webster founders, not least because of the failure of *The Octoroon*. DB's behaviour is typically unattractive where money is the issue.
9 August	Birth of fourth child, Patrice.
22 December	Having altered and renamed Astley's Amphitheatre, DB opens it as the New Theatre Royal, Westminster. The venture makes a shaky financial start.
May 1863	DB's affair with the actress wife of George Jordan becomes public knowledge, and his financial backers abandon the Theatre Royal project.
3 July	DB declared bankrupt, with debts of £31,000.
27 July	Agnes and DB begin a provincial tour in Liverpool.
1864	The touring receives new momentum from the popularity of *The Poor of Liverpool* (or Leeds, or Manchester, or London . . .), and by July DB can afford a new London home at 326 Regent Street.
7 November	*Arrah-na-Pogue*, with DB as Shaun and Agnes as Arrah received with enthusiasm in Dublin.
22 March 1865	*Arrah-na-Pogue* repeats its success at the Princess's.
4 September 1865	Joseph Jefferson persuades Webster to stage *Rip Van Winkle* at the Adelphi. It makes Jefferson's name, and restores the Adelphi's fortunes.
5 November 1866	Henry Irving's success as Rawdon Scudamore in *Hunted Down* at the St James's makes his name known in London. DB was probably responsible for his being given the part.
27 February 1867	Fifth child, Nina (the first Peter Pan), born.
1868	DB and Agnes determine to abandon acting, he to write, she to be with her family.
23 June 1869	Sixth child, Aubrey Robertson, born.
5 August 1869	Controversy over the immorality of *Formosa* helps turn it into a Drury Lane success. The cast included Katherine Rogers, perhaps the most loved of DB's mistresses.
1871	DB and Agnes return to the stage.
1872	The spectacular *Babil and Bijou*, despite its popularity, loses money at Covent Garden for its backer, Lord Londesborough. DB and Agnes return to New York in September. DB takes up residence with Katherine Rogers.
1873	DB and Agnes granted American citizenship, but Agnes returns to her children in England in March. DB tours his plays with Katherine Rogers.

1874	DB employs David Belasco as his secretary during a tour of the west coast.
14 November 1874	Opening at Wallack's of the phenomenally successful *The Shaughraun*, in which DB played Conn. It earned half a million dollars in the United States. DB buys a steam yacht for $75,000.
4 September 1875	*The Shaughraun* opens at Drury Lane, with Agnes in the cast as well as DB. The play flourishes, but the marriage does not.
21 January 1876	On the last night of the run of *The Shaughraun*, Agnes and DB learn that their eldest son has been killed in a train crash near Huntingdon.
August 1876	DB returns to United States, leaving Agnes in England. An attempt at reconciliation fails.
December 1876	DB demonstrates the results of his work on the chemical fireproofing of scenery in New York.
1876–1879	DB tours as actor and dramatist. His new plays do not go well.
4 September 1879	Opens a six-month lease of Booth's Theatre, New York with *Rescued.* The press reaction is part of the emotional stress that leads to a breakdown.
1880–1883	Agnes initiates divorce proceedings. DB contests. They drag on throughout these years, during which DB writes and acts in England and the United States.
18 May 1885	*The Jilt* opens in San Francisco.
6 June 1885	DB sails to Australia, with a company of six actors.
9 September 1885	DB marries the twenty-one-year-old Louise Thorndyke, an actress in his company. Agnes lets it be known that he is a bigamist.
29 July 1886	DB and Louise Thorndyke begin a successful run of *The Jilt* at the Prince of Wales's, London, despite (or because of) public hostility.
1886–1888	DB tours United States, acting in his own plays with Louise Thorndyke.
18 September 1890	Dies of pneumonia, after heart attacks. Louise, who died in 1956, was buried under the same stone, in Hastings-on-Hudson.

A NOTE ON THE TEXTS

Despite his exemplary concern for copyright, Boucicault was careless of his own texts. Those that appeared in his lifetime were published in acting editions, with all the typical faults and virtues of such publications. Scrupulous scholarship may recover better texts – and I have tried to do so – but it would be foolhardy to aim at definitive versions. Boucicault was always ready to fit lines to actors. His plays were vehicles, and he adapted them with the enthusiasm of a skilled mechanic.

The text of *Used Up* is from the Shilling Dramatic Library, edited by Benjamin Webster, where it is ascribed to Dion Bourcicault, Esq. Charles Mathews, who created the part of Sir Charles Coldstream, contested the authorship. The copy in the Library of the University of Kent, 'Marked by Mr. Tony Doyne from C. Mathews Book: Preston, 1856', has a pasted-in newspaper cutting:

> The question of the authorship of this piece has been in Chancery, but the title to it has not been decided. A French piece was translated by a Mr. Bourcicault, who gave it the name of 'Bored to Death'. Mr. Mathews was requested to read and amend it, which he did, and then claimed the whole. The Vice-Chancellor said, it was clear that at one time Mr. Mathews did not claim the copyright. He would not, therefore, grant an injunction against its being advertised as Bourcicault's. The question of ownership might be settled by an action.

There is no doubt that Mathews made suggestions about ways of improving Boucicault's text. I have, therefore, silently included six variants from Doyne's Preston promptbook. The text published here is, then, as close as any can be to the text performed by Charles Mathews during his years of successful touring as Sir Charles Coldstream.

The text of *Old Heads and Young Hearts* is based on that published in French's Standard Drama, No. LXII. I have collated it with the German edition (Leipzig: Hermann Hartung, 1845) in the series Modern English Comic Theatre with Notes in German, which has enabled me to correct two significant misprints.

The text of *Jessie Brown* is that of Dicks' Standard Plays No. 473, word for word (barring misprints) the same as that in Lacy's No. 38, which lacks the admonition about the changed appearance of the actors at the opening of Act III. Neither text is reconcilable with an incomplete manuscript in the Boucicault Collection in the University of South Florida. This is a four-act version (only the first and fourth acts survive), dated 15 September 1863, which seems to have belonged to the actor who played Blount, here called O'Grady, since his part is separately written out. Some of this text is entirely new, much of it re-ordered. Until further research has been done, it remains a mystery.

The text of *The Octoroon* is a collation of the English version in Dicks' Standard

Plays No. 391 and the privately printed American edition as it appears in *Representative American Plays*, edited by Arthur Hobson Quinn (New York, 1953).

The text of *The Shaughraun* differs from all previously published versions. It is based on the prompt copy of the original production at Wallack's Theatre, New York in 1874. It is, in many details, superior to the Lord Chamberlain's copy, as well as to Lacy V.123 and Dicks' Standard Plays No. 390. I am grateful to Dr. Paul Eugen Camp, Associate Librarian of the University of South Florida, for making a photocopy available to me.

USED UP

A petit comedy in two acts

First performed at the Haymarket Theatre, London on 6 February 1844, with the following cast:

SIR CHARLES COLDSTREAM	Mr. Charles Mathews
SIR ADONIS LEECH	Mr. Tilbury
HONOURABLE TOM SAVILLE	Mr. Brindal
WURZEL	Mr. James Bland
JOHN IRONBRACE	Mr. Howe
MR. FENNEL	Mr. Gough
JAMES	Mr. Clark
MARY	Miss Julia Bennett
LADY CLUTTERBUCK	Mrs. Humby

Time of Representation, One Hour and Ten Minutes.

I Charles Mathews as Sir Charles Coldstream in Act I (left) and Act II (right) of *Used Up* (water-colours by James W. Childe)

ACT I

A Saloon in SIR CHARLES COLDSTREAM*'s House, at Kingston-upon-Thames.*
Window: Door leading to Lawn: Door: Folding-doors: Sofa: Ornamental Table etc.
Enter JAMES *with bottle and* IRONBRACE *with basket of tools.*
JAMES: Oh, Ironbrace, you are come!
IRONBRACE: Yes, Master James; what's the job?
JAMES: You see that window? (*Puts bottle on table.*)
IRONBRACE: It's big enough. (*Measures with ruler.*)
JAMES: It looks out upon the river, and that's where the balcony's to be.
IRONBRACE: (*looking out*) Ah, I see; the water flows up to the very wall.
JAMES: This is the deepest spot in the Thames, hereabouts, of any near Kingston:-
    I wonder no balcony has been put up before; I am sure, whenever I am
    obliged to open that window (for it is Sir Charles's favourite smoking spot), I
    get so giddy; and as there's nothing there but a bar of wood – oh, if any-
    body should – oh!
IRONBRACE: I suppose, then, he sent for me to put up a balcony on your account.
JAMES: Principally, I think; for he said he rather liked it himself – it was an excite-
    ment.
IRONBRACE: A what?
JAMES: An excitement – a sensation.
IRONBRACE: I don't understand.
JAMES: Of course not; how should you, you ignoramus? – he's always sighing for
    what he calls excitement: you see, everything is old to him – he's used up –
    nothing amuses him – he can't feel.
IRONBRACE: Can't he? I wish I had him on my anvil for five minutes.
JAMES: But he values my health, respects my feelings; indeed, I am more his confi-
    dant than his valet.
SAVILLE: (*within*) James, you scoundrel!
IRONBRACE: Scoundrel! does he mean you?
JAMES: Ahem! – no, that's Mr. Saville's voice. Sir Charles, you see, is lunching
    within, with a few friends, and amongst friends, you know –
LEECH: (*putting his head out*) James, you rascal! if you don't bring that claret,
    I'll pitch you out of that window. (*Retires.*)
IRONBRACE: Very free and easy! why don't you return the joke, and fling the
    tongs at him?
JAMES: This completes the first dozen. (*Opens door, and discovers* SIR CHARLES,
    LEECH, *and* SAVILLE *at table.*)
SIR C: You may say what you please, but I still maintain the world's a great bore!
    and now let's drop the subject. James, bring in the *patés de foie gras*, which
    arrived from France last week.
LEECH: I rise to propose an amendment.
ALL: Hear! hear!
LEECH: That after the words, 'bring in the *patés de foie gras*', shall be added, 'and
    another case of champagne'.
ALL: Ah! ah! – hear, hear!

LEECH: Carried Nem Con!

SIR C: With all my heart – as you please – it's a matter of perfect indifference to me – James, champagne!

(*Exit* JAMES, *closing door.*)

IRONBRACE: Happy set of devils those rich fellows are! they eat one half their money, drink the other half, and give the rest to the poor. (JAMES *re-enters with bottle of champagne, then exits closing doors.*) That's the trade I should like, only I haven't got the right tools to follow it.

(*Enter* MARY.)

MARY: No one here? – Oh, Mr. Ironbrace, is that you?

IRONBRACE: What, little Mary, niece of old Farmer Wurzel of Copse Hill – how dost do, lass? how's your worthy uncle? he's an old friend of mine. I suppose you have come here to Sir Charles to pay your uncle's rent, eh?

MARY: No – my mother was his nurse, and was very fond of him – indeed, Sir Charles and me used to play together, in this very room, some years ago; but I suppose he has forgotten me by this time.

IRONBRACE: Very likely, or grown ashamed of you, perhaps.

MARY: No, no, for he is too generous and kind for that. When he heard my mother was ill (for the Steward wrote him word of it), though he was somewhere abroad – I don't know where, but very far away – he sent her to say that she should have whatever she wanted. She borrowed £20 – ah! (*Sighs.*) – then she died!

IRONBRACE: Did she require £20 to die with?

MARY: No, it was to pay the doctor's bill.

IRONBRACE: Oh, I see: he got £20 for the killing of her.

MARY: I have made up the sum by shillings and sixpences, and have brought it here to pay him.

IRONBRACE: Come, that's honest, however!

MARY: Besides I have been educated at his expense, because I was his foster-sister. I can read and write, and love music, and –

IRONBRACE: And therefore, of course, hate churning, and washing, and darning, and –

MARY: No, no, I love them, for 'twas by such means I made up this sum to pay him back again. It's a great blessing to be quick at one's needle, Mr. Ironbrace.

IRONBRACE: Is it? I can't say. I never worked at it, but I have often heard talk about it – much *too* often. And now you live with your uncle, eh?

MARY: Yes: he's sometimes a little cross, but very good to me.

IRONBRACE: Ah! I wish I had met you, Mary, about a twelve-month ago; I should now have been a man of substance, instead of the poor devil you see me.

MARY: Indeed!

IRONBRACE: Yes, I should have married you, instead of ruining myself for one who – no matter. Ah, Mary, I have had a severe trial; I have had a blow I shall never recover – a blow that would have felled an ox; but I was rock – I survived it!

MARY: A blow!

IRONBRACE: Ay, a blow! not from a man; no, no, I flatter myself no man dare try that game with John Ironbrace! no, 'twas a woman who dealt it me!

MARY: A woman!

IRONBRACE: Yes, she was a milliner, in a great house in Piccadilly; at that time I had a good iron foundry in Drury Lane; till one fatal night I met her at a ball –

MARY: Oh! a ball! – did you go in that dress?

IRONBRACE: Yes, at White Conduit Gardens; and before I had looked twice at her, her eyes made two holes in my heart as clean as a punch. For eight months I courted her; till as last 'twas agreed we should be welded.

MARY: Wedded, you mean.

IRONBRACE: It's welded in my trade – when, after spending a honeymoon of three months, the very first time I had occasion to leave town, hang me if she didn't run away!

MARY: And didn't you follow her?

IRONBRACE: Ah, I wish I hadn't, for I neglected my business to hunt every corner in London for her – though I might as well have looked for a needle in a bottle of hay; till at last I was lodged in the list of bankrupts, and here I am a poor blacksmith, instead of a master founder. But only (*clenching his fist*) let me catch the fellow who has played me false! – and hammer and tongs!

MARY: Why agitate yourself any more about a woman who did not love you?

IRONBRACE: Not love me? she doated on me!

MARY: And yet she left you?

IRONBRACE: She didn't – I won't believe it – she must have been carried off – she's a prisoner somewhere now!

MARY: D'ye think so?

IRONBRACE: I am sure of it. (*Gets gradually enraged.*) There's some scoundrel at the bottom of it all! I don't know who he is, nor what's his name; but if ever I clap my fist upon him, hammer and tongs! but he shall remember it!

MARY: Oh, Mr. Ironbrace, you should not be so passionate!

IRONBRACE: I'm not passionate! I'm quite cool! But only let me get one thump at him!

MARY: Mr. Ironbrace!

IRONBRACE: He shall take it for the kick of a young horse; he shall say –

MARY: Oh!

IRONBRACE: Stand out of my way – no! I beg pardon, not you, Mary – did I frighten you? – you have nothing to do with it – no, no, it isn't you –

MARY: You shouldn't go on so, Mr. Ironbrace.

IRONBRACE: (*violently*) I can't help it, it's my nature!

(*Re-enter* JAMES.)

JAMES: Sir Charles is coming – Ironbrace, you must postpone your job for an hour or so. You must go now.

MARY: But I want to see him.

JAMES: You! – what an idea! – run away with you directly!

MARY: But where am I to go?

JAMES: Where you like, only you can't stay here; go to the kitchen, or to the garden, or any place you can find, so that you go out of this.

White Conduit Gardens: one of the many tea-gardens that flourished in Islington from the mid eighteenth century. Not for the fashionable, they were part of a cockney day out.

MARY: I won't go till I have seen him, that I am determined.

IRONBRACE: That's right, lass; I like your spirit. Come, we'll go together, and I'll tell you all my sorrows over again. (*Takes her arm.*) It does me good to unload my heart to you; it eases me; and one day I shall fall in with that scoundrel – and then, hammer and tongs!

MARY: Oh, you hurt my arm!

IRONBRACE: Oh, I beg pardon: I fancied I had hold of him.

> (*Exeunt. Enter* SIR CHARLES, SIR A. LEECH, HON. TOM
> SAVILLE, *all laughing, except* SIR CHARLES.)

SAVILLE: Ha! ha! ha! Come, Leech, confess.

SIR C: Fitzackerby, lead the way. (*to guests*) We'll join you directly in the billiard-room. James, cigars. Come, Leech, your confession.

LEECH: With all my heart. I don't care; why should I? She was more than a match for me, and I own it. She was the wife of an ironmonger, or some vulgar thing of the sort – she caught my fancy one day in Long Acre, and my valet, who manages these matters for me, found out her abode, watched the husband out of town, and then hastening to the wife with the news of his sudden death, the bait took, and she followed him to the spot where the accident was said to have occurred.

SAVILLE: Where, instead of the husband, she found –

LEECH: Me! – popped her into a carriage and four, and galloped off with her.

SAVILLE: Bravo! Victory!

LEECH: Not at all: she was in my house above a month, and although she believed her husband dead, and buried too at my expense, she would not listen to me as a lover, but asked me if my intentions were honourable – ha! ha! ha!

SAVILLE: Ho! ho! ho!

LEECH: But you don't laugh, Coldstream! come, man, be amused for once in your life – you don't laugh.

SIR C: Oh yes I do, *mon cher*. You mistake, I laughed twice distinctly – only the fact is, I am bored to death.

LEECH: Bored? what! after such a *déjeuner* as that you have given us? Look at me, I'm inspired – I'm in the seventh heaven of delight!

SAVILLE: You drank more champagne than any of us, and yet you are as dull as a funeral – you are not elated by it.

SIR C: Not the least in the world: why should I? I've drank so much of it in my time – I know it by heart – there's nothing in it.

LEECH: Nothing in it! everything's in it – I'm a King at this moment, and all the world is at my feet.

SIR C: (*rising*) My dear Leech, you began life late – you are a young fellow – forty-five – and have the world yet before you. I started at thirteen, lived quick, and exhausted the whole round of pleasure before I was thirty. I've tried everything, heard everything, done everything, know everything, and here I am, a man of thirty-three, literally used up – completely *blazé*.

LEECH: Nonsense, man! used up indeed! With your wealth, with your little heaven in Spring Gardens, and your paradise here at Kingston-upon-Thames –

Long Acre: this street links St Martins Lane and Drury Lane.
Spring Gardens: a choice spot, at the Trafalgar Square end of the Mall.

SAVILLE: With twenty estates in the sunniest spots in England.

LEECH: Not to mention that Utopia within four walls in the *Rue de Provence* in Paris. Oh, the nights we've spent there – eh, Tom?

SAVILLE: Ah!

SIR C: I'm dead with *ennui.*

LEECH: Ennui! do you hear him, Tom? poor Croesus!

SIR C: Croesus! – no, I'm no Croesus. My father – you've seen his portrait, good old fellow! – he certainly did leave me a little matter of £12,000 a year; but after all –

LEECH and SAVILLE: Oh, come! –

SIR C: Oh, I don't complain of it.

LEECH: I should think not.

SIR C: Oh, no, there are some people who can manage to do on less – on credit.

LEECH: I know several –

SAVILLE: My dear Coldstream, you should try a change of scene.

SIR C: I have tried it – what's the use?

LEECH: But I'd gallop all over Europe.

SIR C: I have – there's nothing in it.

LEECH: Nothing in all Europe!

SIR C: Nothing – oh dear, yes! I remember, at one time, I did somehow go about a good deal.

SAVILLE: You should go to Switzerland.

SIR C: I have been – nothing there – people say so much about everything – there certainly were a few glaciers, some monks, and large dogs, and thick ankles, and bad wine, and Mont Blanc! yes, and there was ice on the top, too; but I prefer the ice at Gunter's – less trouble, and more in it.

LEECH: Then, if Switzerland wouldn't do, I'd try Italy.

SIR C: My dear Leech, I've tried it over and over again, and what then?

SAVILLE: Did not Rome inspire you?

SIR C: (*crossing to centre*) Oh, believe me, Tom, a most horrible hole! People talk so much about these things – there's the Colosseum, now – round, very round: a goodish ruin enough, but I was disappointed with it; Capitol – tolerable high; and St. Peter's – marble, and mosaics, and fountains; dome certainly not badly scooped, but there was nothing in it.

LEECH: Come, Coldstream, you must admit we have nothing like St. Peter's in London.

SIR C: No, because we don't want it; but if we wanted such a thing, of course we should have it. A dozen gentlemen meet, pass resolutions, institute, and in twelve months it would be run up; nay, if that were all, we'd buy St. Peter's itself, and have it sent over.

LEECH: Ha, ha! well said, you're quite right.

SAVILLE: What say you to beautiful Naples?

LEECH: Ay, *La Belle Napoli!*

SIR C: Not bad – excellent water-melons, and goodish opera; they took me up Vesuvius – a horrid bore! it smoked a good deal certainly, but altogether a

---

Gunter's: a pastrycook's in Berkeley Square, whose founder had learned the art of making ices when employed by an Italian.

wretched mountain; saw the crater, looked down, but there was nothing
in it.

SAVILLE: But the bay?

SIR C: Inferior to Dublin.

LEECH: The Campagna?

SIR C: A swamp!

SAVILLE: Greece?

SIR C: A morass!

LEECH: Athens?

SIR C: A bad Edinburgh!

SAVILLE: Egypt?

SIR C: A desert!

LEECH: The Pyramids?

SIR C: Humbugs! nothing in any of them! Have done – you bore me. (*All sit.*)

LEECH: But you enjoyed the hours we spent in Paris, at any rate?

SIR C: No; the *danseuses* were too approachable, and my friends' wives gave me
too much trouble. I was dying for excitement – gambling gave me none, and
women no longer interested me. In fact I've no appetite, no thirst; everything
wearies me – nothing fatigues me.

LEECH: Fatigue you! I should think not, indeed; you are as strong as a lion.

SIR C: But as quiet as a lamb – that was Tom Cribb's character of me: you know I
was a favourite pupil of his. I swear I'd give a thousand pounds for any event
that would make my pulse beat ten to the minute faster. Is it possible that
between you both you cannot invent something that would make my blood
boil in my veins, my hair stand on end, my heart beat, my pulse rise – that
would produce an excitement – an emotion – a sensation – a palpitation? But
no! –

LEECH: I've an idea!

SIR C: You?

SAVILLE: What is it?

LEECH: Marry!

SIR C: Hum! – well, not bad, there's novelty about the notion; it never did strike
me to – oh, but no: I should be bored with the exertion of choosing – if a
wife, now, could be had like a dinner – for ordering.

LEECH: She can, by you – take the first woman that comes: on my life, she'll not
refuse £12,000 a year.

SIR C: The first that comes! Ha, well there's an oddity about that that tickles me.

LEECH: There! didn't I tell you so?

SIR C: Come, I don't dislike the project; I almost feel something like a sensation
coming. I haven't felt so excited for some time; it's a novel enjoyment – a
surprise! I'll try it.

>   (*Enter* JAMES.)

Edinburgh: Edinburgh was familiarly called 'the Athens of the North'.
Tom Cribb: this great bare-fist boxer (1781–1848) became champion of England in 1808. His
two fights with Tom Molyneaux are among the epics of the ring. By 1813 he was landlord of a
London pub.

JAMES: Lady Clutterbuck, Sir Charles, to wait upon you.

ALL: Ha! ha! now's your time.

SIR C: Clutterbuck! – who's that?

JAMES: Our neighbour, sir.

SIR C: Is she a widow?

JAMES: I don't know, sir.

SIR C: If she's a widow, show her up; if she has a husband, show her out. Well sir, why do you hesitate?

JAMES: Beg pardon, sir, but I never knew you object to a husband before.

SIR C: Go away sir! (*Exit* JAMES.)

SAVILLE: Why, you don't mean to say –

SIR C: I do, so away with you!

LEECH: Quite right – the letter of the law – the first that comes – success to Clutterbuck!

SIR C: Away with you, then!

> (*Exeunt* LEECH *and* SAVILLE, *laughing and closing door after them. Enter* JAMES.)

JAMES: Lady Clutterbuck. (*Exit.*)

> (*Enter* LADY CLUTTERBUCK.)

SIR C: She is a widow, then.

LADY C: Sir Charles Coldstream, I presume. I have not the pleasure of knowing you, and I believe you have not the honour of knowing me.

SIR C (*aside*) A good beginning. (*aloud*) May I take the liberty of inquiring, madam – but pardon me – first, I believe you are a widow?

LADY C: Yes, sir. (*aside*) How very odd!

SIR C: Then permit me to offer you – (*Offers his hand; she looks astonished.*) – a chair. (*aside*) I can't propose so abruptly. (*They sit.*)

LADY C: Sir Charles, we will proceed to business.

SIR C: (*feeling his pulse*) No sensation as yet; my pulse is calm.

LADY C: I venture to intrude upon your generosity, Sir Charles, in favour of our infant school; the girls are sadly in want of blue mittens, and the boys of corduroy – a – a – corduroys – any subscription most gratefully acknowledged in the *Morning Post.*

SIR C: (*with his hand on his pulse*) No, not the slightest effect.

LADY C: I beg you won't say that, Sir Charles.

SIR C: Might I ask, madam – we are neighbours, I believe?

LADY C: My house is close to yours – a mere cottage, but I remain there with pleasure, as it was there I lost my poor husband.

SIR C: I understand – the pleasure of memory; and have we bachelors suffered for any length of time the disgrace of your widowhood?

LADY C: Sir!

SIR C: I say, madam, is it long that you have enjoyed your misfortune?

LADY C: Oh, a considerable period. (*Long pause*)

---

corduroy – a – a: Lady Clutterbuck's delicate avoidance of so blunt a word as 'trousers' is typical. 'Unmentionables' and 'unwhisperables' are among the many nineteenth-century euphemisms.

SIR C: A good match, the lamented Clutterbuck?

LADY C: Ah–h, sir, I have been wedded twice.

SIR C: The devil!

LADY C: My first, poor Ironbrace, wooed me from a flourishing business in town.

SIR C: Musical?

LADY C: No, millinery; he was an ironfounder – not handsome, but –

SIR C: Good?

LADY C: No, sir, wealthy; while I had nothing to offer him as dowry but my virtue.

SIR C: Ah! little enough!

LADY C: Sir!

SIR C: I simply remarked that, in this money-making age, mere virtue – unfortunately – but pray proceed.

LADY C: Three months after marriage news reached me of his death. I immediately quitted London with what fortune I possessed, to hide my tears at a watering-place, where I met Sir Stephen Clutterbuck, a little wizen old gentleman, who wore powder; but one couldn't look upon that as a physical objection, you know, sir –

SIR C: On the contrary, madam.

LADY C: He offered me his hand and heart – a heart of five-and-fifty is rather –

SIR C: Tough!

LADY C: A hand of half a century seemed to me a –

SIR C: A paw – I catch the idea! well, you sighed, thought of your unprotected state, and took the heart and the –

LADY C: Exactly; besides, he kept his carriage, and his family was good – his name a pretty one – you think Clutterbuck a pretty one, don't you sir?

SIR C. *Distingué*, madam.

LADY C: When what, sir, do you think I discovered, a week after our marriage?

SIR C: That he had a ready-made family?

LADY C: Worse, sir!

SIR C: A couple of other wives?

LADY C: Worse again – sir, he hadn't a sixpence.

SIR C: Just now, you said he had a carriage.

LADY C: So he had, but no horses – 'twas only jobbed.

SIR C: Oh, *Corpo di Bacco* – then 'twas a swindle?

LADY C: He soothed my indignation – for he had a good heart withal – by making me the only atonement in his power.

SIR C: I see – he left the country.

LADY C: No, he died.

SIR C: He died – well that was handsome of him at any rate.

LADY C: Yes. However, notwithstanding his behaviour, I mourned him the regular time.

SIR C: It does honour to your head and heart, madam.

LADY C: (*rising*) But, in your delightful conversation, I forgot the object of my visit.

---

jobbed: hired.   *Corpo di Bacco*: literally, 'body of Bacchus' – an Italian drinker's oath.

SIR C: (*putting chairs up*) Your pardon; my steward will give you a cheque for twenty guineas.

LADY C: You are generosity itself – good morning, Sir Charles!

SIR C: Permit me; delighted to have made the acquaintance of so lovely a neighbour – farewell! (*Rings bell. Exit* LADY CLUTTERBUCK. SIR CHARLES *yawns.*) Rather an odd woman, that, and rather amusing for a short time – but stay – by Jove! I forgot to propose to her. (*Runs upstage.*) Hollo! I beg pardon, madam – yes – you – madam! – one moment, if you please. (*Comes downstage.*) She's coming – positively, she amused me so, that she drove the idea of marriage out of my head.

(*Re-enter* LADY CLUTTERBUCK.)

LADY C: Sir Charles –

SIR C: I beg ten thousand pardons – I omitted to mention a small matter – a – a – you – you – are positively very good-looking still.

LADY C: Oh, Sir Charles!

SIR C: I never pay compliments; but of all the women I ever adored (that is, in the days when I did adore), out of about two hundred, I may say, who have possessed my heart, there were several who could not in justice compare with you.

LADY C: You are very polite, I'm sure, Sir Charles.

SIR C: Do me the favour to look at me – observe me critically – how old am I?

LADY C: Dear me, how odd! – I should say about seven or eight and twenty.

SIR C: Lady Clutterbuck, do you remember the comet of 1811?

LADY C: The comet?

SIR C: You cannot be old enough – don't answer, perhaps the question is indelicate; but if that comet still existed, we should be precisely of the same age.

LADY C: You and I, Sir Charles?

SIR C: No, madam! I and the comet. (LADY CLUTTERBUCK *counts her fingers.*) I am thirty-three, madam.

LADY C: Is this what you called me back to tell me, Sir Charles?

SIR C: It was, madam.

LADY C: Oh!

SIR C: Madam, I am by nature melancholy.

LADY C: You? – why, you have been saying all manner of funny things to me this half hour.

SIR C: You are mistaken; they were melancholy truths, positively. Why, 'twas only last week I made my will, left all my property amongst some friends, who are now on a visit here, before I carried out a fancy I had entertained for some time, of hanging myself on a tree.

LADY C: Hanging yourself on a tree!

SIR C: Or throwing myself into the river: I've a window here convenient – the water flows to the wall.

LADY C: Oh, you are joking!

SIR C: But, since I have seen you, my mind is changed: I have taken up another fancy, one in which you can assist me.

---

twenty guineas: i.e. £21. A guinea was twenty-one shillings.

LADY C: (*aside*) What does he mean? – me!

SIR C: You! listen: I have a house in town – estates in the three kingdoms, and one for a freak in the Isle of Man – I've a shooting box on the banks of the Mississippi; three carriages – a – with horses – £12,000 a year, and I offer you my hand.

LADY C: Your hand to me!

SIR C: I am, as I have told you, only thirty-three; and, according to the highest female authorities, this cannot be designated a *paw*. (*Holds out his hand.*) Will you accept it?

LADY C: Sir Charles, you amaze me! is this intended for a declaration of love?

SIR C: Quite the contrary – it is a proposal of marriage.

LADY C: But –

SIR C: Excuse me; I have had so much love-making in my time, I am sick of it – there's nothing in it – the same thing over and over again – I prefer coming to the point at once: will you have me? – if you accept me, you will do me a favour, and I shall be able to say I have a charming wife; if you refuse me, it will be precisely the – I shall then simply say I have a charming neighbour. Turn it over in your mind, my dear Lady – excuse my memory.

LADY C: Clutterbuck.

SIR C: Lady Clutterbuck – give it your serious reflection; and pray don't allow my violent arguments to alarm you into matrimony.

(*Enter* MARY *at back.*)

MARY: There he is!

SIR C: Who's that?

MARY: 'Tis I, Sir Charles – Mary Wurzel – you remember little Mary?

SIR C: (*crossing to her*) Perfectly: you were my college bedmaker.

MARY: No – do you forget twelve years ago?

SIR C: Twelve years ago – forget! – is there any human being can remember twelve years ago? The exertion must be Herculean – my dear, do you think my brain a parish register, or the minutes of the House of Lords? (*Takes* LADY CLUTTERBUCK*'s hand.*)

LADY C: Go, child: don't you see Sir Charles is busy at this moment?

MARY: (*aside*) He forgets me – Ironbrace was right – I came, sir, to pay a debt.

SIR C: A debt! that was twelve years ago, I suppose – don't remember it. Good morning!

MARY: But my mother, sir –

SIR C: Give her my regards, and say I'm engaged. (*to* LADY CLUTTERBUCK) In ten minutes I will return to know if I am to be, or not to be – whether husband, or neighbour?

LADY C: Ten minutes! – that's sudden.

SIR C: Twelve, if you like – oh, take your own time, I entreat; don't hurry on my account.

MARY: What does he say?

(*He goes upstage, humming an air; suddenly stops and returns.*)

SIR C: Lady Clutterbuck – with horses! (*Exit.*)

---

shooting box: a small country house near a game-shooting area.

MARY: Pray, madam, might I pay this money to you, on Sir Charles's account?

LADY C: In a few days you may – we are not married yet.

MARY: Married! and to you?

LADY C: Can you oppose any objection, moral, physical, or legal?

MARY: (*aside*) Dear me, what a strange effect this news has upon me! and yet it is quite natural he should marry, of course. I ought to rejoice; but I did not expect to find him so changed – how I have thought of him, ay, every day, and he could not even remember me – thought I was his college bedmaker!

LADY C: (*aloud, but to herself*) Hum! – of course I shall accept him; he's handsome –

MARY: Oh, very – I hope, madam, you will take great care of him; he's very melancholy sometimes, and then you must be sure and –

LADY C: Heyday, child! – are you going to instruct me how to take care of a husband? What is your business here?

     (*Enter* SIR A. LEECH.)

LEECH: Where is Sir Charles?

LADY C: Sir Adonis Leech!

LEECH: Mrs. Ironbrace, by all that's cruel!

MARY: Ironbrace!

LEECH: Have you forgiven me yet? (*They talk apart.*)

MARY: (*aside*) Ironbrace! – it must be his wife, going to marry my foster-brother! – I'll run down and ask him if that's proper. I'm sure he won't allow it. (*Exit.*)

LEECH: And you are going to marry him?

LADY C: What can I do?

LEECH: (*aside*) I wonder if Ironbrace is still alive – no matter: if he turns up, it will make a splendid paragraph for the *Post.* (*aloud*) Where is the victim?

LADY C: He retired to that room, to relieve his anxiety during my deliberation.

LEECH: Egad! we'll acquaint him with his good fortune.

LADY C: No, not yet.

LEECH: Relieve his sufferings – (*Throws open door, discovering* SIR CHARLES *asleep.*)

LADY C: Asleep! the wretch!

LEECH Ha! ha!

LADY C: Leave us.

LEECH: He's dreaming of you. (*Sings.*) 'Oh, there's nothing half so sweet in life as Love's young dream.' (*Exit.*)

LADY C: I'll awake him. – Hem! Sir Charles! (*Shakes chair.*)

SIR C: (*starting*) Eh? what! – oh, is it you, my dear madam! You destroyed the most delicious dream. I was dreaming of you.

LADY C: Oh!

SIR C: Yes, I dreamt that you refused me.

LADY C: But dreams go by contraries, you know, Sir Charles.

SIR C: Alas! yes.

LADY C: What!

SIR C: I meant, it was agitating – I was wretched! – but still it was something to be that – it was a sign of existence.

LADY C: Yes, Sir Charles, I awoke you to say –

SIR C: What?

LADY C: That the ten minutes are past.

SIR C: What ten minutes? – eh? – oh! – ah! – beg pardon; of course, I remember my proposal.

LADY C: I have considered, and –

SIR C: You refuse me – well! – (*Walks to sofa and throws himself upon it.*)

LADY C: I accept.

SIR C: Aha, good! – (*Puts up his legs.*)

LADY C: That surprises you, I believe.

SIR C: Not in the least. We'll fix the happy day as soon as you please. (*Takes out a cigar case.*)

LADY C: Is that all the effect it produces upon you, Sir Charles?

SIR C: Why, what effect would you have it pro– will you allow me? – I beg pardon, may I offer you one?

LADY C: Not before dinner, thank you.

SIR C: Perhaps you are right. (*Smokes.*)
    (*Enter* IRONBRACE.)

IRONBRACE: (*aside*) Ha! there they are at last! yes, I think that I have got him now.

SIR C: Come here, my dear; sit down beside me, and we'll talk over the matter.

LADY C: With pleasure.

IRONBRACE: No, you don't. (*Moves between them.*)

LADY C: Alive!

IRONBRACE: Yes, alive! – flesh and blood! Oh, you unfortunate, undone woman!

SIR C: It seems my intended knows this gentleman.

LADY C: What shall I do?

IRONBRACE: Yes, I – I who have sought you all the world over, now my turn is come.

LADY C: Before Sir Charles! –

SIR C: Good – go on – oh, don't mind me: settle your little matters, Mr. What's-your-name?

IRONBRACE: My name! – my name is Ironbrace – I'm not ashamed of it, though I ought to be.

SIR C: Ironbrace! damme, this is the blacksmith's wife – this is going to be amusing.

IRONBRACE: And is this animal the thing for which you deserted me? this –

SIR C: (*opening his eyes*) Heyday!

IRONBRACE: This threadpaper – this fine-whiskered wig-block, that I'll flatten on the earth, like a tenpenny nail on an anvil.

LADY C: Oh, good gracious!

SIR C: My good friend, will you allow me to inquire who is the individual you propose to flatten in so agreeable a manner?

IRONBRACE: You! – hammer and tongs!

SIR C: Me! – hammer and tongs!

IRONBRACE: As for you, degraded woman, I despise, and leave you to your conscience; but for you, villain! (*seizing* SIR CHARLES *and dragging him off sofa*) – we will settle our accounts another way.

LADY C: Oh, mercy on me!

SIR C: Don't, I beg. *Per Bacco*, this is becoming decidedly exciting! (*Feels his pulse.*)
An unquestionable pulsation! This is what I wanted – yes, my heart beats
fast – hem! – I think you will leave this room.
IRONBRACE: I'll give you the finest drubbing you ever got.
LADY C: I shall faint.
SIR C: Pray don't, till I polish off your friend, I entreat. (*to* IRONBRACE) Leave
the room, or I must force you out.
IRONBRACE: Force me! ha, ha, ha!
SIR C: Leave the room, I say, by the door, or I'll throw you out of the window.
IRONBRACE: Ha! you! – I should like to see you do it.
SIR C: Would you? you shall – this is the first little bit of excitement I've had for
a very long time.
IRONBRACE: I've been waiting above a twelvemonth for this.
SIR C: (*sparring*) This is about the thing, I believe.
IRONBRACE: Oho! a bruiser! then here's Cornwall for you – here's a pair of
pincers at your service.
SIR C: I regret that I have only a pair of tweezers to offer you in return, but you
are welcome. (*to* LADY CLUTTERBUCK) Do me the favour. (*Gives her his
watch.*) Thank you; will you excuse me for a moment? (*Leads her to door.*) I
can't fight before ladies – I will be with you immediately. (*Locks her in.*)
Now, sir, since you will have it. (*They engage.*)
IRONBRACE: Oh! his grip is like a vice!
SIR C: I could choke you if I liked, but let us prolong the fun.
IRONBRACE: Damme – I've caught a Tartar! (*By this time, they have wheeled up
to the window.*)
LADY C: (*within, ringing bell*) Help! help!
    IRONBRACE *and* SIR CHARLES *disappear through the window –
a loud crash heard. Enter* JAMES *and* MARY – LEECH *rushes in
from door.* SAVILLE *unlocks door and releases* LADY CLUTTER-
BUCK.)
ALL (*but* LADY CLUTTERBUCK): What has happened?
MARY: Where is Sir Charles? ⎫ *Together*
JAMES: And the blacksmith? ⎭
LADY C: Oh! I don't know – out of the window!
JAMES: Then they are drowned.
    (LADY CLUTTERBUCK *faints, and falls into a chair.* MARY *falls
lifeless – a general confusion. Tableau.*)

ACT II

The Interior of WURZEL*'s Farm House. Balustrade across, with stairs leading to it.
Doors leading to Balustrade. Doors at the back. Door at left. Tables and chairs of a
rustic pattern.* WURZEL *discovered, seated at table writing, with a large register.*
WURZEL: Joe! Joe! where can that stupid dolt be? Mary!

Cornwall: obscure – perhaps a reference to the saying that a woman who cuckolds her husband
has sent him to Cornwall without a boat.

MARY: (*appearing on balustrade*) Yes, uncle.

WURZEL: What are you doing up there?

MARY: I am ironing, uncle.

WURZEL: A very pretty fellow that Joe is! here he has been gone above two hours.

MARY: He will be back directly, uncle; I am looking down the lane for him.

WURZEL: If you had not told me that Sir Charles had recommended him, I should have turned the lazy dog out a week ago.

MARY: Why, uncle, you know he brought you a letter from Sir Charles himself, which I saw the poor gentleman write on the day of that dreadful accident, three weeks ago.

WURZEL: A dreadful accident, indeed! I hope it was an accident: people don't think so. It's very lucky, I think, that Sir Charles was drowned, as well as poor Ironbrace. Baronet as he was, he might have been hanged for the murder.

MARY: Oh I am sure, uncle, poor Sir Charles never meant to drown him; but the night was so dark, and there was such a fog on the river, it was impossible to give any assistance.

WURZEL: Well, they haven't found either of them yet, though they've been dragging the river daily; but when they do, there'll be a crowner's quest on them; and then you'll see if they don't bring in a verdict of wilful murder against Sir Charles, that's all.

MARY: What! though he's drowned too?

WURZEL: To be sure. Justice is blind, you know; she's not to know whether he's drowned or not; and Mrs. Ironbrace, or Lady Clutterbuck, or whatever she calls herself, swears she hears Sir Charles say he would fling the blacksmith out of the window. That shows the malice aforethought – oh, I know the law.

MARY: Well, but uncle –

WURZEL: Don't tell me – go, watch for Joe, and finish your ironing.

(*Exit* MARY. *Enter* IRONBRACE – *rushes to* WURZEL, *and throws himself into his arms.*)

IRONBRACE: Save me, my dear friend! save me!

WURZEL: Ironbrace! not drowned?

IRONBRACE: No.

WURZEL: And Sir Charles?

IRONBRACE: Food for the fishes.

WURZEL: Ha! he is dead, then!

IRONBRACE: I'm a wretch, farmer! but I didn't mean it; it was more his fault than mine, after all. I've been wandering about the country ever since, an outcast; I dare not return home, the police would be after me; – save me!

WURZEL: What can I do for you?

IRONBRACE: Hide me somewhere, that's all I ask, till the body's found, and the verdict made public.

WURZEL: What here! on Sir Charles's own farm?

IRONBRACE: This his farm?

WURZEL: Yes; and his heirs and executors are coming here this very day to take possession of the estate.

---

crowner's quest: coroner's inquest.

IRONBRACE: What then? They won't carry it away?

WURZEL: Well, my poor fellow, I'll tell you what I'll do for you – hush – (*Goes to a trap-door and lifts it up.*) – what do you say to that? you'll be snug enough there.

IRONBRACE: What! in that black hole?

WURZEL: I chose it for this reason: this farm was the Manor House of the estate, and in old times these secret recesses were made for the purpose of concealing the Jacobite people, so they say; and the nook is only known to me, now old Sir Arthur Coldstream is dead.

IRONBRACE: But, as I'm not a Jacobite, I'd rather –

WURZEL: Well, well, let me see: – you can hide here, in the wood-room for the present. (*Points off.*)

MARY: (*opening door above*) Uncle! uncle! here's Joe, uncle.

WURZEL: In with you – hide behind the brambles.

IRONBRACE: I'll warrant you I'll creep into a rat-hole, if necessary. (*Exit.*)

MARY: Here's Joe, uncle! – here's Joe. (*She comes down and opens door. Enter* SIR CHARLES, *in the dress of a ploughboy. He advances leisurely, as if weary, and flings himself on a chair.*)

SIR C: Phew!

WURZEL: Why, you impudent dog! is that the way you sit down before your master?

SIR C: No, no, it isn't that – only – oh Lord, I'm tired to death!

WURZEL: A pretty ploughboy, indeed! – tired to death with a few yards.

SIR C: What do you mean by a few yards? – half way to London and back, that's all – twelve miles, I'll bet a hundred!

WURZEL: Bet a hundred! – a hundred what? peas? He talks like a gentleman! Damn me if he could open his mouth wider if he were landlord of the whole estate.

SIR C: You're quite right: Mary, my dear, bring me a basin of soup.

WURZEL: Not a spoonful – go about your business.

SIR C: Well, but damn it!

MARY: Hush!

WURZEL: What's that you say?

SIR C: Nothing, master.

WURZEL: If you had been home at a proper time, you would have had dinner – bacon and cabbage; but it's all gone.

MARY: (*aside*) I've put you a slice by.

SIR C: You're an angel! I'm famished – I've had nothing but a bit of brown bread and an onion all the morning.

WURZEL: Well, did you deliver the letter right?

SIR C: Yes, master.

WURZEL: Then go and put Baldface in the cart, and take that load of hay down to Farmer Beech.

SIR C: Yes, master.

WURZEL: And bring back a load of lime for the corner field.

SIR C: Yes, master. (*to* MARY) I suppose I must go.

MARY: Yes, Joe.

SIR C: I'm nearly done up. Please mayn't I take a lump of bread and cheese to eat by the road?

WURZEL: Not a crumb, you gluttonous rascal; get out!

SIR C: That's the way I'm treated. (*aside*) Mary, dear, crib me a bit, and throw it out of the window. – I'm going, master – oh, *quel inexorable condition – sacre bleu!*

WURZEL: What outlandish Welsh are you jabbering there, you stupid bumpkin! Follow me, sloth; and unless you want to feel the cart-whip, be quick. (*Exit.*)

SIR C: Very pleasant, upon my soul! The respect I meet with from my farmers is quite delightful!

MARY: I won't be an instant with the soup – I've kept it hot on the copper; it was washing-day. It does my heart good to see you so gay – I won't be a moment. (*Exit.*)

SIR C: Gay! it's quite true, I am gay – it's a melancholy thing to reflect upon, but I certainly *am* gay, and yet how can it be? I work like a nigger, and yet I'm as hearty as a buck! When I was – what I was – that is, when I was myself – my table loaded with all the luxuries of the season, I could not eat; the most exquisite wines, and yet I could not drink – I was a puny weakling. Now I drink nothing but spring water, and I drink like a fish; and as for digestion, it's positively horrible to think how I digest – I must have the stomach of an ostrich. It's curious – very curious, I haven't a moment to myself, yet I never feel *ennui*, I'm never bored – I'm never languid; – I breathe – I live again – I exist! It's a very curious thing.

(*Enter MARY, with soup.*)

MARY: Here's the soup!

SIR C: Oh, what a thimble-full! – why, here isn't a pint and a half, I'm sure!

MARY: Yes – but there's the bacon coming.

SIR C: And the cabbage – he said there was cabbage.

MARY: So there is, but do make haste – excuse me, Sir Charles.

SIR C: Hush! – you forget I'm Joe.

MARY: Then, Joe.

SIR C: Dear Joe, if you like.

MARY: Then, dear Joe!

SIR C: There's a darling!

MARY: When you speak to my uncle, try not to use the language of gentlemen, but be a ploughboy in thought.

SIR C: I am, in appetite. (*eating voraciously*)

MARY: You see, I stole you a piece of nice white bread; I made it myself. Oh, I like to see you here so much better than at your fine house. I wish I could render this hard life more agreeable to you.

SIR C: 'Tis beautiful! (*tasting soup*)

MARY: Can you think so?

---

crib: steal (thieves' slang).

quel inexorable condition: what a cruel way of life – by all that's holy. (This is a loose translation of Sir Charles's loose French.)

SIR C: Too much pepper!

MARY: Your life?

SIR C: No, the soup. As for my position, there's but one thing that hangs like a
blight over my life: I've destroyed that of a fellow-creature – that horrible
blacksmith haunts me like the statue of Don Juan – do you know the opera?

MARY: No, dear Joe.

SIR C: In white marble.

MARY: No.

SIR C: Mozart's music. Well, the figure of the wretched blacksmith, he stands
between me and my rest – Hush! – why, 'twas only two nights ago I heard a
noise – looked round – beside me stood –

MARY: Ironbrace!

SIR C: He! – he uttered a hollow moan; – I gasped for breath – stooped my head to
put out the horrid vision, and rushed towards the spectre.

MARY: It was a dream.

SIR C: Not at all, for I broke my head against him or something.

MARY: But, after all, you are not guilty – it was only an accident!

SIR C: I know it; but my conscience conjures up dreadful things; at night, I see
figures – hear voices denouncing me.

MARY: Oh, if I had not paid your steward the £20 I owed him, you might have left
the country with it.

SIR C: I don't want to leave the country; I am happy here; besides, Mary, did you
remark yesterday that I pressed your hand?

MARY: No, I didn't.

SIR C: I did – I pressed it. (*Gets up.*) Fly the country, indeed! – no, Mary, I could
not leave you.

MARY: I have nothing to fear; they wouldn't hang me for concealing you, would
they?

SIR C: Would you wish me, then, to go?

MARY: To go – to – no – but – no – I could not – do not – go, unless, perhaps, you
would fly to her you love.

SIR C: Her I love! (*Approaches her.*) Mary, do you know there's something very
remarkable going on here?

MARY: (*looking round*) Where?

SIR C: No, not there – here! (*touching his heart*)

MARY: What is it?

SIR C: I'll tell you all –

MARY: Hush! (*Puts bowl off.*)

                    (*Enter* WURZEL.)

WURZEL: Joe, Joe, quick, they are here! set the place to rights; the lawyer is
coming, Mr. Fennel, and the gentlemen.

MARY: What gentlemen, uncle?

WURZEL: The heirs and executors!

SIR C: (*aside*) The devil take 'em. (*aloud*) What heirs?

---

the statue of Don Juan: the reference is to the marble statue which brings retribution to the
dissolute hero of Mozart's *Don Giovanni*.

WURZEL: The heirs of Sir Charles Coldstream, who is dead, of course.

SIR C: What!

WURZEL: What's the matter with that fool! – don't you know that Sir Charles is dead, blockhead?

SIR C: Oh, yes, poor devil!

WURZEL: What do you mean, then?

SIR C: Nothing, master. (*going*)

WURZEL: Stop, you idle dog! you are always going when work begins.

MARY: (*aside*) He will be recognised.

SIR C: The letters I took, then, this morning –

WURZEL: Were to appoint his heirs and executors here, to divide the property.

SIR C: (*aside*) I only wanted that to complete me – I shall have to assist at my own cutting up.

WURZEL: Here they are.

SIR C: (*aside*) Will they penetrate this disguise?

(*Enter* FENNEL, LEECH, *and* SAVILLE.)

WURZEL: Welcome, gentlemen! There, Mary – Joe, you dog, place chairs – make haste, you lazy villain!

SIR C: Yes, master. (*He places chairs awkwardly – running against each person, hiding his face.*)

WURZEL: Idle vagabond!

SIR C: Yes, master.

WURZEL: And one at the table, for Mr. Fennel, too. (SIR CHARLES *does so and moves to the side.*) Excuse this awkward booby – he's only a clod – has no idea above sheep-washing.

FENNEL: Don't mention it. To business, gentlemen. Ahem! Gentlemen, Sir Charles Coldstream is dead.

ALL: Hear! hear!

SIR C: The butchers!

FENNEL: The law says it; and, indeed, if he were alive, the law would make him dead, for the law never lies. He would have a bad cause to defend; so, although his body has not been found, I believe he may be considered dead to all intents and purposes.

ALL: Dead, decidedly!

SIR C: (*aside*) Dead as a door-nail! – carried *nem. con.*

LEECH: Everything's for the best – his temper was perfectly insupportable!

SIR C: (*aside*) Good. Go on!

SAVILLE: Proud as Lucifer!

SIR C: (*aside*) Beautiful! Go on!

LEECH: Unfit for our society altogether!

SIR C: (*aside*) In that I perfectly coincide.

FENNEL: Gentlemen, this sealed will was found amongst the papers of the defunct.

SIR C: (*aside*) Here present.

FENNEL: The formula is perfect; after, it then proceeds – 'I leave to Sir Adonis Leech, Capitalist –'

LEECH: Ha!

MARY: (*to* SIR CHARLES) Capitalist! is he rich, then?

SIR C: Not a penny – he inhabits the Capital.

FENNEL: 'My estates in Scotland. To the Honourable Thomas Saville, and the said Adonis Leech, my estates at Kingston-upon-Thames, to be divided equally among them.' – The rest he leaves to his heir-presumptive – a distant relative.

SAVILLE: Well, this is the only reasonable act in his life.

LEECH: Except his death – ha! ha!

SIR C: (aside) Damn his impudence!

SAVILLE: He never enjoyed his money.

LEECH: We did, for him.

SAVILLE: He was a great ass!

SIR C: (aside) 'Pon my soul, this is pleasant! (Takes out snuff-box.)

SAVILLE: Well, Farmer, at what do you value this property?

WURZEL: Not much, sir. Sir Charles said to me, 'Wurzel, my dear fellow –'

SIR C: (aside) The old scoundrel! never saw him in my life before I came here.

WURZEL: 'I must reduce your rent.'

SIR C: What a thumper!

WURZEL: What's that you say?

SAVILLE: Let us view the estate; and suppose we begin with this house: come, Farmer, show us the premises – what's this? (Goes to the door where IRON-BRACE is concealed.)

WURZEL: (aside) The devil! Ironbrace is there! (aloud) I have not the keys with me, gentlemen – I will find them against your return. There, Joe, show these gentlemen over the farm.

SIR C: Me!

MARY: Stay here, I'll go with them – this way, gentlemen. (Exeunt.)

WURZEL: Now to let out the blacksmith. (Exit into wood-house.)

SIR C: So, these are heirs-apparent! – very pretty treatment towards a poor defunct gentleman, who has left them everything! It's enough to disgust any man with drowning himself for the rest of his life. But I won't stand it. – Oh, if I wasn't dead, I'd – stay – ha! – I have it – THE WILL! – here's a brilliant idea! (Runs to table and writes.) So, a codicil on the reverse page – signed – so – now, my friends – date – let's see, on what day was I drowned? – on the 20th – so – the 19th – ah! – there! By-the-bye, there must be two witnesses; let me see – Paul Jones and Jack Robinson.

(Re-enter WURZEL, with IRONBRACE.)

WURZEL: Now to – ha! Joe! (Shuts door on IRONBRACE quickly.) What do you here?

SIR C: Me, master?

WURZEL: You, you dog! To work, sirrah, to work!

SIR C: Ah! I'm going. (aside) Oh, if ever I live to be alive again, I'll double your rent, you old rascal! (Exit up stairs – WURZEL opens door.)

WURZEL: Here, Ironbrace, quick! (Enter IRONBRACE.) You must go down into the secret cellars. They will be back in a moment.

IRONBRACE: It's devilish dark! – you will let me out again?

WURZEL: Yes, yes; but haste.

IRONBRACE: You'll bring me something to eat?

WURZEL: Every moment is full of danger – make no noise – quick! (*They lift trap, centre-stage, and* IRONBRACE *descends.*)

IRONBRACE: I say, that young ploughman of yours is after your niece – take my advice, and –

WURZEL: (*slamming down the trap*) They are here.

(*Enter* FENNEL, LEECH, *and* SAVILLE.)

SAVILLE: I say it shall be.

LEECH: Shall! – Mr. Saville, I have as much right to that expression as yourself.

SAVILLE: Then I'll take legal opinion, sir.

LEECH: Take what you like, but you don't take more than a just half.

FENNEL: (*who has been looking over the will*) Gentlemen, gentlemen, you needn't trouble yourselves to quarrel – look here, is it possible I could have overlooked it?

ALL: What!

FENNEL: A codicil, upon the reverse page.

ALL: A codicil!

FENNEL: Dated the 19th – the day before his death. (*Reads.*) 'As I may do something desperate tomorrow, I hereby annul all my former bequests, and leave my entire real and personal estates to Mary Wurzel, whom I hereby constitute my sole heiress.'

WURZEL: My niece! Tol de rol! (*Dances.*)

LEECH and SAVILLE: This is a fraud!

FENNEL: It is in the handwriting of the defunct, and part of the same deed which made you his legatees. If part is fraud, all is fraud. (*They all look over the will.*)

(*Enter* MARY *with a tray, bearing wine etc.*)

MARY: Allow me, gentlemen, to invite you – here is some fresh cream, and brown bread, and strawberries.

SAVILLE: (*aside*) Ha! a pretty girl! I may regain the fortune.

LEECH: (*aside*) The heiress! – I'll try my luck – why not? I've lost the legacy, but the girl is attackable – here goes.

FENNEL: (*aside*) I was married last week!

SAVILLE: (*to* MARY) I cannot permit one so lovely to serve me.

LEECH: (*on the other side*) Miss Mary, might I beg a look – a –

MARY: What does this mean?

SAVILLE: This is disgusting, Sir Adonis Leech. Never mind, my dear, allow me –

LEECH: The nectar must be delicious, which is served by so charming a Hebe.

MARY: Nectar! – Hebe! – what do you both mean?

WURZEL: Mean? – why, that you are sole heiress to Sir Charles Coldstream's fortune.

MARY: I! (*Suddenly leaves the tray between* LEECH *and* SAVILLE. SAVILLE *leaves hold* – LEECH *is much embarrassed what to do with it – at length puts it on table.*)

WURZEL: So, now you will leave your old uncle?

MARY: Leave you, never! (*Crosses to him.*) But heiress – am I his heiress?

FENNEL: I was Sir Charles's man of business – will you honour me with your orders?

WURZEL: Only assure me that you will not marry.

ALL: Cruel! not marry? what barbarity!

MARY: Where's Joe? – Joe!

LEECH: Who the devil is Joe?

WURZEL: My ploughboy!

SAVILLE: She's in love with him.

(*Enter* SIR CHARLES, *at back.*)

SIR C: (*aside*) So, the fun's begun, it seems.

MARY: (*aside*) Here he comes – they'll recognise him. (*aloud*) Love him? nonsense! Love Joe – a common ploughboy? – besides, he is not worth a shilling,
while I'm an heiress!

SIR C: (*aside*) Ha! – just in time – *Et tu Brute*!

MARY: An ugly clod.

SIR C: Go on.

MARY: A sulky bumpkin!

SIR C: (*aside*) Don't spare me, I'm used to it.

MARY: I certainly might have cast my eyes upon him when I was only a dairy-
maid – but now – oh, no!

SIR C: Can wealth so poison the purest heart? – what a precious world we live in!

MARY: Gentlemen, I must consider your claims – you are both deserving; but if I
must choose a husband at once –

ALL: Undoubtedly!

MARY: Permit me a few minutes' reflection alone.

WURZEL: This way, gentlemen. (*Exeunt* FENNEL, LEECH, *and* SAVILLE. *As
they are going out, each turns to get a look at* MARY; LEECH *returns, kisses
her hand, and exits, followed by* WURZEL, *who returns.*) Don't give up your
liberty. There is not one of them but would spend your fortune in three
weeks, and you would be deserted before the honeymoon was out. Promise
me that you will never marry, but will always remain with your poor uncle.

MARY: I promise nothing at present; wait here a moment for my decision. (*aside*)
Now to find Sir Charles. (*Exit.*)

(SIR CHARLES, *who has hidden himself on the stairs, comes down
and seizes* WURZEL, *who is going.*)

WURZEL: What do you want, Joe? are you mad?

SIR C: I am, nearly.

WURZEL: Mad! – what does the fool mean?

SIR C: There's no longer any fool in the case – excuse me for saying so in your
presence. Listen to me, old Wurzel.

WURZEL: Old!

SIR C: Ay, old as the hills – superannuated!

WURZEL: Me! I am dumb with astonishment!

SIR C: Consent at once to your niece's marrying whom she pleases, or I'll break
every bone in your body.

WURZEL: What!

SIR C: We are alone here.

WURZEL: Well!

SIR C: You are not strong.

WURZEL: And would you take advantage of a feeble old man?

SIR C: Oh, what! you are old now, are you? (*Seizes him.*)

WURZEL: Stay, Joe, you're a good lad, I believe.

SIR C: I am.

WURZEL: Brave.

SIR C: Very.

WURZEL: But rather –

SIR C: Exactly.

WURZEL: I consent to anything you wish.

SIR C: Honour!

WURZEL: Honour! there's no resisting you.

SIR C: I know it. Now, you must forbid those gentlemen thinking of her.

WURZEL: But, my dear Joe, how can I?

SIR C: (*seizing him*) That's your affair.

WURZEL: Well, well, I promise – there!

SIR C: Now you may go.

WURZEL: There's a good lad. (*aside*) The rascal! I'll trounce him for this. Good bye, Joe.

SIR C: Good bye. (*Exit* WURZEL, *shaking his fist behind* SIR CHARLES*'s back.*) Ungrateful girl! on whom I lavished riches – whom I loved! Now, indeed, I feel the lack of that existence which I thought I experienced when I was wealthy.

(*Enter* MARY, *seeing him.*)

MARY: Oh, my dear Joe! what an excellent idea it was to think of disinheriting those wretches.

SIR C: Indeed! do you think so?

MARY: I saw you coming, and feared for your detection. Believe me, Joe, I will most jealously guard your fortune.

SIR C: I've no doubt.

MARY: 'Til means can be found to restore it to you. You can now escape, and gain some foreign country – live free, free!

SIR C: What!

MARY: If I do not seem happy at the thought of your departure –

SIR C: Why, Mary, did you understand, then, that I merely transferred my fortune to your hands for my own use?

MARY: Of course: but fly at once – leave me.

SIR C: Say, before I go, that you love me.

MARY: Love you!

SIR C: You do?

MARY: We shall be overheard.

SIR C: Then here I stop for ever.

MARY: Well, then, I do.

SIR C: She loves me! she loves me! (*Embraces her, and feels his pulse.*) But you love me for myself, not for dinners? (*aside*) How could she – she never was at any of 'em.

MARY: They are coming – what shall I do? they will expect me to choose a husband.

SIR C: Very well, choose me. (*She turns to him, he seizes her in his arms, and kisses her.*)

(*Re-enter* SAVILLE, LEECH, *and* FENNEL.)

SAVILLE: Well, fair lady!

LEECH: Have you made your choice?

ALL: (*seeing* SIR CHARLES *embracing her*) Hollo!

MARY: Permit me, gentlemen, to introduce my future husband.

SAVILLE: Why, surely –

LEECH: Tom!

SAVILLE: Leech!

LEECH and SAVILLE: It's Sir Charles himself!

FENNEL: The defunct!

SIR C: Yes, gentlemen.

LEECH: Not dead?

SIR C: No, I am not, lucky for me; and if I were I should consider it my imperative duty to re-visit you. (LEECH *and* SAVILLE *approach to shake hands.*) Avaunt! Begone, vampires!

FENNEL: (*crossing to him*) Sir Charles Coldstream, excuse me – your position, when you were dead, was a most excellent one, but –

SIR C: (*aside*) The devil! I forgot the damned blacksmith.

FENNEL: But since you are alive –

SIR C: But I am not! I'm dead – dead as a door-nail – dead in law!

FENNEL: My duty is to secure your person.

MARY: Heavens!

SIR C: What for?

FENNEL: Additional evidence has been found against you today.

SIR C: Today! – by whom?

FENNEL: By yourself. Listen: John Ironbrace was drowned on the 20th of August.

SIR C: Well –

FENNEL: On the 19th, you write in your will – 'As I may do something desperate tomorrow – '. I regret to state that you are in an awkward position.

ALL: Oh!

SIR C: I've done it now, that's certain – committed suicide in spite of myself.

LEECH: But Mr. Fennel, surely –

FENNEL: Gentlemen – I must trouble you to clear the room; it shall be guarded until the arrival of the rural police. Farmer Wurzel's now gone for them.

MARY: My dear Joe!

SIR C: I am stunned – that damned codicil! a happy idea!

MARY: And I have been the cause! But I will save him still.

FENNEL: Come, madam. (*Exeunt all but* SIR CHARLES – *the door is shut and bolted.*)

SIR C: It's – it's all over with me! – just as happiness was at last within my grasp. I wish you a good morning – it faded like a spectre from my arms. Poor Mary, 'tis for her sake I suffer. Night is closing in; I shall be left alone here; solitude is hateful to me – since a certain event – especially in the dark: then the spectre rises up before me – a candle end – a sad emblem! we shall last about the time – unhappy analogy! – is there no means of escape? none! Stay! –

surely – yes – I remember my old nurse, Mary's mother, used to tell me tales of this very house – the old Manor House – of the subterranean passages that were underneath the hall, to conceal Jacobites in the rebellion. The hall! this must be it. (*Searches about floor.*) If I could hit on the entrance – stay, here is something like. Let's try – yes, it moves – it is. (*Lifts trap, centre.*) How devilish dark and cold. It's anything but inviting. No matter, I'll go down uninvited. (*Goes down a step and comes up again.*) I tremble in every limb. The idea of a blacksmith not knowing how to swim – it's perfectly ridiculous. (*Exit down trap.*) Help! help! get out! ho! (*They are heard beneath.*)

IRONBRACE: Ha! dog! assassin! Oh, Lord, – oh, dear!

> (*After much confused noise*, SIR CHARLES *lifts up the trap, leaps out, stamps it down, and stands on it.*)

SIR C: Oh, Lord, he's there! I've seen him! I've seen his ghost. There was a rusty, smoky smell about it. I felt the ghost of his arm seize me. I heard the ghost of his voice call me assassin! Through the dim twilight I saw his blue features glaring on me; and then we began just such an infernal waltz as that which preceded our last water excursion – round we spun in the dark, until at last – oh Lord, the thought! – I dealt him a severe punch on the ghost of his head. Oh, Fate, what hast thou next in store for me!

IRONBRACE: (*lifting a trap, right*) So, I'm out at last.

SIR C: No, you don't. (*Rushes to trap, slams it on him, and sits on it.*) Horrors accumulate on me – oh, if this is only the force of my imagination, I wish it would take another subject to amuse itself with!

IRONBRACE: (*raising a trap, left*) Shall I ever get out of this?

SIR C: Never! (*Runs over and slams the trap down.*) He has as many holes in the house as a rabbit warren!

IRONBRACE: (*raising trap, centre*) Here's another!

SIR C: (*slamming it down*) Down! down, perturbed spirit! The ground's drilled like a cullender! What shall I do? I only drowned one, after all, not fifty. I'm on a volcano – an eruption of blacksmiths! (*noise without*) Here comes the police. I won't go – I won't be taken – they shan't remove me – I'm part of the fixtures. I'll stay here in spite of the universe.

> (*Enter* WURZEL, SAVILLE, LEECH, FENNEL, *and* MARY.)

MARY: Where is he? Where is Sir Charles?

LEECH and SAVILLE: Where is our dear friend?

WURZEL: Sir Charles, my dear landlord, you are free.

SIR C: Free!

WURZEL: Ironbrace is preserved.

SIR C: Yes, in spirits – Eugh!

WURZEL: He is no more drowned than you are – see! (*Goes to lift trap, centre.*)

SIR C: Don't – don't! He's there. I saw him – it's his ghost!

WURZEL: His ghost! nonsense! I'll let him out, dead or alive. (*Lifts trap, and* IRONBRACE *ascends.*)

IRONBRACE: Alive, if it's all the same to you.

SIR C: Alive! are you quite sure? Let me touch you. Oh, by Jove! my good friend, you have no idea how pleased I am to see you. Give me your hand.

IRONBRACE: There it is. I am glad enough to see *you* alive, too, I can tell you.

SIR C: Are you pretty well? I've often thought of you. (*aside*) Well, I thought it was very dirty for a ghost.

LEECH: What happiness to recover our friend!

SAVILLE: Joy! joy! (*They cross to him.*)

SIR C: Joy, indeed, my good friends! and, as I am sure you would not like it to be incomplete, do me one favour.

LEECH and SAVILLE: Anything, my dear Sir Charles!

SIR C: Never let me see your faces again.

LEECH and SAVILLE: What!

LEECH: A man of no refinement!

SAVILLE: A perfect brute!

LEECH: Sir Charles, I have the honour – perhaps, when you feel bored with your own company, we shall hear from you?

SIR C: I promise that.

SAVILLE: We shall hear from him tomorrow.

LEECH: Today!

SIR C: Never! And now, with the wisdom and good sense peculiar to Englishmen who have fought – I will explain. I never saw your wife in my life, till the moment you found us together.

IRONBRACE: No!

SIR C: Consequently, your fury was misdirected. Would you know the proper object for your vengeance?

IRONBRACE: I should – hammer and tongs!

SIR C: There he stands! (*Points to* LEECH, *who runs off.*) Don't trouble yourself; he's not worth caring for.

IRONBRACE: You're right: nothing's worth caring for, I believe – the world's a bad one.

SIR C: Pshaw, man! don't talk nonsense. The world's a beautiful world, if people will but think so; isn't it, Mary?

MARY: Yes; but when people run too much after excitement, they may chance to get more than they bargain for.

SIR C: I am a living instance: but my sufferings are now repaid, thanks to the disinterested affection of an artless girl. I've found within this lowly farm what I've sought in vain amidst the dissipation of Europe – a home. Yes! I've had a good lesson. A man's happiness, after all, lies within himself. With employment for the mind, exercise for the body, a domestic hearth, and a mind at ease, there is but one thing wanting to complete his happiness – the approbation of his friends, without which there is nothing in it.

OLD HEADS AND YOUNG HEARTS

A comedy in five acts

First performed at the Haymarket Theatre, London on 18 November 1844, with the following cast:

EARL OF POMPION	Mr. Tilbury
LORD CHARLES ROEBUCK	Mr. H. Holl
COLONEL ROCKET	Mr. Strickland
LITTLETON COKE	Mr. C. Mathews
TOM COKE	Mr. Webster
JESSE RURAL	Mr. W. Farren
BOB	Mr. Buckstone
STRIPE	Mr. T. F. Mathews
RUSSELL	Mr. Carle
COUNTESS OF POMPION	Mrs. W. Clifford
LADY ALICE HAWTHORN	Madame Vestris
MISS ROCKET	Miss Julia Bennett

The Costumes are those of the present day.

ACT I

The Temple. The interior of LITTLETON COKE'*s Chambers, meagerly furnished.*
COKE *is discovered at breakfast, reading the paper.* BOB, *cleaning a Meerschaum.*
LITTLETON: (*reading*) Express from China – um – um – police – um – fashionable
    arrivals. Ha! – at Mivart's, Lord Charles Roebuck, from Paris – my school-
    fellow and college chum – perhaps he has written to me – Bob!
BOB: Sir.
LITTLETON: Any papers for me this morning?
BOB: Yes, sir; one, for the income tax.
LITTLETON: Do we pay that, Bob?
BOB: No, sir, I wish we did.
LITTLETON: (*rising, and coming forward*) How comes it, that during five years'
    hard labour at the bar, I never have had anything to do?
BOB: Yes, sir; law is quite as unprofitable to us now, as it would be to our clients,
    if we had any.
LITTLETON: Have I not angled daily in Westminster Hall?
BOB: While I carried after you a red bag, fat with your unpaid bills, like a landing
    net.
LITTLETON: Without a nibble. (*half apart*) I could almost repent that nature had
    not left me in the insignificance of my birth. What right had the son of a hard-
    working Yorkshire coal-owner to flaunt it at Eton and Oxford, and all
    because my mother, before my birth, dreamed of a woolsack, and so would
    call me Littleton? And yet, while my suppers and stables were declared
    unique – when tufted lordlings exchanged Christian names with me – I
    thought . . . Ha! I see my error – mistook my money for myself. Why was I
    given so keen a sense for enjoyment, and so limited a power of gratifying it?
BOB: But your father, at his death, sir, left you £700 a year.
LITTLETON: To support 7000 appetites he bequeathed me at my birth; so, un-
    fortunately, through life my wants have ever exceeded my means.
BOB: Ah, sir, but wants are the servants of genius.
LITTLETON: Say its masters, rather.
BOB: Your brother in Yorkshire is rich.
LITTLETON: Thanks to my extravagance that made him so; I have mortgaged
    every acre of my land to him.
BOB: If you were to write to him, sir.
LITTLETON: I have done so; (*Postman's knock.*) there's the answer. (*Exit* BOB.)
    It was my last resource.
            (*Re-enter* BOB.)

Mivart's: the most expensive hotel in London during the Regency. It was here that Lady Byron
set up her defences after leaving Byron in 1816.
Westminster Hall: the chief courts of law of England from the thirteenth to the nineteenth
century.
dreamed of a woolsack: a reference to George Lyttelton (1709–73), friend of Pope and
Fielding, who was chancellor of the exchequer in 1756.
tufted lordlings: a reference to the tuft, or golden tassel, worn on their academic caps by titled
undergraduates at Oxford and Cambridge.

BOB: (*weighing the letter*) It feels promising, sir.

LITTLETON: (*Opens and reads.*) 'Dear brother Littleton – Your favour of the 21st
ultimo has duly come to hand – am most happy to find you have not forgot
Sykes Hall, and those in it. Tabby sends her love, and the Rev. Mr. Rural his
blessing – the collieries win fairly – corn is at 50s. and mutton is looking up;
and I am your affectionate brother,

THOMAS COKE.'

BOB: Lord, sir!

LITTLETON: 'Postscript. As to your debts, I can neither afford to give champagne
suppers to your friends, nor pay for the spavined horses they have to sell you;
had you moderated your vanity in the entertainment of a pack of spunging
spendthrifts, you had not now to stoop your pride to a set of honest trades-
men.' (*Tears up the letter.*) I deserved it: let him keep his gold.

BOB: They say he is generous enough on occasion.

LITTLETON: Oh, yes! (*bitterly*) Builds charity schools and endows lying-in hospi-
tals, while his own flesh and blood may rot in a jail! Curse his generosity! his
is all newspaper charity and mouth virtue. Yes, I will apply to my friend:
Bob, did you take that note to Lord St. James?

BOB: Yes, sir; I found him at Mr. Deuceace's.

LITTLETON: (*half apart*) It was but for £20. Well, where is his answer?

BOB: He sent down his compliments, that he was gone to Florence.

LITTLETON: The paltry – Here's a fellow, now, who used to swallow my dinners
and jokes in sunny times, to take away at the first post.

BOB: Yes, sir, swallows always were summer birds.

LITTLETON: No impertinence!

(*A double knock.*)

BOB: (*chopfallen*) Are you at home, sir?

LITTLETON: Yes. (*Exit* BOB.) Home! mine is a sarcasm on the word.

(*Re-enter* BOB.)

BOB: Lord Charles Roebuck, sir. (*Retires upstage.*)

(*Enter* LORD CHARLES ROEBUCK, *and crosses to centre.*)

LITTLETON: Charles, my dear fellow. (*shaking his hand*)

ROEBUCK: The same as ever – I can almost believe myself at College again – and
Bob, too.

BOB: Yes, my lord, promoted from gyp to lawyer's clerk.

ROEBUCK: It seems but a month ago since I roasted you for courting the bedmaker – do you remember?

BOB: Remember! Your lordship tied me along a form before the fire, went out,
and forgot me.

ROEBUCK: You found that night's roasting a cure for love, eh? Well, I'll remember
you this time: there (*giving him a note*) is a plaster for your sore memory.
Vanish!

(BOB *looks at money, and exits.*)

LITTLETON: Why, your long residence in Paris has transmuted you from a model

---

gyp: Boucicault has slipped up here. A gyp was a college servant or bedmaker at Cambridge.
'Scout' is the Oxford equivalent.

for young England into the type of *jeune France*. Some time since we parted
at Alma Mater.

ROEBUCK: Three years; I started immediately for Paris, where my brother was
ambassador plenipotentiary; my father wished me to graduate in diplomacy
under his able *surveillance*.

LITTLETON: And your respected sire, the Home Secretary?

ROEBUCK: I have not seen the Earl since my return.

LITTLETON: How?

ROEBUCK: No! to be candid with you, I'm in a scrape, so I naturally hastened to
you.

LITTLETON: I have, at your service, a stock of advice, generously subscribed by
my friends when I revealed to them the bottom of my purse – proceed.

ROEBUCK: The most ancient of maladies.

LITTLETON: Oh, love?

ROEBUCK: To distraction.

LITTLETON: How? vulgarly, with a woman – or fashionably, with yourself?

ROEBUCK: Listen and judge. Ten days ago, as, in obedience to my father's man-
date, I was on my route from Paris – my chariot was arrested on the Dover
Road, by a spill illustrated with oaths and screams.

LITTLETON: Heroics – by Jove!

ROEBUCK: Post-boy whipping – horses kicking – old gentleman cursing – young
lady screaming and fainting alternately.

LITTLETON: Lucky dog!

ROEBUCK: I disengaged the senseless fair, threw off her bonnet, and unveiled a
face – oh, Coke, such a face! she gasped for breath.

LITTLETON: You lent her some of yours?

ROEBUCK: I did – but she relapsed again.

LITTLETON: Naturally – so you kept her alive by repeated application?

ROEBUCK: Till her father came up.

LITTLETON: She recovered then?

ROEBUCK: Immediately. He thanked me, tucked my angel under his arm, they
re-entered the righted vehicle, and drove on.

LITTLETON: Is that all?

ROEBUCK: Forbid it, Venus – no – with incredible trouble I traced them. The
father – the dragon who guards this Hesperian fruit, is an old East-Indian
Colonel, as proud as Lucifer, and as hot as his dominions. I hovered round the
house for a week.

LITTLETON: Successfully?

ROEBUCK: I saw her once for a second at the back garden gate.

LITTLETON: To speak to her?

ROEBUCK: I hadn't time.

LITTLETON: No? – Oh!

ROEBUCK: No. So I gave her a kiss –

LITTLETON: Excellent economy! and her name –

Hesperian: western. The daughters of Hesperus, in Greek mythology, guarded with the aid of a
dragon the garden in the Isles of the Blest in which grew the golden apples.

ROEBUCK: Is Rocket. Her father, an eccentric old bully, turns his house into a
    barrack – mounts guard at the hall-door – the poor girl can't move without a
    sentry, and I believe her lady's maid is an old one-eyed corporal of artillery.
LITTLETON: Is she rich?
ROEBUCK: She is fair.
LITTLETON: Possibly – a thing to be admired in a *danseuse* or a friend's wife; but
    in the matrimonial stocks, done on our Western 'change, the fairest hue we
    recognise is yellow.
ROEBUCK: Does virtue go for nothing?
LITTLETON: Oh! no; character is indispensable to servant maids, but virtue as a
    word is obsolete; we have, indeed, a French one like it, *vertu*, yes – ladies of
    vertu might signify articles of rarity.
ROEBUCK: Does the lexicon of fashion, then, abjure the sense?
LITTLETON: Certainly not; virtue signifies the strength in a bottle of salts.
ROEBUCK: And vice?
LITTLETON: A – a fault in horses.
ROEBUCK: And religion?
LITTLETON: A pew at St. George's.
ROEBUCK: So 'twould appear that beauty is invested in bank stock, grace consoli-
    dated with the landed interests, while reputation fluctuates with the three
    and a half per cents.
LITTLETON: Exactly; gold is the Medean bath of youth, possessing also a magnetic
    attraction for every cardinal virtue, while all the plagues of Egypt are shut up
    in one English word, and that is *poverty*; the exhibition of which, like that of
    the Gorgon's head, turns the hearts of your dearest friends to stone.
ROEBUCK: Can Mayfair legislation so repeal the laws of nature? by Jove! the West
    End at last will cut the sun because it rises in the east, and live by wax light.
LITTLETON: You, perhaps, may never see the world as I do, Charles, because I am
    poor; but a rich man's view of life is bounded by his parasites – he feels but
    through his glove, and thinks all things are soft.
ROEBUCK: Then I am lost, for my angel is penniless.
LITTLETON: Right, angels are the only things who can be poor and lovely; but to
    marry thus before you have given the worshipful company of mamma brokers
    a chance, is against all rule.
ROEBUCK: Would you have me marry a thing whose mind is bounded by her
    bonnet, a soul perfumed with foreign sentiment – as guiltless of old English
    virtues as her tongue is of their native names. No! I'll have a heart that beats
    with blood – a cheek that's red with it – and be no slave of such a thing of
    scent and paint – but strike one blow for love and human nature.
LITTLETON: Oh, you luxurious dog! (*Embraces him.*) Oh–h! if I could only afford

---

our Western 'change: Boucicault may here be contrasting the Stock Exchange in the City, *east*
of Westminster, with the marriage market in the fashionable *West* End.
vertu: an appreciation of the fine arts and of curios.
St. George's: this church in Hanover Square, built by John James in 1713–24, was particularly
sought after for fashionable weddings.
Medean: Medea restored Jason's father Aeson to youth by boiling him in a cauldron filled with
magic herbs.

to marry a woman instead of a banker's account – but what obstacles oppose your epicurean intentions towards Miss Rocket?

ROEBUCK: I hear my father intends for me the double honour of a seat in the house, and a wife – my cousin, Alice, the wealthy young widow of Lord George Hawthorn.

LITTLETON: Lady Alice – who shook the very apathy of the opera last week, by demanding to be balloted into the omnibus box!

ROEBUCK: Such a wife – why do they not give her a commission in the blues, at once?

LITTLETON: She flashed into our fashionable system like a new comet, whose eccentricity defied all known law, and quickly drew after her a train that obliterated all the constellations of St. James's, and the heavenly bodies of Mayfair.

ROEBUCK: You know her, then?

LITTLETON: A Polka acquaintanceship! I've been introduced to her waist; we know each other in the houses of our mutual friends – but of what use can I be here?

ROEBUCK: The greatest. My father has arranged my nomination for Closeborough; I shall be obliged to advocate his political principles in the house, to which party old Rocket is a virulent opponent.

LITTLETON: What's to be done?

ROEBUCK: My father – and thus; oblige me by opposing my election, and I will answer for your success.

LITTLETON: Ha! ha! help me to your borough – why, you rascal, would you make the Home Secretary purchase in a talented member for the opposition?

ROEBUCK: Consent.

LITTLETON: With all my heart; I see but one obstacle – the qualification!

ROEBUCK: The three hundred a year – that's true – stay – Coke, at Eton you were considered a fellow of great pluck.

LITTLETON: You flatter.

ROEBUCK: You look tenacious of life.

LITTLETON: Ha!

ROEBUCK: I'll make you a present of the widow.

LITTLETON: Lady Alice?

ROEBUCK: If she have not, ere this, volunteered to Morocco or Macao.

LITTLETON: Charles, to oblige you I accept the borough – for your sake I'll encounter the widow and the five thousand a year.

(BOB *rushes in.*)

BOB: Sir – sir – they are come –

LITTLETON: They – who?

BOB: Two of the fattest clients, sir, you ever saw.

---

omnibus box: the name given to the large and capacious boxes, introduced at the Paris Opera by Dr Veron in 1831, and soon imitated by the English.
Polka: the polka's popularity dates from *c*. 1844.
three hundred a year: the property qualification for a member of parliament was £300 per year in income from land ownership.

LITTLETON: Clients? You are mad, or a fool.

BOB: Neither, sir – but I think they are both.

LITTLETON: Stay – come here. Bob – (BOB *crosses to* LITTLETON.) what are they like?

BOB: One, sir, is a very respectable old gentleman in black, white hair –

LITTLETON: Scriven, the attorney and money lender. The other?

BOB: A responsible – sort of – sporting character.

LITTLETON: Craft, the bailiff – I'm ruined!

ROEBUCK: What's the debt? perhaps I –

LITTLETON: No, Charles – to be honest with you, my hopes are too slender to bear an obligation. I'm as low in pride, now, as I am in pocket, and cannot afford to turn a friend into a creditor.

BOB: They are just on this landing, sir.

ROEBUCK: Come with me. I can offer you a room at my father's till your election is over.

BOB: Step inside, sir; while they come in, you can go out by the other door.

LITTLETON: Farewell, fond visions of the woolsack: Bob, give up my chattels, let them take possession.

BOB: All right, sir; a table, two chairs, a bed, and a boot-jack. (*Exeunt at the back centre, followed by* BOB. *After a pause, knocking is heard, left. Enter* RURAL.)

RURAL: Littleton! Littleton! Litt – eh! – bless me, nobody! Tom, come in.
           (*Enter* TOM COKE.)

TOM: I'm here, minister; so these be brother Littleton's chambers – well, they don't look prodigal, neither.

RURAL: No, no, but where is he?

TOM: And they ca' this the Temple, eh? It'll be moire loike a coil hoile aboove ground than owt else a knaw; well, minister, you would coome up to town wi' me; here we are – what next?

RURAL: My dear boy, I know that you feel an old man like me a burthen on you – now you are a great man, a member of parliament.

TOM: That's onkind of yaw, minister, and you're not given to say cruel things; why, isn't your face the very first thing in the world I can remember? haven't you been a father to us since we were left orphans? a burthen! that's the hardest word you spoke since you taught us catechesm wi' brother Littleton sitting on one knee and I on t'oother.

RURAL: Think of that, Tom, do; and to see you united again is my prayer.

TOM: But wha couldn't yaw wait until we had set down quietly in the Earl of Pompion's house, according to his invitation? 'Twas main kind of him, minister; he's the Home Secretary, and the next post after I was made member o' Parliament brought me a hearty invitation to his house: that's hospitality.

RURAL: But where is Littleton?

'The language used by Tom Coke is written in a broad dialect, to distinguish the character, but should be acted with an accent only; and in Provincial Theatres, should not be given to the gentleman performing Yorkshiremen, but to the eccentric comedian.' (Note in French's Standard Drama No. LXII, p. 14)

TOM: I'll tell ye: – in bed, sleeping off his last night's debauch, or wi' flushed and haggard cheek, still leaning over the gambling table.

RURAL: No, Tom, no! my little pupil, my child! a gambler! – no! he was wild, sensitive, but you know he was never –

TOM: I know no more than this – I remember him, the rapture of my poor mother, the hope of my father – and you, you always loved him best.

RURAL: Tom, Tom, don't reproach me!

TOM: Reproach! nay, not so – Nature gave him a great mind, me only an honest one. He was born for greater things than I, and so he had all that wealth could lavish on him – I didn't grudge it him – he fed from the silver plate, I from the wooden platter – I cared nuaw't for that; but at his grand school, why did he find the houses of my lord this, and marquis that, more welcome than his own home? I don't reproach, mind – but – but when our mother died I stood alone by her – and her last breath prayed for him. I wasn't jealous, minister; but in my father's will, the part that gave me my inheritance was writ in the hard hand of a lawyer's clerk, while the gift to Littleton, with a blessing, was penned by the trembling fingers of my father, and blotted wi' his tears. I've tried to hate him.

RURAL: Tom!

TOM: I did, but I couldn't. The same strange love you all showed for him, I shared wi' you – a'most against ma will – and when those short heartless letters would come, containing nowt but calls for money – money – money – I could ha' freely *given* ten times what I *lent*, for but four words of heart's blood in 'em, if 'twor but 'God bless ye, Tom'.

RURAL: And he will say so when he sees you – he will. Think what a dear child he was – so clinging, affectionate, innocent. (*spoken very affectionately*)

TOM: Ye forget, that was fifteen years ago.

RURAL: Was it? – bless me – so it was – but you remember how generous, and kind, and wild he was – how I doted on the trouble he used to give me; and how clever – quite overpowered my faculties. I could never teach him anything but cat's cradle.

      (*Re-enter* BOB.)

      Oh, here is his servant.

      (BOB *advances, whistling, and sits on the table.*)

TOM: Where be thy measter, lad?

BOB: Beyond your clutches, vampire! Oh, you may stare!

TOM: What dost mean?

BOB: Why, that the paltry debt I suppose you come to sue for, will be paid.

TOM: My debt? he knows me, then?

BOB: Unhappily, he does.

TOM: Is this his welcome when a come to tak him by the hand?

BOB: By the collar, you mean – oh, there, seize – seize! – your sort don't refuse even two-pence in the pound.

TOM: This is too much. (*Attempts to get at* BOB.)

RURAL: Stop, don't be rash! let me see the boy. (*Crosses to table, and puts on his spectacles.*) My good boy, I'm sure you will tell me where your master is. (*looking* BOB *in the face affectionately*)

BOB: Oh, you precious old rascal!

RURAL: Good gracious!

BOB: Aren't you ashamed of yourself?

TOM: Let me at him.

RURAL: (*holding* TOM) No! no! Tom, I insist.

BOB: I say it again – you *are* vampires, leeches, and, though I am nothing but a poor servant, before I would do a day's work like this, I'd see all the gains your trade has ever wrenched from misery sunk to the bottom of the sea – ach! (*Exit slamming the door.*)

TOM: Well, minister, ar't satisfied now?

RURAL: He never could intend –

TOM: Intend – didn't he know us – he spoke of my debt – oh, 'twas done by his orders – let us go.

RURAL: He called me an old rascal – and asked me if I wasn't ashamed of myself – ashamed of – coming.

TOM: Come, come, your errand's over – forget him.

RURAL: To me – to me – my hopes – my fond, fond hopes of seeing him again – of reconciling – of – oh, Tom!

TOM: And I, too – but no matter – I loos him off for ever – you shall return today to Yorkshire.

RURAL: No, not yet – there's some – some mistake – forgive him.

TOM: I cared nowt for what he said o' me, but to insoolt you, his old friend, his father!

RURAL: Yes – but he could not mean to – to –

TOM: Why, dommed if ye beant crying. The villain – coom – don't take on so – the – the –

RURAL: No – never mind.

TOM: I wouldn't – if I could only get one crack at his poll, I'd forgive him.

RURAL: Don't be violent. I can't – I won't believe my ears against my heart. I'll see him – I'll talk to him as I used.

TOM: The heartless reprobate.

RURAL: (*sternly*) Tom, I'll not allow you to speak so of your little brother.

TOM: Nay, 'taint bad enough, that's sure.

RURAL: God bless me! there – your violence has made me swear – I declare I shall be angry: now, my dear Tom – if you will only leave it all to me, and have patience, you will see that I am right. (*going, followed by* TOM *grumbling*)

TOM: Go on – defend him again –

RURAL: If only you will be quiet.

TOM: T'ould man's getting crazy, I'm thinking.

RURAL: And have patience – now only a little patience.

>   (*Exeunt*, RURAL *crying and expostulating, followed by* TOM, *grumbling.*)

ACT II

LADY POMPION's *Boudoir. Decorated in Arabesque, furnished very richly in buhl and marqueterie, divans, priedieux, causeuses, bergères and dormeuses, covered in chintz; tambour frame, and work tables – ornamental writing table – alabaster French clock – Indian screen, etc.* LADY POMPION *discovered reclining on a bergère, with her feet shawled on an Ottoman, and a spaniel in her lap.*

LADY P: (*yawning and closing a book*) Really, parliament ought to do something for that dear creature, Eugène Sue. I'll speak to the Earl about it! (*Strikes a gong.*)

> (*Enter a richly liveried* SERVANT.)

Has Willis sent out those invitations?

SERVANT: Yes, my lady.

LADY P: I am not at home this morning to anyone.

SERVANT: Lord Charles Roebuck, my lady, is expected every moment.

LADY P: Oh, true! Charles does arrive today from Paris: well, tell him the number of my box at the Opera, and my hour in the ring. I dare say we shall meet – my nerves are not equal to receiving him now.

> (*Loud and peculiar knock.*)

Good heavens! can that be he?

SERVANT: No, my lady! that is Lady Alice Hawthorn's tiger.

LADY P: I'm not at home – I could never survive that girl an hour.

> (*Enter* LADY ALICE HAWTHORN.)

LADY A: Then prepare to die, my dear aunt, for here I am for the day – ha! ha! (*to the* SERVANT) Tell my groom to bring my carriage at nine. (*to* LADY POMPION) You will excuse my leaving your table at so early an hour, but I never miss the last act of the Barbiere.

LADY P: My head – my head – the salts – the restoratives.

LADY A: Tom – bring the liqueur case. (*Exit* SERVANT.) Ha! ha! well, my dear, I heard of Charley's arrival, so I have come to dine with you – tell me, what is he like? – partiality apart – is he worth making love to?

LADY P: Charles has not yet arrived home.

LADY A: Why, I saw by the *Post* that he arrived in town last night.

LADY P: Indeed! ah! well! – he might as well have sent a card.

LADY A: A card! has he not rattled you up at four in the morning – broken in your knocker panel, and pulled up the bell by the roots? Hasn't he dislocated your wrist and kissed you into an asthma? Hasn't –

LADY P: Lady Alice, my son has not the manners of Abdel-Kader to take my

---

Eugène Sue: French novelist and playwright (1804–57), who trained as a naval surgeon, got involved in several scandals, and wrote the enormously successful *Les Mystères de Paris* in 1843.
in the ring: the Ring in Hyde Park was a display ground for high fashion on horseback and in carriages.
tiger: a liveried groom, or footman.
Barbiere: Rossini's *Barbiere di Siviglia* (1816) was one of the outstanding favourites of the English operatic stage in the nineteenth century. Boucicault would have remembered the Queen's visit to it on 20 July 1843 at Her Majesty's Theatre, when the basso Luigi Lablache (active in the London opera from 1830 to 1852) and the soprano Giulia Grisi (active in the London opera from 1834 to 1861) were among the singers.
Abdel-Kader: perhaps a reference to the Algerian national leader Abd al Kader (1808–83), whose resistance to the French from 1832 to 1844 made him a religious hero. After his defeat at the battle of Isly in 1844, the Moslem cause was lost. Boucicault presumably thought of him, as he later thought of Nana Sahib in *Jessie Brown*, as an oriental savage.

establishment by such a surprise, and I trust he always leaves bells and
knockers to the servants.

LADY A: Does he? then Charley's occupation's gone indeed. But *apropos*, Georgy,
what fun I had with your old Earl last night at Almack's, ha! ha! ha!

LADY P: My old Earl!

LADY A: He came in, thawed with a decent dinner; the premier's Steinburg had
given the *cadavre* a bloom; 'pon my life he talked impudence to me.

LADY P: The Earl of Pompion!

LADY A: It would have delighted you to watch such signs of restored animation.
A knot of politicians had nearly secured him – politics at Almack's – I darted
in amongst them, crying 'treason', seized Pompey himself, and whirled him
into the most delirious polka. (*Hums a polka.*)

LADY P: A polka!

LADY A: Toe and heel, as I'm a widow and a sinner; we threw Jullien into extacies,
till I restored the Home Secretary to his party, a wiser and a better man.
(*Enter* LORD POMPION.)
Didn't I, Pompey?

LORD P: Lady Alice *est toujours gaie*. Where's my countess?

LADY A: Not up yet, look! (*Points to* LADY POMPION, *who is pulling her
spaniel's ears.*) Or stay, she is making Bichon's toilette.

LORD P: I forgot to mention that I expect Mr. Coke, of Yorkshire, on a visit: he
has lately been returned for Ashby, and I want his interest and a loan to
secure Charles for Closeborough – we must show him attention.

LADY P: Very well, write down his name, and I'll send it to the housekeeper.

LADY A: Long live old English hospitality.

LORD P: He has some of his family with him.

LADY P: They can have the britzska, and you must manage something for their
Opera – leave it to the housekeeper.

LADY A: Talking of visitors, I have invited a couple to you.

LADY P: To us!

LADY A: Yes – Colonel Rocket and his daughter; old friends of mine. My *bonbonnière* in Brook Street only holds me and my plagues, but, fortunately, having
a card of yours in my case, I thought how glad you'd be. I mentioned six as
your dinner hour. Don't be anxious – they'll be here in a minute.

LORD P: How rash – he may be of the opposition.

LADY A: An East India Director, with two boroughs. (*aside*) Rabbit ones.

LADY P: Is the girl presentable?

Almack's: this great ballroom in King Street had its heyday as a fashionable resort during the
Regency.
Jullien: Louis Antoine Jullien (d. 1860) established promenade concerts in England. His social
successes as a musician led him into debt and decline. He died insane after a spell in prison.
britzska: open carriage with folding top and reclining space.
bonbonnière: a fancy box for holding sweets, here used figuratively to describe a 'little bijou
residence'.
Brook Street: a fashionable street, joining Hanover Square and Grosvenor Square, and crossing
Bond Street on the way.
rabbit ones: the pun on boroughs/burrows tells us something about received pronunciation.

LADY A: Met them at Devonshire House –

LORD P: Two boroughs! my dear Alice, you are rash, but you mean well.

LADY A: Of course I do – only think of two boroughs, Pompey. (*aside*) A half-pay colonel, with less interest than a treasury clerk, but a glorious old fellow. I'll bet he'll kiss the Countess in a week – what fun!

> (LADY ALICE *and* LORD POMPION *retire upstage. Enter a* SERVANT.)

SERVANT: Lord Charles Roebuck.

> (*Enter* ROEBUCK, *followed by* LITTLETON COKE.)

ROEBUCK: My dearest mother!

LADY P: Ah! Charles, how d'ye do, dear? (*Lifts her eye-glass.*) Bless me, how brown you're grown – for heaven's sake, take care of Bichon, there. (*Shakes his hand over the dog.*) Have you brought me the Eau de Cologne?

ROEBUCK: Yes, everything – but, my dear mother –

LADY P: Dear – how old he looks for a son of mine.

LORD P: (*advancing*) But undoubtedly improved.

ROEBUCK: My dear father, forgive me! (*offering both his hands*)

LORD P: (*regarding him*) A Pompion, decidedly.

LADY P: Tell me, Charles, your Italian is Roman – and – ah! I see you wear *Bouquet du Roi*. I understand that *esprit d'Isabella* was the court scent at the Tuilleries, just now.

LORD P: Of course, your present appearance is the remains of a diplomatic compliment to the Court of Versailles – very judicious.

LADY P: I trust, Charles, you have picked up no foreign immoralities – I mean, you go to church sometimes; we have a pew at St. George's – and, apropos, have *glacé* silks gone out yet, in Paris?

ROEBUCK: Really, dearest mother, I didn't notice.

LADY P: Ah! boys are so thoughtless.

LORD P: You don't make yourself remarkable in dress or equipage, Charles?

LADY P: I hope you have no *penchant* for *liaisons* with public people or unmarried women, dear?

LORD P: Every notoriety, which is not political, is hurtful.

LADY P: I trust you don't swear, Charles – I mean in English; and excuse the anxiety of a mother – you continue to use the almond paste I wrote to you about?

LORD P: Apropos – you'll find in my room a list of the doubtful ones of our party, so that you may know where to lose your money, at Crockford's – of course, you will not enter any of the lower gaming clubs – and, by the bye – be cool to Vernon.

ROEBUCK: My dear father – my schoolfellow, Dick Vernon, once saved my life.

LORD P: Possibly – but he voted against us on the Barbadoes Bill, and he has

---

Devonshire House: only the gates remain of this Whig stronghold in Piccadilly. The sixth Duke of Devonshire (1790–1858) was a celebrated party host. That there was much gambling at his 'parties' is clear from a well-known Rowlandson print.

Crockford's: this club in St James's Street was at the height of its fashionable notoriety in the 1830s. The gaming-room was its nerve-centre. When 'Crocky' died in 1844, he had made £1,200,000 out of high-society losers.

talked of conscientious principles, and in presence of the Premier – in short –
he was omitted in the Premier's dinner yesterday – of course, you speak
German?

LADY P: Do you bet?

LADY A: Do you polk?

ROEBUCK: Blest voice – surely – it is –

LADY A: Your cousin Alice – how are you, Charley? (*He hesitates.*) All right – go
on – (*He crosses to her.*) I'm human nature! (*He kisses her.*) What's your
friend's name? We are acquainted, I know – but I can't recollect who he is!

ROEBUCK: (*aside*) Coke – I had almost forgotten him – what can he think of my
cold reception? how frigidly they will receive him – I am fairly ashamed to –
(*Brings* COKE *down.*) My lord and lady, mother, allow me, Mr. Coke.

LORD P: Coke! of Yorkshire? (*Crosses to him.*)

LITTLETON: Yes.

LORD P: Ashby?

LITTLETON: The same.

LORD P: (*heartily*) My dear sir, I'm delighted to see you! (*shaking him by both
hands*) delighted! this *is* an unexpected pleasure, to find in you a friend of my
son's; allow me – the Countess – Mr. Coke, of Ashby.

LADY P: Mr. Coke, of Ashby! Take care of Bichon, ha! ha!

ROEBUCK: Mr. Coke – Lady Alice Hawthorn, with whom the whole world is in
love.

LADY A: Speak for yourself, sir.

> (LADY ALICE *speaks aside with* LITTLETON. LADY POMPION
> *sounds a gong, and a* SERVANT *enters, unwraps her feet and wraps
> the dog in the shawl.*)

LORD P: You will excuse me, Mr. Coke – the business of the nation – till dinner,
eh? *sans adieu!* (*Shakes his hand.*) Charles, I can spare you a moment; follow
me to my study. (*Exit.*)

LADY P: Adieu, Charles! *au plaisir*, Mr. Poke – bye-bye, Alice.

LADY A: Adieu, Bichon.

> (*Exit* LADY POMPION, *followed by* SERVANT *carrying the dog.*)

ROEBUCK: What can this mean? Coke received with such fervour – and this – this
is my return, after three years' absence! well! (*going*)

LADY A: I say, Charley, are *glacé* silks out in Paris?

ROEBUCK: By heaven!

LADY A: Ah! ah! I hope you don't swear – I mean in English! ah! ah! ah! (*Exit*
ROEBUCK. *Aside*) So! a pair of recruits to my staff.

LITTLETON: (*aside*) And this glorious creature is the deadly widow whom Roebuck
gives up without a sigh.

> (*A pause*)

LADY A: Well, Mr. Coke, if you have nothing droll to say, give us your maiden
speech; on what question do you come out?

LITTLETON: To love, or not to love!

LADY A: I'll settle that – to love – carried, eh?

LITTLETON: Without a division. (*Kisses her hand.*)

LADY A: (*aside*) Hang the fellow's impudence. – Well, if you can't say something funny, make me cry; I haven't cried since my marriage, except with laughing. You are on a visit here, eh? you will find it a horrid bore.

LITTLETON: I can view it only as a paradise at present; when your ladyship leaves it, I may see in it a desert.

LADY A: Are you an old friend of my cousin's?

LITTLETON: Lord Charles and I entered Eton on the same day, and never parted for nine years – I may say we are brothers.

LADY A: I have a secret with which I mean to electrify the old folks here – I want a partner in the scheme – can I trust you?

LITTLETON: With your whole heart.

LADY A: Miss Rocket, a friend of mine, is in love with my cousin Charles here – don't stare! – I found it out, and have asked her on a visit.

LITTLETON: To supplant yourself! – why, the Earl sent for Roebuck home, to – expressly – to – marry you.

LADY A: Me! oh, the old fox! Ha! ha! so – so! – so much the better: I'll teach him to keep his intrigues within Whitehall. To begin, then, let's be friends.

LITTLETON: Ah! beware, Lady Alice! the friend of a young and lovely woman should have sixty years, at least, and holy orders for his qualification.

LADY A: Young man, take my advice; a woman never likes her lover to be more careful of her character than she is herself, or too provident in his heart's economy; your sex arrogates too much on the solitary advantage which nature has given it over ours.

LITTLETON: What is that?

LADY A: You are born without reputation. – What club owns you?

LITTLETON: None!

LADY A: Right – allow neither your opinions nor your society to be dictated to you; – what clique claims you?

LITTLETON: Only one – (*aside*) the Queen's Bench – (*aloud*) but they are too exclusive and confined for me.

LADY A: You love liberty?

LITTLETON: As a mistress likely to be lost.

LADY A: You are a man after my own heart.

LITTLETON: I am, and I trust soon to come up with it.

LADY A: What is the world?

LITTLETON: A gentler synonym for vice in town.

LADY A: It seems to me that your sex is capable of but two characters – selfish politicians or reckless gamesters. Did modern chivalry erect new orders, one half nobility would range under the folds of a minister's tablecloth, while the other would canonize Crockford.

LITTLETON: Fair play, Lady Alice, or I must assert my sex.

LADY A: A challenge! tell me, as this sex of yours has adopted every effeminacy of soul in its desire to change genders with ours, when will you assume the fan and flacon?

---

flacon: smelling-bottle.

LITTLETON: When ladies who have already engrafted the whip on the parasol, revel in tops and inconceivables.

LADY A: Women must adopt your habits, if left at home to exercise those duties of husbands which you are performing in every house but your own.

LITTLETON: At home! are ladies ever 'at home', except, indeed, when under that pretext they invite the world to see their houses turned out of doors.

LADY A: To exhibit a satire upon men who regard matrimony as a ministerial sinecure.

LITTLETON: (*half apart*) The duties of which are only known to the deputy.

LADY A: True; men, whose friendship means a design against a wife's heart, and whose honor only retains its existence for the convenience of swearing by: – spirit represents to them but a contempt of morality, while to pay has reference to nothing but visits.

LITTLETON: Ahem! (*aside*) she's becoming personal.

LADY A: Aha! (*aside*) that hit him in the conscience.

LITTLETON: Were I a woman, such a contemplation of society would almost drive me to suicide.

LADY A: A fashionable alternative and genuine French. I've thought of it – but decided on *not* doing the world the honor of cutting it.

LITTLETON: (*aside*) What a gorgeous creature. Can I believe that such an angel could ever be my property?

LADY A: Now you are puzzling whether to propose to me next week or the one after – delay it. Meanwhile, make most of your time. I'll send you a voucher for Almack's – I'm a patroness, you know – here's my polka card – let's see; I'm engaged for the first, fifth, ninth, and seventeenth. (*Sits on ottoman.*)

LITTLETON: Put me down for all the rest. Enchantress, you divine my very heart. (*Sits by her.*)

LADY A: What wonder, when you are going to swear that I possess it.

LITTLETON: Ridicule me, if you will. Yes, I confess it. I came here to see you – to woo you – perhaps to mock – be merciful, for see (*Sits on the ottoman at her feet.*) – I remain to pray.

LADY A: (*opening his hand and applauding on it with her own, as she eyes him through her glass*) Bravo – not bad – get up now, there's a dear man. I promise not to flirt with anyone else for one calendar week – there, don't be vain; I once patronized a boy in the guards for two days, and now he won't enter the pit of the opera during an aria for fear of engaging the attention of the house.

LITTLETON: (*seizing her hand*) Torturess – (*He pauses.*)

LADY A: Go on.

LITTLETON: (*looking at her hand*) You leave it in mine?

---

tops: the turned-over uppermost part of a riding-boot – or a broad band of material simulating it.

inconceivables: I assume this to be a euphemism for trousers, though I have traced only 'indescribables', 'unspeakables', 'unmentionables', 'inexplicables', 'unwhisperables', and 'unutterables' to the first half of the nineteenth century.

LADY A: Certainly, till you have kissed it – (LITTLETON *kisses her hand. They come forward.*) Hang the fellow, he does not think I'm gone so far in love with him as to snatch it away.

LITTLETON: I know not what to think, but this I know, that I'm the happiest wretch you ever doomed to misery.

(*Enter* COLONEL ROCKET.)

ROCKET: Aha, my little congreve – I've been looking for you everywhere.

LADY A: So, Colonel, I proved a sort of invisible shell, eh?

ROCKET: Only twice as mischievous; I do believe one like you would unman a whole fleet. Ah! your friend in the army?

LADY A: On my own staff! Colonel Rocket – Mr. Coke.

(ROCKET *crosses to* LITTLETON.)

ROCKET: Coke! any relation to Cook of the 23rd? no! ah! sorry for it! brave fellow – cut in two by a chain shot at Pullinabad; was knocked down by his top half myself – gallant fellow – bought his kit for 100 rupees.

LADY A: Where's Kate?

ROCKET: I picqueted her in the hall with the baggage – happy to make you acquainted, sir – brought her up for a soldier's wife – perfect in her facings as a light company, and can manoeuvre a battalion with any adjutant in the service; look at her walk, thirty inches regulation pace – head up – left leg forward – perfection! that's the way to put a girl into the hands of a husband, sir.

LADY A: (*aside to* LITTLETON) She twists the old fellow round her finger like a purse!

(MISS ROCKET *screams without.*)

ROCKET: Hollo! that's her discharge – she is retiring upon her supports.

LADY A: Here she comes, as wild as game in July.

ROCKET: Observe how steady she will file in – right wheel.

(KATE ROCKET *runs in, her bonnet hanging on her neck.*)

KATE: He's here – I saw him – I –

ROCKET: Hollo! fall in – halt – the devil – discipline!

KATE: Yes, my dear father, presently – but I believe he lives in this very house.

ROCKET: Report yourself! Who?

KATE: The gentleman who kissed – I mean, who assisted me when we were upset. He rushed up to me in the hall here – and I was so – I screamed – I – here he is.

(*Enter* ROEBUCK.)

ROEBUCK: Can I believe my eyes? (*aside, seeing* ROCKET) Old Chili vinegar, by Jove!

ROCKET: Steady, Kate – stand at ease – now, sir, might I ask why, sir – you – you – damme, sir – why do you drive in my picquet in this way?

ROEBUCK: Really – sir – I – I –

LADY A: (*advancing*) Permit me, Colonel, to introduce to you Lord Charles Roebuck, son of the Earl of Pompion, who is too happy in being your host.

---

congreve: a rocket for use in war, invented in 1808.
facings: the cuffs and collar of a military jacket, of a different colour from the jacket itself. Rocket may be using the word in its military sense of 'turning to face in another direction'.

ROCKET: Sir, your hand. No apology enough – I accept the quarters. Roebuck, in the army? – no! – any relation to Rover of the 81st, retired on full pay and two wooden legs, after Nepaul? No! no matter – my daughter, Kate Rocket – Bombay Cavalry.

ROEBUCK: Allow me to apologise. (*aside*) Whom have I to thank for this? (*crossing to* KATE)

LADY A: (*aside*) Me! I'm in the secret – she has confessed all to me – I invited them here – am I not an angel?

ROEBUCK: (*aside*) A divinity! How do you find Coke?

LADY A: As impudent as an heiress!

ROEBUCK: My father mistook him for his brother, whose arrival has rectified the error – I have left him closeted with the Earl. (*Goes up to* KATE.)

LADY A: Now, Colonel, to introduce you to Lady Pompion – your arm? (*taking* ROCKET's *arm*)

ROCKET: Kate, present arms to our host, and follow.

LADY A: Executed with wonderful dispatch.

ROCKET: Discipline!
　　　　　(ROEBUCK *and* KATE, *in earnest tête-à-tête, go upstage.*)

LADY A: Only they are marching without orders.

ROCKET: Hollo! halt – attention! (ROEBUCK *and* KATE *go out, still conversing, without apparently hearing him.*) It's nothing – a mere manoeuvre – but we mustn't club the battalion. We only constitute the reserve, instead of the advance – a clever movement of Kate's?

LADY A: Very –

ROCKET: What we call a diversion.

LADY A: Yes, very diverting indeed – ha! ha!
　　　　　(*Exeunt.*)

LITTLETON: So now, fate, I'm thy worshipper forever – do with me what you will: this morning I arose with fewer hopes than a Pennsylvanian bondholder; my belief in hearts was restricted to the thirteen in a pack of cards – and here I am, in a few hours, domiciled in Grosvenor Square, with expectations beyond a new railway company.
　　　　　(*Enter* RURAL.)
Strange, too – hum!

RURAL: They tell me Littleton is here – in this house – if I could only – this gentleman, perhaps, might – pray, sir?

LITTLETON: (*throwing himself into a chair*) Come what may to Thomas Coke, I'll never sign myself a brother.

RURAL: Thomas Coke! let me look – (*Takes out his spectacles tremblingly.*) yes, yes, it is he – it is – he stares at me – he won't know me now.

LITTLETON: What a strange old gentleman!

RURAL: I tremble to – to – ask him; if he should meet me as a stranger – or – how altered he is – in form: perhaps he's changed in –

LITTLETON: (*starting up*) By heaven! I know that face.

RURAL: Mr. Coke – I – ventured – I – you don't forget your tutor – friend – Jesse Rural.

LITTLETON: (*running to him and taking both his hands*) Forget you! may Heaven forget me when I do!

RURAL: Ha! ha! ha! (*embracing him*) bless you, my child – God bless you! I knew it – I knew you wouldn't – no – let me look at you – yes – it is you!

LITTLETON: Tell me, how came you here, in town, and in this house?

RURAL: Tom came up to Parliament – you know he is member now for Ashby.

LITTLETON: (*aside*) Ha! that accounts, then, for the Earl's warm welcome – mistook me for him.

RURAL: So I accompanied him to town.

LITTLETON: And he is in this house?

RURAL: Yes, he is dressing for dinner. I heard that you were here, and could not contain myself – came to bring you to him; he is unaware of your presence.

LITTLETON: What, creep on my knees to his purse like a prodigal son! In what have I injured him? He has my land. I wrote to offer to sell him the mortgages he held – he refused me.

RURAL: The same wild, violent spirit he always had – just the same, ha! ha! Littleton, listen to me, my dear boy; Tom loves you, you don't know him. When we went to your chambers this morning –

LITTLETON: You, you! (*aside*) It must have been them whom Bob announced, and I mistook for Scriven and Craft.

RURAL: Tom was prepared to forgive you.

LITTLETON: Forgive! 'tis I who claim that office.

RURAL: Ha! he! there he flies out again – the dear boy!

LITTLETON: Let him ask my pardon! – I entreat you will not attempt a reconciliation; it would only sever us more certainly.

RURAL: But listen – my darling child, listen – Tom always meant to give you the money you asked for – (*aside*) God forgive me! (*aloud*) See, here is the very, very sum – look – bless you, take it! (*Takes out a pocket-book.*)

LITTLETON: How – and – (*aside*) this is impossible – ha! I see – 'tis the old man's savings with which he would conceal Tom's parsimony. (*aloud*) No, no – not a farthing! (*aside*) How can I refuse it? (*aloud*) It comes too late.

RURAL: Too late! why? (*aside*) I am so delighted to find at last some use for these things. (*aloud*) Here comes Tom.

LITTLETON: Do not attract his notice to me; let me manage this meeting – the Earl supposes we arrived together – hush!

> (LITTLETON *sits with* RURAL. *Enter* LORD POMPION *and* TOM COKE, LADY POMPION, ROCKET, LADY ALICE, *dressed for dinner, followed at a distance by* ROEBUCK *and* KATE.)

LORD P: Your observations, Mr. Coke, are full of justice and originality.

LADY A: Hardly adapted for the House, then, my lord.

ROCKET: In the army, Mr. Coke?

TOM: Nay, sir, I'm it yeomanry, if that'll do, though a trust I shall never require ta know ma duty.

ROCKET: How, sir, are you nervous?

I'm it yeomanry: perhaps an attempt to register the north-country accent. The more normal form would be 'in t' yeomanry'.

TOM: Nay, not so; it requires courage to tak the life o' an enemy, but it wants more than that to be called on to strike at the heart of a neighbour – I confess, I look with more pity than pride on the ranks of brave fellows, marked out for slaughter, with red on their backs, like my sheep.

LORD P: Necessity, Mr. Coke.

TOM: Not the less sad for that, my lord.

ROCKET: Who would not die in defence of such a city as London? How did it strike you?

TOM: As big – but not enough to hold the evil done in't.

LORD P: But you admired its buildings?

TOM: Yes – Whitehall, the Nelson Pillar, the Fire Offices, the Duke of York's Pillar, the National Galleries, and the triumphal arches.

LORD P: Ah, sir, an immense sum they cost.

TOM: But what puzzled me was, no one seemed to know who lived in any of 'em.

LORD P: Why, you see – a – nobody lives in them.

TOM: Then I have no hesitation in saying 'nobody' is the best housed man in the country.

LADY A: Surely, sir, you consider our streets are splendid?

TOM: Yes, but not as glorious as the heaven they shut out. Since I came into this city I haven't seen a fair inch of blue sky, or a blade of green grass. Stop – I did, though – yes, I did see a puir sickly plot penned up in a place they called a square, looking as if they'd put nature in a pound for straying into town.

LADY A: Ha! ha! sir, yours will be a distinguished voice in the House.

TOM: And yours is the most musical and honest one I've heard since I left Yorkshire.

LADY A: Here's a hand belonging to it.

LITTLETON: (*aside*) By Heaven, can she be smitten with him already?
            (*Enter* BUTLER.)

BUTLER: Dinner, my lady.

LORD P: Colonel Rocket, her ladyship – permit me. (*Leads the way, followed by* ROCKET *and* LADY POMPION.)

TOM: (*to* LADY ALICE) You'll favour me. (*Offers his arm to her.*)

LITTLETON: (*starting up*) Lady Alice, my arm is at your service. (*Offers on the other side.*)

TOM: Ha! – it – it – must be!

LADY A: (*looking suprisedly from one to the other*) Your – brother, I believe.

TOM: Here – and I – dom it – I canna help it! (*affectionately*) Yes, it – is my brother. (*Offers his hand.* LITTLETON *bows coldly.*)

LITTLETON: I fear, your ladyship, they wait for us –

LADY A: (*looking with reproof on him*) True – they do. (*Takes* TOM's *arm and goes out with him.*)

LITTLETON: My brother and my rival! be it so! (*Walks violently up and down, followed by* RURAL.)

RURAL: Don't be violent, my dear boy –

LITTLETON: Yes – I will not let her see how she can wound me – and him – 'twould be too deeply gratifying. (RURAL *takes his arm.*) I will go – yes.

RURAL: That's right.

(LITTLETON *takes fierce strides,* RURAL *running to keep up with him – he suddenly stops.*)

LITTLETON: Yet can I endure without betrayal? I must. (*Exits rapidly with* RURAL.)

BUTLER: Ahem! dinner, my lord. (*A pause. He goes behind the causeuse.*) Dinner, my –

(ROEBUCK *and* KATE *start up confused.* ROEBUCK *looks sternly at the* BUTLER, *and they exeunt, followed by* BUTLER, *bowing.*)

ACT III

The Drawing-Room in LADY POMPION's *house. Central arch, draperied and surmounted with a rich cornice, discovering an inner Drawing-Room with a fireplace. Fireplace and fire, windows draperied in rich crimson damask and gilded valances. The room is decorated in white and gold, with a bouquet pattern, a brilliant chandelier, branches between the windows, and divans and consoles. Mirrors and chandelier in the inner room.* LADY ALICE *is discovered playing at a piano,* TOM COKE *leaning over it.* RURAL *is seated on a priedieux, reading a pamphlet.* LORD POMPION *and* COLONEL ROCKET *are walking up and down in the inner room.* LADY POMPION *is lying on a sofa opposite the fire; a* SERVANT *is offering her coffee on a salver, while another* SERVANT *waits with liqueurs.* LITTLETON COKE *is playing with her spaniel, but watching* LADY ALICE *and* TOM. ROEBUCK *and* KATE ROCKET *are seated on a flirting vis-à-vis, pretending to play écarté on a small ornamental table.*

ROCKET: My opinion is, that a submarine battery is attracted to the keel of the vessel, and exploded by concussion.

LORD P: Bless me! had Guy Faux lived in these times, what would become of the House of Peers?

ROCKET: Pooh! vote me a hundred thousand pounds, and I'll undertake to blow up both houses.

(*They move upstage conversing.*)

ROEBUCK: I propose.

KATE: I won't let you, I've a beautiful hand.

ROEBUCK: I've been admiring it. (*Plays.*)

KATE: I take your heart. (*Takes a trick.*)

ROEBUCK: I wish you would take my hand with it. (*Plays his last card.*)

KATE: I do, the game's mine; – what were we playing for?

ROEBUCK: For love –

KATE: Exactly – that means for nothing.

(*They flirt aside.* LORD POMPION *watches them, while* COLONEL ROCKET *joins* LADY ALICE.)

RURAL: (*to* LADY POMPION) Your ladyship, may I entreat your sympathy and beneficence in favour of a subscription I am raising for a poor creature, a widow with eight children?

LADY P: Widows never appear to have less – have I seen the case in the *Morning Post*?

RURAL: Not that I am aware of.

LADY P: Pray, sir, let me see your list – what people of importance have sub-
     scribed? (*to* LITTLETON) One gets one's name mixed up with such *canaille*
     in these charities. (*to* RURAL) In whose name, sir, is it raised, pray?
RURAL: In that of the most bountiful Dispenser of all Good.
LADY P: Ah! sorry – we are not acquainted. (*Turns away and takes coffee from*
     SERVANT.)
LORD P: Colonel Rocket, a word.
ROCKET: My lord?
          (LORD POMPION *takes him into a corner to speak apart.*)
LADY A: (*to* TOM) Ha! ha! you strange creature – I declare I will storm Sykes Hall
     next September.
LITTLETON: (*aside*) This is done to torture me – and succeeds.
TOM: We will show you old English sports.
LADY A: Suppose, after my invasion, I should determine to occupy.
TOM: I'd ask no better.
LITTLETON: The devil! (*Nearly chokes the spaniel, who howls.*)
LADY P: Mr. Coke, my poor Bichon! (*Snatches it up.*)
LITTLETON: Really, I – (*aside*) Damn the dog! I can suffer this agony no longer –
     although she may despise my want of pride in suing her after my exhibition
     of ill-temper – what would I give to be able to affect her indifference? No!
     after all my oaths to bring her to submission first – Here I go. (*Joins* LADY
     ALICE.)
LORD P: (*aside to* ROCKET) In a word, Colonel Rocket, your attentions are
     thrown away – My dear sir, recollect – the son of a peer!
ROCKET: My – daughter.
LORD P: With all respect – I have other views for him, and excuse my candour –
     but the Pompions came over after the Battle of Hastings, and have never yet
     mingled with anything but Norman blood.
ROCKET: Damn it, my lord, Kate Rocket need not look up to blood royal – her
     mother was the Begum of Currypore, princess of the first caste; she was the
     only one of her family my guns had left alive – I took her in a brisk charge
     after she had shot two horses under me. No offence, my lord – but her lady-
     ship don't show such blood as that.
LORD P: No! My Countess is not of a fusileer family – pardon me, I feel my
     honesty is almost plebeian, but should your daughter's name suffer by contact
     with my son's, don't blame him. (*Moves away.*)
ROCKET: Blame! certainly not, I'll blow his brains out! Kate!
KATE: (*rising*) Colonel! (*Joins him.*)
ROCKET: (*aside*) We leave this house to-morrow.
KATE: (*aside*) To-morrow! (*Looks at* ROEBUCK.)
ROCKET: Orders given, no appeal – duty – damme – ha! ha! that peer is as proud
     of – of the Norman puddle that stagnates in his heart, as if his country had
     ever seen any of it – ha! Battle of Hastings! ha! a pretty affair that must have
     been, when there's no mention of it in the Army List! ha! damme if I think
     there ever was such a battle.
ROEBUCK: (*to* LORD POMPION, *who has been speaking aside to him*) Be careful!
     wherefore, my lord?

LORD P: I have discovered that all the Government interest he possesses is confined to 3 per cent on £5000, and he is no more an East India Director than my valet. Need I say more? (*Goes.*)

> (LITTLETON *leaves* LADY ALICE, *who has been devoting herself to* TOM.)

LITTLETON: 'Tis useless. I have yielded up my will, soul, and all to her – I cannot escape her torture – struggling wounds me more than patient suffering. Heaven – to what despicable slavery can manhood be reduced!

RURAL: (*joining him*) My dear boy, what's the matter? why do you look so darkly at Tom? is he not your brother?

LITTLETON: Is he so? Why then has he crossed me through life – has he not devoured my inheritance – am I not a begger?

RURAL: No – not while a roof and crust are mine. Littleton – listen to me – I left my cure, my people in the country, for the holy purpose of uniting you again: I entered this wilderness to bring back a lost sheep.

LITTLETON: Then you should have come unaccompanied by the wolf – I care not to avow it – I am madly in love.

RURAL: My goodness!

LITTLETON: Servilely – despicably – meanly – infatuated – willing – anxious to exchange degrading worship for contempt, to return blind grovelling adoration for indifference!

RURAL: The dear impetuous boy.

LITTLETON: Look around you, and judge if I have cause for misery. (*Goes upstage and seats himself.*)

RURAL: Misery – cause – let me see! (*Puts on his spectacles, looks round, sees* ROEBUCK *and* KATE.) Oh! oh! oh! there it is – well poor Littleton! perhaps I can do something here! it may not be hopeless.

TOM: (*coming downstage*) 'Tis my opinion there's honest nature in that girl, and wholesome feeling, too – I'll wait, and see if it be his lordship's Burgundy, or my reason, that's at work upon my heart – Minister!

RURAL: (*advancing*) Well, Tom.

TOM: You noticed yon blithe lass, I'm thinking.

RURAL: I did, Tom.

TOM: Do't again – I'm not clear about it; but it's more than likely I'm in love.

RURAL: Bless me, how very remarkable!

TOM: I have hesitated, minister, because I thought Littleton did seem that way inclined.

RURAL: Thank heaven, I can answer no to that! – no, Tom, he *is* in love, but 'tis there. (*Points to* KATE.)

TOM: Ar't sure?

RURAL: He owned it to me.

TOM: 'Tis loike him – to drag a poor, trusting, loving girl from comfort here – to share his discontent. (*Goes upstage.*)

RURAL: I'm determined – yes, that will do – the bequest left me by the father of these boys I have never thought of till this moment – 'tis not a fortune, but with my vicarage – enough – enough – Littleton shall have her – I – I – will provide for all – they shall come to me, and my happiness will be too much – more than I deserve; then Tom will relent. I know his good heart, and I shall be blessed in their union once again! – how shall I begin? (*Thinks apart.*)

(*Enter the* GROOM OF THE CHAMBERS, *with shawls.*)

GROOM: The carriage waits, my lady.

LADY P: I had almost forgotten the opera.

LORD P: (*advancing*) Mr. Coke, a seat in our box is at your service.

TOM: Oh, too happy. (*Crosses to* LADY POMPION *and shawls her, then crosses back to* LADY ALICE.) Does your ladyship accompany us?

LADY A: I don't mind, though I have a box of my own on the pit tier – Russell, have they sent my Brougham?

GROOM: Not yet, my lady.

LADY A: Then I'll follow you, for I hate three in a chariot.

LADY P: Charles, dear, do take Bichon to his valet. I think he's sleepy.

LORD P: Colonel, shall we stroll down to the House?

ROCKET: Your lordship's pardon – I've an appointment at my club – the Oriental.

LADY A: Here, one of you men, run and see if my carriage is come. (*to* LITTLE-TON) You'll do, and ask my footman if the *lorgnette* is in the pocket. There, do go, run. (*Exit* LITTLETON.) Colonel, (*taking* ROCKET'*s arm*) suppose you propose me at the Oriental.

ROCKET: Would you not prefer being a member of the Jockey Club?

LADY A: No; I could amuse myself with your old drolls, but nothing appears to me so slow as your *soi-disant* fast man. Come, do propose me.

ROCKET: You would kill us all off with laughing in a week.

LADY A: Do, now!

ROCKET: No, no.

(*Exeunt talking.* LADY POMPION *and* TOM *go out.* KATE, *following* ROEBUCK, *with dog shawled up, is going.*)

ROEBUCK: (*dropping the dog*) Miss Rocket, one word.

KATE: Don't detain me! – (*aside*) I must let him know how valuable his time is, or he will let me go. (*aloud*) Let me say farewell, my father leaves town to-morrow.

ROEBUCK: To-morrow! – then there is no time for delicacy.

KATE: Not a mom– that is, I mean, let me go – how I tremble.

ROEBUCK: Lean on me!

KATE: Thank you. I am so faint –

ROEBUCK: Do – if we are discovered!

KATE: I will. What am I saying?

RURAL: (*aside*) How very extraordinary – here's more love. It appears to me that the young people in this house don't do anything else.

ROEBUCK: (*while* KATE *hides her face in her hands*) Kate – dear Kate – need words pass between us, doesn't this speak for itself? Your father's tyranny will defeat itself, and excuse this precipitation of an avowal.

---

on the pit tier: between the pit tier boxes and the pit stalls was the notorious 'Fop's Alley', where habitués lounged and ogled.

Brougham: a closed one-horse carriage, seating one or two.

KATE: My father's tyranny! – you mean that of the severe and haughty earl.

ROEBUCK: No, dearest, fear nothing from him – I am his son, 'tis true, and, as such, will yield him the obedience I ought. But 'tis to my children, not to my father, that I am answerable for the choice of my heart – I claim, therefore, my freedom and your hand – assure me that I have won it.

KATE: Spare me a reply – but, my father –

ROEBUCK: On what pretext can he withhold his consent?

KATE: On the earl's dislike to our union.

ROEBUCK: Ha! I see – my father has already spoken to the colonel – that accounts for his sudden departure.

KATE: I fear so – but don't mind papa, he's nobody –

ROEBUCK: How – are not his orders peremptory?

KATE: Yes – so is his obedience – he's a dear, noisy old man – the worst-tempered, best-hearted creature in the world; he's fond of reviewing, so I let him burn his powder, and then I march him home again – ha! ha!

ROEBUCK: I took him for a tyrant.

KATE: He? why he has the heart of a woman – when my mother died, before I was two years old, I've heard that he would watch me like a nurse – fearing to touch me, but envying the Ayah to whom I was confided.

ROEBUCK: But you had some female relatives?

KATE: Not one – nor did I feel their absence. I felt myself, as our mess-room used to toast me, 'the fair colonel'. Oh Charles, you will love him so – could you have seen him as I have, under the scorching sun of India, pacing along the ranks, trying to inspect the men with a regulation frown, and swearing down their honest murmurs of 'bless his old wig and spurs', till, suffocated with their benedictions, with tears in his eyes, he'd cry – 'Get out of the sun, you mutinous rascals! Dismiss! I'll flog every man of you – march – God bless you, boys.' Oh, I could have cried with pride.

ROEBUCK: And when you leave this, where do you go?

KATE: To our villa at Closeborough.

ROEBUCK: The very seat which I was to represent; the election, or rather the nomination, occurs to-morrow.

KATE: Another obstacle – my father's politics.

ROEBUCK: I am a martyr to them – I abdicate the honour in favour of Littleton Coke – but have you no excuse by which your departure might be retarded?

KATE: I – yes – my father's gout has prevented him lately from accompanying me in my daily ride; he has consented to allow me a groom of my own; I have not yet selected a –

ROEBUCK: A groom? A moment – ha! will you take one of my recommendation? one in whose confidence you may rely as in my own?

KATE: What do you mean?

ROEBUCK: Rely on me – I mean all for the best.

KATE: I have no will but yours.

ROEBUCK: My angel! (*Kisses her.*)

(*Enter* COLONEL ROCKET.)

Ayah: Indian nurse.

ROCKET: Hollo, there – Kate – recover arms – the devil!

KATE: My father!

ROCKET: You – you – you – here's mutiny! and you, sir, how dare you, against general orders?

ROEBUCK: Hush! my father! – should he overhear.

ROCKET: Don't think your Norman blood will –

KATE: ⎫ (together) ⎧ Hush! I entreat – the Earl!
ROEBUCK: ⎭   ⎩ We shall be ruined.

ROCKET: (still enraged, but under his breath) What do I care whether he hears or not? I hope he will – pair of disaffected mutineers. (gradually breaking out) Don't imagine I want to steal a recruit from your family into mine – because I'd see it –

KATE: ⎫ (together) ⎧ My dear father! he's only in the next room.
ROEBUCK: ⎭   ⎩ The Earl – for Heaven's sake –

ROCKET: (under his breath) Very well, then – don't Earl me – who's the Earl? – you? – harkye, sir, (KATE throws her arms round his neck.) you may have come over after the Battle of Hastings – though I can't say I see much glory in arriving when the fight's done – but I can count scars for every branch in your genealogical tree – so look ye, if you think there's any ambuscade here to catch your lordship, fall back – your retreat is still open; but if you try a surprise on my baggage here, damme, look out for a warm reception.
      (KATE stops his mouth with a kiss.)

RURAL: Don't be alarmed, Colonel, I heard it all.

ROEBUCK: (aside) Ruin – ruin – nothing can prevent this simple old fellow from committing our secret with my father.

ROCKET: You have brought on a twinge of the gout, you have, you graceless baggage – then what do you care – you'd run off with the first fellow whose grandfather came over after the battle of Hastings, and leave your infirm old father with nothing to swear at but his crutch. If I had a family poodle to leave my money to, damme I'd cut you off with a rupee – give me a kiss – I would, you – oh! don't laugh at my sufferings – oh! (Exit, assisted by KATE.)

ROEBUCK: My dear old friend, one word. (aside, bringing RURAL forward) What shall I say? (aloud) You never thought I was making love to that lady?

RURAL: It did strike me, but if not, what were you making?

ROEBUCK: Why, can't you guess?

RURAL: No! making love is very unlike anything else I know of.

ROEBUCK: You are right – I was – but – but – not on my own account.

RURAL: Oh!

ROEBUCK: I pressed the suit for – for a friend – in fact, for Coke.

RURAL: For Littleton?

ROCKET: (without) Don't tell me –

KATE: (without) No – but –

ROEBUCK: You must be aware that I am destined by my father for Lady Alice – and – of course – I – I am devoted to her.

---

ambuscade: ambush.

RURAL: And Littleton was jealous of you! generous young man! how he will repent when he is aware of his unjust suspicion; I know my dear boy is in love with the lady, he has confessed it to me.

ROEBUCK: (*half aside*) The devil he has!

RURAL: Now, leave the rest to me –

ROEBUCK: Oh! there's some mistake here.

RURAL: I will get the Colonel's consent – I'll do it at once before I see Littleton – not a word to him. Let me surprise him with it. Oh, Littleton! (*Exit.*)

(*Enter* LITTLETON, *through another door.*)

ROEBUCK: My dear fellow, you must aid me.

LITTLETON: In what?

ROEBUCK: Old Rocket leaves this to-morrow, taking Kate with him. I have determined to accompany them.

LITTLETON: How?

ROEBUCK: The lady wants a groom.

LITTLETON: You never mean to undertake the place.

ROEBUCK: When I have removed these foreign decorations from my chin and lips, I'd defy the eyes of Argus to know me.

LITTLETON: But the election to-morrow?

ROEBUCK: Egad! that's true – and my father expects Mr. Bribe, his solicitor and parliamentary agent, every moment to arrange accounts for my nomination. What's to be done?

LITTLETON: We must prevent the interview.

ROEBUCK: How?

LITTLETON: I'll engage him at a larger fee. But we must find some one to represent a partner in his firm, who is unknown by sight to your father.

ROEBUCK: Crawl's the man.

LITTLETON: Then Crawl shall enjoy an honest reputation for a day, in the person of Bob.

ROEBUCK: Is he equal to it?

LITTLETON: I'll back him with odds at anything, from winning a kitchen wench, to a speech from the woolsack.

ROEBUCK: He is here – where shall I find him?

LITTLETON: Have you any spot in the house dedicated especially to the maids and mischief? If so, raise your voice in that quarter.

(*Enter* BOB, *cautiously.*)

BOB: Sir! sir! (*Looks about.*)

LITTLETON: Here he is.

BOB: I've sent your address to the *Closeborough Independent*, sir.

LITTLETON: My address!

BOB: To the free and enlightened electors – you'll find it sharp and undecided, sir – I've been rather abusive in my allusions to your lordship, but one cannot be political without being personal; therefore, when I refer to your lordship from the hustings to-morrow as only falling short of a fool by being born a knave, and the disgrace you are to the aristocracy – (*to* LITTLETON) oh, sir, I've not read the debates for nothing – (*to* ROEBUCK) your lordship will understand me to speak professionally.

ROEBUCK: Why – you – you –

LITTLETON: (*crossing to* ROEBUCK, *and aside*) Never mind, wait till I can afford
to pay him his wages, I'll not forget you. (*to* BOB) We require you to adopt
the name and character of a gentleman who is expected here, and to per-
sonate him before Lord Pompion: can you do it?

BOB: That depends upon whom he is.

ROEBUCK: Crawl, the attorney and agent.

BOB: (*to* LITTLETON) I thought you spoke of a gentleman.

LITTLETON: Nonsense, sir; can you play the attorney?

BOB: *Facilis descensus Averni*, as Virgil said when you were at college, sir. I'll
adopt the character, but I'm afraid my honesty will show through and spoil
the assumption.

LITTLETON: No fear of that. Accompany Lord Charles, he will give you instructions.

ROEBUCK: 'Tis a fearful alternative, but there is no time to invent; (*to* BOB) this
way. *Gare!* here comes the widow! (*Exit with* BOB.)

LITTLETON: The widow, and once more alone, ha! I feel that if I could mask my
impetuosity for a moment, I might at least discover my position, but my love
is in its own way, and –

(*Enter* LADY ALICE.)

Here she is.

LADY A: (*aside*) I thought he had gone without me – ha! I almost believe I like the
fool. (LITTLETON *sits and writes*.) I must discover why these brothers do
not speak. – I was thinking of trying the opera for an hour, Mr. Coke.

LITTLETON: Not a bad idea – (*writing*) my distracted love is too perceptible –
(*aloud*) the opera, ay! (*aside*) Could she have refused to accompany Tom and
the Countess to secure a tête-à-tête with me? I dare not hope it. (*writing*) 'In
the fond hope'.

LADY A: (*aside*) Why, I do believe the fellow is writing a love letter.

LITTLETON: (*still writing*) 'Grisi' – yes – ah – eh – I beg your pardon – you'll
allow me to ring for your carriage.

LADY A: (*aside*) So he thinks he is sure of me – oh! yes – hang his smirking self-
sufficient grin – that letter is to me – now, if I liked him less, I would torture
him till – why – he is not going to seal it!

LITTLETON: (*burning the wax*) Lady Alice, I remarked a minute signet ring on
your lovely hand: will you favour me with it for an instant?

LADY A: Nonsense; it bears the motto, 'L'amour est'.

LITTLETON: Love defunct – excellent. You keep it to seal your death warrant to
the heart of a discarded lover. (*Seals the letter.*) Spirituelle – ha! (*Kisses the
ring, and returns it to her finger, kissing her hand.*)

Facilis descensus Averni: the descent to Hell is easy.
Gare: look out!
Grisi: more likely a reference to the romantic ballerina Carlotta Grisi (1821–99) than to the
singer Giulia Grisi.
'L'amour est': the motto is almost as unsatisfactory as Littleton's translation of it. A word –
perhaps 'mort' – may be missing here.

LADY A: Well – ahem – (*aside*) He does not give it to me – (LITTLETON *writes.*) he directs it – really, I – (LITTLETON *extinguishes the taper and advances.*) feel very – oh, here he comes – ha! he was too nervous to speak – I –

LITTLETON: Lady Alice –

LADY A: (*aside*) His voice trembles – ha! (LITTLETON *walks round her, and takes up a shawl.*) He's swimming round the hook.

LITTLETON: You were talking of the opera –

LADY A: (*aside*) The float sinks.

LITTLETON: Allow me, before you go –

LADY A: (*aside*) I have him!

LITTLETON: – to shawl you.

LADY A: Sir! (*aside*) He's off.

LITTLETON: (*folding the shawl, aside*) Happy shawl! – Blest cashmere! – why was I not born amongst you to be continually hugged round such a lovely form as this? (*shawling her*) Allow me to ring for the carriage.

LADY A: (*aside*) Hang the fellow, I'll have that letter if I die for it. – A warm correspondence that of yours, if I may judge by your escaped expression.

LITTLETON: (*aside*) Aha! 'tis a bite, as I expected – now I'll play with her a little. – Warm! oh, yes; and, apropos, you may be of some assistance to me.

LADY A: Assistance!

LITTLETON: Yes, you might deliver the letter. I am sure the interest you took in me this morning will excuse the confidence I ask you to give us.

LADY A: Us!

LITTLETON: Yes. (*Gives the letter.*) I'm an humble aspirant to –

LADY A: (*reading*) Miss Rocket!

LITTLETON: You seem surprised.

LADY A: Surprised! and the lady – she encourages you?

LITTLETON: Look at me, and don't wound my feelings by reiterating the question.

LADY A: And your – your – ha! ha! – your protestations to me –

LITTLETON: Egad, that's true. I forgot – oh, don't mistake me – when I offer Miss Rocket my hand, allow me to express at the same time my wild adoration of your ladyship, in the abstract – It's a fearful mania of mine.

LADY A: Ha! ha! and you thought I reciprocated your empty expression of – Oh! (*aside*) I shall choke! (*aloud*) Perhaps, you even imagined I was in love with you.

LITTLETON: I did.

LADY A: Disabuse your mind of it, I beg – you flatter yourself!

LITTLETON: You are not in love with me?

LADY A: Not in the least.

LITTLETON: Ah, true – how could one expect Heaven to endow you with beauty and sense at the same time?

LADY A: And do you imagine, sir, that I will permit my friend to remain in ignorance of your treachery?

LITTLETON: Quite the contrary. I feel convinced you will instantly apprise her of the fact – Oh! I don't wish to take her at any disadvantage – I wish to owe nothing but to the unaided dynamics of personal appearance.

LADY A: (*aside*) The egregious puppy – my heart should disinherit him – cut him off with a sigh – but that I feel it has quitted this world (*touching her heart*) without a will.

LITTLETON: (*aside*) She loves me, and now begins to feel it. As I proceed I gain more confidence. – You seem rather animated! sorry that I'm compelled to leave you alone with your feelings – excuse the imputation. (*eyeing her*) I see you possess those inconveniences; they impart expression, and are amusing enough to observe – but must be very troublesome in their manufacture.

LADY A: (*aside*) I would esteem this man a brute, but 'twould be a libel upon quadrupeds, for he wants their animation.

LITTLETON: You are bored, I see – regret I can't amuse – possessing only the ability to be amused. Shall I ring for *your* dog or *my* brother?

LADY A: Don't trouble yourself! were I inclined to laugh at anything, you would do very well. (*aside*) I *could* cry, but I won't.

LITTLETON: Farewell! I tear myself away. (*Looks at his watch.*) I'm agonized with the necessity, but I see the ballet has commenced, and I would not miss the *Truandaise* for a thousand. (*Lounges out, humming an air.*)

LADY A: Can this be real? – what need I care? – I'll go to the opera and find fifty lovers there, make each commit fifty follies, and revenge myself on the sex. (*Throws herself on sofa.*)

(*Enter* RURAL.)

RURAL: What a fearful mistake I had nearly committed – the Earl has just been speaking of his son's projected marriage with this lady; I must find Tom, and tell him so – poor fellow! 'tis well he has not known her long enough to feel her loss. But how delighted Littleton will be to hear that his suspicions were unfounded; now, now, I can conscientiously promote their happiness.

LADY A: (*apart*) Yet, his fervour was so natural, I could not be mistaken in his honesty – he *does* love me – on my life he does.

RURAL: (*aside*) I must get some assistance in my plot, these young hearts are such strange things. – My dear young lady, I want your help in a little plot of mine; you understand these matters better than I do, and will assist me – Littleton has fallen in love.

LADY A: (*aside*) Bless this dear old man, he's always in the wrong. – Ha! he has confessed it to you, then?

RURAL: He is as open-hearted as a child; but you will not mention it?

LADY A: I think I was his first confidant, sir.

RURAL: Then, you will join me in trying to reconcile these dear children, and recovering to my affection my favourite – I mean, my dearest hope.

LADY A: I will. (*aside*) I thought it was affectation – but I am too happy to think of revenging it. Yes, yes, yes, my dear, dear sir – I will be all you wish – all he wishes.

RURAL: What a kind, warm heart it is.

LADY A: Where is he?

---

ballet: the popularity of ballet as a curtain-raiser to the opera was at its height in London in the 1840s, but waned rapidly after the opera debut of Jenny Lind in 1847.
Truandaise: the reference is to Jules Perrot's ballet *La Esmeralda* (based on Hugo's *Notre Dame de Paris*), in which Carlotta Grisi danced the title role.

RURAL: I dare say, like young folks – ha! he has stolen to her.

LADY A: To her – who?

RURAL: Miss Rocket – bless me, are you ill?

LADY A: Miss Rocket! Has he then –

RURAL: Confessed to me his love for her – yes – his grovelling adoration – servilely, meanly, despicably infatuated – bless his impetuous heart!

LADY A: And Lord Charles? –

RURAL: Nobly presses his suit.

LADY A: I cannot believe it.

RURAL: My dear child, his lordship told me so himself.

(*Enter* KATE.)

LADY A: Kate – tell me – are you deceiving me?

KATE: What do you mean?

LADY A: Mr. Coke is in love with you?

KATE: With me!

LADY A: He has been confessing it all over the house – to me – to him – to Lord Charles –

KATE: Why, it can't be – what means Lord Charles's declaration to me?

RURAL: My dear young lady, he means nothing to you: you mistook his intentions – he was wooing for his friend, who was ridiculously jealous of him – Lord Charles told me just now that he was betrothed to her ladyship, and devoted to her – the earl has since said the same thing – therefore it must be true.

LADY A: Kate!

KATE: Alice!

LADY A: That villain Charles wished at once to deceive his friend – destroy you – and cheat me.

KATE: Destroy me – oh, Alice! (*They embrace.*)

RURAL: Tears! what strange things young hearts are.

LADY A: Stay, this note will decide it. (*drawing out the note*) No, I can't do it – I – at least, not yet – when we are alone, I may find courage.

(*Enter* a SERVANT.)

SERVANT: Your ladyship's carriage waits.

LADY A: Kate – be a woman –

RURAL: She is – she is a woman.

LADY A: These pair of wretches are doubtless in the stalls at the opera, directing a *lorgnette* battery against all the beauty in the house; let us go and show them we can be as heartless as they. (*Goes to table, and gets an opera-glass.*)

RURAL: Yes – exactly – what can it all mean? There is nothing so puzzling to an old head as a young heart.

(LADY ALICE *takes one of* RURAL'*s arms, and places the opera-glass in his hand.*)

There! my dear child – don't weep. (*He is going to apply her handkerchief to her eyes when* KATE *takes the other arm and checks him.*) Well! woman is a wonderful and mysterious thing!

LADY A: Wretches – both.

RURAL: Ah!

KATE: Villains!

RURAL: Yes – (*aside*) I wonder where I'm going to.

> (LADY ALICE *and* KATE *go out dejectedly, with* RURAL *between them.*)

ACT IV

The same as Act III. Enter COLONEL ROCKET *with a newspaper.*

ROCKET: Here's news! A copy of this evening's *Closeborough Independent* has been despatched to me. (*Reads.*) 'We gladly issue a second edition, to give the earliest publicity to the following address, which reached us after going to press:–

> *To the Independent Electors of Closeborough*
>
> Gentlemen – In reply to a requisition from a numerous and highly respectable body of your townsmen, I too happily accede to your wishes, and shall be proud to represent your opinions in Parliament, which I cannot but suppose are violently adverse to those of my noble friend and antagonist, Lord Roebuck, whose character, speaking publicly, I must despise – but whose private character, generally, I know nothing about. I am, gentlemen, your obedient servant,
>
> Littleton Coke.'

Hurrah! now I can show fight! now I've outflanked his Norman Lordship. My villa at Closeborough, Ghuznee Lodge, and its estate, gives me the influence of thirty votes – ha! ha! ha! I'll not sleep another night beneath this noble roof – I've despatched orders to Corporal Stripe to have the guard out, in their old uniforms – my travelling carriage will be here in two hours – I'll canvass the whole town before breakfast. Ho! ho! damme, I've never been so excited since Bhurtpore!

> (*Enter* RURAL.)

RURAL: Had I been the first-born of Richelieu, and the favourite pupil of Machiavel, I could not have surrounded myself with more intrigues, plots, and difficulties. Those two dear girls took me to the opera; they beguiled the way by crying, and endeavouring to discover which could invent the worst name for her lover. When we arrived, I found myself amongst soldiers and footmen; then labyrinths and lights; then in a little closet with one wall out, apparently for the admission of noise and glare. I was astonished into the place, and amazed out of it, and thankful I am to get here again. – (*aside*) Here's the Colonel – I'll venture to – to sound him about his consent to the marriage. – My military friend, will you allow me to ask – has Littleton acquainted you with – his intentions?

ROCKET: No, sir – I wish he had – however, accident has revealed them to me.

RURAL: And dare he hope that you will grant your consent?

ROCKET: Grant! I'll secure his success. He shall have Jack Rocket's interest, sir.

RURAL: (*astonished*) Then you approve of his offer?

ROCKET: I could not have selected from all England a finer fellow – more after my own heart.

RURAL: He is – he is –
ROCKET: Noble souled.
RURAL: Princely.
ROCKET: Honest, free –
RURAL: God bless you!
ROCKET: No stiff-backed pretension –
RURAL: What a kind soul you are.
ROCKET: I'll lay a thousand *his* father was *at* the Battle of Hastings.
RURAL: But, your daughter –
ROCKET: Kate! ay – she'll go with him, heart and soul!
RURAL: She will; she has said as much.
ROCKET: Bless her heart, it always says right.
RURAL: My dear benefactor, don't – don't overcome me with gratitude; what shall
    I say or do – may I run and tell Littleton?
ROCKET: Tell the rascal I'll never forgive him not coming to me at first.
RURAL: At first, ha! ha!
ROCKET: Tell him my carriage is at his service – my house at his command.
RURAL: Ha! ha! I shall do something very foolish for joy when I get out!
ROCKET: Advise him to lose no time: he should clinch the affair before breakfast
    to-morrow.
RURAL: To-morrow! isn't that rather – rather early, eh?
ROCKET: Too late, sir – I like despatch.
RURAL: But the lady?
ROCKET: Kate! pooh! you don't know the girl; she'll spring up at five in such a
    cause.
RURAL: Bless me!
ROCKET: No more – I'm off. Remember my carriage will be at the door in two
    hours; let him use it.
RURAL: Use it to –
ROCKET: Not a word – orders given – ho! great guns! this is glorious!
RURAL: Miraculous!
ROCKET: I'm in the saddle again, huzza! (*twinges*) Oh! the gout! – I'm a rusty old
    arquebuse, only fit to hang up for a show of old times; but no! I'll be charged
    and primed, and damme I'll go off once more, if I'm blown to the devil for
    it! – Hurrah! eh! ha! ha! hurrah. (*Exit.* RURAL, *very excited, joins feebly in
    his boisterous shouts.*)
RURAL: Hurrah! bless me, how exciting all this is; – ha! ha! (*He runs about.*) I'm
    inclined to do something very frantic – Huzza!
                (*Enter* LORD POMPION.)
LORD P: My dear sir. (*aside*) What is the old man about? – Will you have the kind-
    ness to inform Mr. Coke –
RURAL: Certainly, in two hours –
LORD P: I mean the member, sir; that I would be happy to see him here –
RURAL: Before breakfast –
LORD P: On parliamentary business –
RURAL: Of course. Tell the rascal I'll never forgive him.
LORD P: Mr. Rural – will you –

RURAL: Spring up at five in such a cause.

LORD P: (*aside*) He is possessed –

RURAL: Great guns! this is glorious! Hurrah! hurrah! (*Exit.*)

(*Enter* SERVANT)

SERVANT: Mr. Crawl, my lord.

LORD P: Show him in. (*Exit* SERVANT.) Charles informs me that Bribe sends word that he is engaged against us by the opposing candidate; but he has proved himself a trustworthy fellow, for he has despatched an intelligent and junior partner in his firm, whom he feels assured will carry all before him. We must do something for Bribe – fidelity should be rewarded.

(*Enter* SERVANT.)

SERVANT: Mr. Crawl.

(*Enter* BOB, *dressed in black. Exit* SERVANT.)

LORD P: Mr. Crawl?

BOB: Of the firm of Bribe, Crawl, and Treatem.

LORD P: Fame speaks highly of you, Mr. Crawl, and parliament has its eye on you. Fortune favoured me when, twenty years ago, I selected your firm for my solicitors.

BOB: I remember the era. Its date – I think – is on your lordship's first mortgage to us.

LORD P: A tenacious memory – be seated. (*Points to chair.*) How fortunate for us that Bribe is secured to our opposing candidate.

BOB: He's a treasure –

LORD P: So are you –

BOB: Oh, I'm a mint, my lord, a perfect mint – I'll coin you votes that shall pass current with any Committee of the House – I'll put you in for any borough in Great Britain, and return you with any majority you may please to pay for – I'll qualify you with three hundred a year landed property, for fifty pounds, and show more voters in your interest unpolled than there is population in the country.

LORD P: My dear Mr. Crawl!

BOB: Oh, my Lord – that's nothing.

LORD P: I may conclude my son elected, then?

BOB: Chaired – and has returned thanks in a neat speech, which I have already prepared.

LORD P: Then I may venture to dismiss anxiety from my mind – and enter on other topics.

BOB: (*aside*) Other topics – master didn't prime me for other topics.

LORD P: Fifteen years ago –

BOB: (*aside*) Oh, lord!

LORD P: It may be in your tenacious recollection that I confided to the care of Mr. Bribe – a boy.

BOB: Oh! perfectly – a perfect child – a – a mere – a – boy – a – oh, I perfectly –

LORD P: The – the – son of an old and valued servant.

BOB: Female?

LORD P: No – my butler.

BOB: Oh!

LORD P: I promised to – to – protect – to educate – my – I mean, his child – and confided the responsibility to Bribe's charge.

BOB: (*aside*) Oho! – the Earl has been a gay deceiver in his youth – ahem! – not much of the Lothario left!

LORD P: I – I left England shortly after this occurrence, as ambassador to the court of Lisbon – since my return – business – a –

BOB: Of course. I see. – Oh, yes – I know the boy – a fine fellow he has grown – an universal favourite.

LORD P: Indeed!

BOB: His name is Robert, but we call him Bob, familiarly.

LORD P: Yes, yes.

BOB: I do assure you, there's no one for whom I possess a higher esteem – whose interest I have more at heart.

LORD P: It does you honour.

BOB: I got him into the service of Mr. Littleton Coke.

LORD P: Coke! what a strange coincidence.

BOB: But, to-day he has obtained the situation of groom to a Miss Rocket.

LORD P: Miss Rocket! why, that lady is now in this house.

BOB: Indeed! then so is Bob.

LORD P: Could I – I – see him?

BOB: Of course; permit me to ring. (*Rings bell on table.*) By the way, if you will excuse the idea, I can't help thinking that there is a considerable resemblance between his features and those of your son – our candidate.

LORD P: Ha! ha! what a strange notion. (*aside*) Can it be so striking as to betray me?

> (*Enter* SERVANT.)

BOB: Tell Miss Rocket's new groom to step up. (*Exit* SERVANT.) So, Lord Charles, you roasted me once, now I'll give you a turn.

LORD P: (*aside*) How agitated I feel.

> (*Enter* ROEBUCK, *dressed as a groom, with his moustachios and beard cut, and his hair cropped.*)

BOB: Step forward, young man – my lord, this is Bob.

ROEBUCK: (*aside*) My father – the devil – (*Threatens* BOB.)

LORD P: (*aside*) I dare not look at him –

BOB: His lordship is good enough to take an interest in you, Bob – for which you will feel duly grateful – ahem – I've no doubt that he will even do something handsome for you – you see the reward of virtue: – I promised you, that by steady and persevering conduct, I should be able to give you a turn when you least expected it.

ROEBUCK: (*aside*) Expected it – the fellow is roasting me now with a vengeance!

BOB: Do you hear?

ROEBUCK: I – I heartily thank his lordship.

LORD P: (*aside*) The voice – the Pompion voice – I could swear to its haughty

---

Lothario: the Lothario who reluctantly seduces Camilla in *Don Quixote* was transformed into the libertine ('gay Lothario') he has remained in Rowe's play *The Fair Penitent* (1703).

tones amongst a million. (*Looks at him.*) Mercy! he will betray me. Blindness
would know him to be Charles's brother.

BOB: Bob, are you ready to experience his lordship's generosity?

LORD P: Young man – I – take some – little interest in your – Robert – I – (*Checks
himself.*) Mr. Crawl, you will expend this hundred pounds for Robert's benefit. (*Gives money.*)

BOB: I feel it as a gift to myself – every shilling of it shall be conscientiously spent
on that individual. Bob, have you no tongue? mercy on me – no gratitude –
there you stand – do you see, sir, 'tis one hundred pounds – thank his lordship.

ROEBUCK: (*aside*) Oh, the scoundrel!

BOB: Thank him on your knees, sir.

ROEBUCK: (*bowing*) Oh, you – your – lordship – I – I – scarcely know how to –
(*aside*) Damn that fellow's impudence.

LORD P: Farewell, Mr. Crawl; you will let me hear of this young man from time
to time. (*Takes a last look at* ROEBUCK *from the door.*) Fatal image – poor
boy – Sarah Jane – oh, memory! (*Exit.*)

ROEBUCK: (*Sits across a chair and looks at* BOB, *after a pause.*) So, sir, you have
the daring impudence, not only to ring me up for your special amusement,
but to rob my father before my face.

BOB: Perquisites, my lord, nothing more; besides, if I am to injure my character by
adopting that of a lawyer for half an hour – the least I may be spared is the
lawful plunder of the profession. Consider the risk.
> (*Enter* RURAL.)

RURAL: I can't find him anywhere.

ROEBUCK: Mr. Rural.

BOB: (*aside*) The old money-lender – he has dogged us – the bailiff can't be far off -
– I must find my master. (*Exit cautiously.*)

RURAL: Why – surely –

ROEBUCK: (*aside*) He detects me – better make him a confidant, or he may betray
me. – Yes – yes – he – he – you look surprised – this dress –

RURAL: But where's all this? (*touching his chin*)

ROEBUCK: Ha! sir! my judicious compliment to the court of Versailles – hush! –
I'll tell you – it's a freak –

RURAL: Law!

ROEBUCK: Nothing more – (*aside to* RURAL) you see – (*aside*) aid me, Mercury,
god of lies – I told you I was assisting Coke to the hand of Miss Rocket.

RURAL: You did – so am I.

ROEBUCK: They – they are off to-night.

RURAL: I know it – ha!

ROEBUCK: The deuce you do – well – I'm going to ride postillion, that's all.

RURAL: Going down as his groom?

ROEBUCK: No! as hers – but hush – I implore – not a syllable – could I but find
Kate without meeting my father – I have secured the servants. (*Exit.*)

RURAL: Well, I had heard of young noblemen turning coachmen – but this is the
first instance of one turning groom – I –
> (*Enter* LORD POMPION.)

LORD P: They have gone, sir – the persons who were here this instant, do you know, have they left the house?

RURAL: You saw them?

LORD P: Certainly!

RURAL: (*aside*) Oh! then he is in the secret. – You know then – you are aware –

LORD P: Of what?

RURAL: That Miss Rocket has got another groom.

LORD P: Y–e–s.

RURAL: A new character for your rogue of a son.

LORD P: Ah! hush! (*Seizes his arm, and looks round.*)

RURAL: Eh! what's the matter?

LORD P: My dear sir, you have gained, I know not by what accident, the possession of a secret of the deepest importance. Yes, I confess it – the person who is now engaged in the menial capacity you mention, *is* my son.

RURAL: Of course, he is – he is going to, ha! ha! ride postillion; what will he do next?

LORD P: You will conceal this secret?

RURAL: If you desire it, certainly; I had suspicions that Miss Rocket was in love with him, but –

LORD P: Miss Rocket! is it possible – my dear, dear sir, you transport me – could you but conclude a match between them.

RURAL: Good gracious!

LORD P: (*aside*) Young ladies have eloped with their grooms before now.

RURAL: Why, my lord?

LORD P: I know – you would start objections, I anticipate them. Listen – should this desirable event take place, it may be politic for me to show some temper, you understand –

RURAL: Certainly not.

LORD P: To be angry – but do not heed it – 'twill only be in compliment to the colonel, and to conceal my relationship – Remember, there's a valuable benefice in my gift: it is just vacant. All I can say is – consummate my hopes, and ask me for what you will, it shall be yours. (*Exit.*)

RURAL: But, my lord – Lady Alice – What can this mean? – an hour ago he told me that he designed Lord Charles for Lady Hawthorn. Now, he would given anything to see him married to Miss Rocket. This is all very strange – if he agrees to the match between his son and her ladyship, and the colonel consent to Littleton's proposals, and the young people love each other – why make any mystery? Ha! here is my boy – he seems annoyed – a – (*Seats himself, and watches.*)

(*Enter* LITTLETON. *He walks up and down after a pause.*)

LITTLETON: I don't think there was a fool in the house whom she did not flirt with through her opera-glass. Everyone noticed it – she swept over the stalls, smiling at every eager eye that was fixed on her – damme, she appears intimate with the whole subscription – and then the omnibus boxes – oh, that

---

subscription: a subscription system for the financing of opera in London began in 1708. In 1793, 25 guineas bought attendance at fifty performances of the Italian Opera.

was awful – why, every man in 'em went round into her box – they went by twos, relieving each other every five minutes, like sentries before Whitehall. She made herself the focus for every lorgnette in the pit – and not content with that, she goes round into Lady Pompion's box, turns her back full upon the stage and me, and flirts with Tom, as if she had only six hours to live. I was obliged to groan in the middle of one of Grisi's finest arias – and nearly got turned out.

RURAL: Littleton, fortune smiles on you – my dear boy, I give you joy – she is yours.

LITTLETON: Is she?

RURAL: The colonel says his carriage and house are at your service, and that the affair ought to be settled before breakfast to-morrow.

LITTLETON: (*aside*) In all this excitement I had almost forgotten my election, and the colonel – of course! Roebuck told me he was violently opposed to his politics. He will aid my return – I'll accept his offer.

RURAL: His carriage will be at the door in an hour.

LITTLETON: Then it shall bear me from this fatal scene of enchantment, and you will accompany me.

RURAL: May I – oh! what, with you! (*embracing him*)

LITTLETON: Forgive me, if in my moments of passion I have slighted your affection.

RURAL: Slighted! let me hear anyone say you slighted – my dear boy, you have been all love, and – let's go – (*aside*) I'll write to Tom to follow, ha! ha!
(*Enter* TOM *and* LADY ALICE, *with letters, laughing.*)

LITTLETON: Ha! they follow to outrage me even here. I'll remain. (*Retires upstage.*)

LADY A: (*to* LITTLETON) Oh! Mr. Coke, did you hear Lablache in the finale? ha! ha!

LITTLETON: (*aside*) She must have seen me leave the house in disgust before it; I felt every eye was upon me.

LADY A: Ha! ha! he was too droll to bear. I would not hear or see anything after that – 'twould be a sacrilege.

LITTLETON: (*aside*) She can be amused, too!

TOM: (*aside*) She loves me – I felt it – I am too full of happiness to remain unforgiving: my heart has been knocking against my will all day long. I could not look at him wi'out a blush. – Brother Littleton, a word wi' you. (LITTLETON *bows aside, and advances a little.* TOM *hesitates.*)

LADY A: (*aside to* RURAL) Go, leave them to me.

RURAL: Bless you, angel that you are – that is – that you will be – join those young hearts and gain an old man's last prayers. (*They retire into the inner room.*)

TOM: Brother, a'm not goin' to reproach you, but – but – no matter what you've been – forgive and forget. Littleton, we are brothers – flesh and blood do tingle against our parting this way – you are my father's son – the child of my

---

Lablache: Luigi Lablache, a huge man, was leading basso of the English Opera from 1830 to 1852.

mother – don't look from me, brother Littleton – because there are tears in ma eyes that a'm not ashamed of – you tremble – so do I – 'ave got my hand out, though you don't see it – you'll take it?

LITTLETON: This charity seems strangely sudden – to what do I owe it?

TOM: To her.

LITTLETON: Lady Alice!

LADY A: (*coming downstage*) Well!

LITTLETON: (*aside*) She loves him.

LADY A: I've taken a fancy to see you two shake hands: whoever begins shall be rewarded with my waist for the first polka at Rochester House to-night; do you hear, you statue? (*She goes to* LITTLETON, *who is standing, with his back towards his brother* TOM.) Come, give me your hand.

LITTLETON: His hand will suffice your ladyship for the present.

LADY A: (*aside*) Aha! have I reduced you to submission? now I'll try on him if I have learned by heart the lesson he taught me an hour ago. (*aloud to* TOM) Will you favour me with a moment's *tête-à-tête* with this amusing creature?

TOM: You command me. (*Exit.*)

LITTLETON: Will your ladyship excuse me?

LADY A: No – I want you – don't go, I beg.

LITTLETON: (*aside*) She entreats – she repents. (*He pauses. She draws out a letter.*) She takes a letter from her breast – 'tis to me. (*She opens it.*) No – she opens it – she reads it – (*She sighs.*) she is affected – what can it mean?

LADY A: Mr. Coke – I – I hurt my hand this evening, and am unable to write – would you have the kindness to answer, for me, this letter, and write as I tell you?

LITTLETON: Write as! – (*aside*) What does she – perhaps 'tis from Tom – it is – I –

LADY A: (*having settled the writing materials for him*) Pray be seated. (*He sits.*) Now, will you promise me to write as I tell you?

LITTLETON: (*aside*) She smiles, ah! – (*aloud*) I'll swear it.

LADY A: 'My dear' – let's see – yes – 'dear sir' –

LITTLETON: Two adjectives?

LADY A: Ye–s! 'If (*reading letter*) fondest hopes' – poor fellow! – 'if you imagine my treatment of you to be cruel' –

LITTLETON: (*aside*) Damme, if she isn't making me write a love letter to somebody; oh, that's too good! (*Rises and throws down pen.*)

LADY A: Bad pen? don't stir, here's another. (*Offers a pen; he looks at her, and sneaks back.*) 'You will forgive me, your letter now before me, so full of deep affection' – (*Reads letter.*) mad affection – ah! – 'has touched me to the heart.'

LITTLETON: If I write that, may I –

LADY A: Your promise, sir!

LITTLETON: Go on – your ladyship is very kind – proceed.

LADY A: 'Let me confess, that I am at this moment inflicting upon you a torture, which, although you deserve, I am too feeling to continue. Rather than see you suffer longer, let me own myself, for ever, yours.'

LITTLETON: Is there any more?

LADY A: Yes, the direction.

LITTLETON: Ha! who's the inf– gentleman?

LADY A: 'To Littleton Coke, Esq.'

LITTLETON: (*starting up*) Myself – could you –

LADY A: Ha! ha! ha!

LITTLETON: That letter –

LADY A: Take it. (*Gives him the letter.*)

LITTLETON: Blank! – ha! my own to Miss Rocket.

LADY A: Ha! ha! ha!

LITTLETON: And you love me?

LADY A: Let me sign that letter.

LITTLETON: Which? – a – this – oh! yes, true.

LADY A: (*looking over it*) Why, it's blank, too: you did not write a line, then?

LITTLETON: Not a syllable; and for such a document I would have given my life; stop, we'll begin again.

LADY A: No, no! had you kept your promise, you would now have possessed mine to be for ever yours. (*Goes to table and sits, ready to write.*)

LITTLETON: I won't occupy you long; we'll come to 'I'll be for ever yours' at once; eh! sign a new lease of life to me.

LADY A: No, leave the document for me to look over.

LITTLETON: While suspense is making me feel like one great pulse.

LADY A: There is a prescribed time to wear mourning for a husband, and a certain time to wear reserve to a lover. I cannot throw it off so early – think how short is our acquaintance.

LITTLETON: But how much can be done in it, by hearts like ours; you are no slave to society, nor am I. (*Embraces her.*)

LADY A: You impetuous wretch – release me.

LITTLETON: One word, then.

LADY A: Hush! someone.

　　　　　(*Enter* BOB.)

LITTLETON: Bob!

BOB: (*aside to him*) Sir – sir – Craft's –

LITTLETON: Craft!

BOB: On the premises, saw him myself, and dressed like a gentleman – so he's serious, and means to have you – get out of the house.

LITTLETON: But how?

BOB: By any way but the hall door; it's old Scriven's debt.

LITTLETON: And it's above £20. Ruin! – in twelve hours I should have been a Member of Parliament, and free. Bob! go to the top of the staircase – watch – prevent him from coming up, by any means, tumble on him, pitch him over the bannisters accidentally, any way. (BOB *goes out.*)

LADY A: Who is that?

LITTLETON: A – a – my agent; he tells me that I must start for Closeborough immediately – every moment's delay is an agony to him.

LADY A: Closeborough?

LITTLETON: Yes – the poll takes place to-morrow. I must be there to-night.

LADY A: An election without me – that's enough to unseat the candidate – and only a few miles from town, too.

LITTLETON: 'Tis not too late – with your voice in my favour.

LADY A: Oh, if I could but escape! the Earl considers me bound to canvass for Charles – ha! ha! fancy me stealing a march on Pompey, turning Closeborough into a modern Pharsalia, to run away, like Cleopatra, when the battle began, and leave Pompey in the minority. Ha! ha! ha!

LITTLETON: Not run away, only desert to the enemy.

LADY A: That's true – I'll do it – consider yourself M.P. for Closeborough – ha! ha! ha! I'll be off at once.

LITTLETON: Hark! your carriage is driving round into the stables.

LADY A: Let the horses be kept in it; I shall be ready before the earl can return.

LITTLETON: Can you afford Mr. Rural a seat?

LADY A: With pleasure.

LITTLETON: And me?

LADY A: Impertinent – certainly not!

LITTLETON: Outside?

LADY A: Don't dare to approach me, by a mile.

LITTLETON: But you go to Ghuznee Lodge, where I am invited also.

LADY A: Then you must occupy the village inn, while I am there. Now the fellow pouts again; listen: must I not preserve my reputation intact, even from you, before marriage, or you may call it in question with yourself after it? Send to me your dear old friend – good bye.

LITTLETON: But stop one moment, this letter –

LADY A: Well?

LITTLETON: 'Twas written and directed, but unsealed –

LADY A: You want my ring again – love defunct.

LITTLETON: No, I'm alive – thus (*kissing her hand*) Paradise is regained. (*Exit* LADY ALICE.) She loves me; there is not the slightest doubt on the point – I am beloved by an angel and five thousand a year – do I remember awaking this morning?

(*Enter* ROEBUCK, *in a postillion's jacket and cap.*)

Charles! – what's this?

ROEBUCK: Old Rocket's carriage has just driven up to the door – a thought struck me – I'll use it to elope with his daughter.

LITTLETON: Where to?

ROEBUCK: To Closeborough; I have not the courage to argue with my father, or with hers. I'll make a demonstration – I'll ask Lady Alice to accompany her; for form's sake I shall leave her at the Lodge, and to preserve the reputation I prize beyond my own. I will not compromise it by showing myself to the servants, but, without dismounting, return to the Rocket Arms, in the village.

LITTLETON: You're five minutes too late: she's engaged to me on the same road.

ROEBUCK: To elope?

LITTLETON: Very near – own brother to the fact.

ROEBUCK: Ha! ha! you're jealous of my speed in love – you're distanced – look, this is a suit of our family livery; I'll rattle down to Ghuznee Lodge in two hours and forty minutes.

(*Enter* BOB.)

LITTLETON: (*crossing to* BOB) Run down to the stables, and slip a saddle on the near-horse in the Brougham fly. (*Exit* BOB.) All right. Lady Alice is going down on my interest with Rural – she refused me a seat inside her carriage: damme, I'll take one outside on her horse and give Craft the slip – this is glorious – where is the livery? in the harness-room? I know – all right.

    (*Enter* RURAL.)

My dear old friend, give me your hand. (*Shakes it violently.*) You said fortune smiled upon me – a mistake – she roars – don't ask me to explain – I couldn't. There's Roebuck, ask him – he's in his senses – shall I survive it? (*Runs out. RURAL approaches* ROEBUCK, *who is walking hastily up and down.*)

RURAL: Tell me, what does it mean?

ROEBUCK: It means rapture – success – madness.

RURAL: Yes, I see that – but –

ROEBUCK: You – you take Lady Alice down to her carriage, and mum – do you understand?

RURAL: Not quite! but never mind.

ROEBUCK: While the colonel's carriage waits below.

RURAL: I know it does, for his lovely daughter – yes.

ROEBUCK: (*aside*) Ha! the old gentleman is deeper than I thought – he sees through our plot. – Then, my dear sir, two of the happiest dogs in London will whirl down two of its loveliest denizens to Closeborough.

RURAL: What an extraordinary preface to marriage. Had I not heard of its approval from the lips of the old gentleman, I should have considered it too wonderful to be correct.

    (*Enter* BOB, *breathlessly.*)

BOB: It's all ready, sir; saddled complete.

ROEBUCK: To your conduct is confided Miss Rocket.

BOB: (*aside*) Oh! I thought it was an elopement my master was about.

ROEBUCK: Hush! she is here; run to her lady's maid, and get her shawl; I'll not give hesitation a chance.

    (*Enter* KATE.)

BOB: (*looking at her*) Oh, that's the lady – well – he has my consent. (*Exit.*)

RURAL: This appears very strange.

ROEBUCK: My dearest Kate!

KATE: Charles! and in this dress!

ROEBUCK: Do not waste our precious time in wonder; I will explain it presently.

KATE: I have suspected you unworthily, wickedly, but Alice has made me ashamed of my folly; let me suffer something to gain your pardon.

ROEBUCK: I will. Your carriage waits: suffer me to fly with you.

KATE: Fly!

ROEBUCK: Only to your own house – 'Twill be enough to show our tyrants that their opposition would be vain. Bob will conduct you to your carriage.

KATE: Bob!

ROEBUCK: Ha! oh! I never – Crawl, Bob Crawl – Alice is going –

KATE: To elope –

ROEBUCK: With Coke. (*aside*) Nothing convinces a woman or a judge like a precedent.

KATE: I dare not – how – to --

ROEBUCK: I will waft you both down like a zephyr. (*to* RURAL, *who is approaching*) My dear sir, join your prayers to mine – she refuses to go.

KATE: But my father? –

RURAL: My dear young lady, if that's all, your father desires it – commands it – declares that the affair must be settled before breakfast to-morrow.

KATE: That's he – I must credit you.

RURAL: He ordered the carriage – have no scruples – he assures me that you would not.

KATE: Can I believe my ears?

RURAL: You may; it's extraordinary, but you may.

          (*Enter* BOB, *with the shawl and bonnet.*)

BOB: Here they are, sir: only cost me a kiss and a few promises.

KATE: I'm in a dream.

RURAL: So am I. (*Goes upstage with* KATE *and* ROEBUCK.)

BOB: (*aside*) The old money-lender here, and on such a job – ah! gets his bill out of her fortune. I must make something. Excellent! a paragraph in the *Morning Post*. Elopement in high life – Littleton Coke, Esq., with the great heiress and lovely daughter of Colonel Rocket. Bilious father – it's in time for to-morrow's impression – they'll make an express of it. Let's see, I'll ask a small percentage on the magnitude of her fortune – I'll try twenty thousand a year. I may get five pounds; besides, 'twill civilize the creditors.

ROEBUCK: Be assured, dearest; confide in my devoted love, and farewell. Enough – (*to* BOB) I leave her to your care; farewell, dearest – now for the saddle, and I'm off – hurra for the road! (*Exit.*)

LITTLETON: (*appearing in the dress of a postillion*) Is she ready?

BOB: Very near, sir: all right.

LITTLETON: Make haste!

BOB: That's for you to do, sir –

LITTLETON: True – I'll introduce the turnpikes to fourteen miles an hour. (*Exit.*)

KATE: I tremble –

RURAL: So do I, my dear child.

          (*Enter* LADY ALICE.)

LADY A: Kate!

KATE: Alice!

BOB: (*aside*) Hollo! here's –

LADY A: What does this mean?

RURAL: Exactly – now – we'll have it.

KATE: My meaning, I believe, is yours.

LADY A: I – I – I'm – give me a kiss, Kate; we are both a pair of fools, dear.

RURAL: Well, 'tis no clearer now – my dear – he waits.

BOB: (*aside*) Extraordinary express – another elopement. Lord Charles Roebuck with the Lady Alice Hawthorn. Ten pounds –

RURAL: 'Tis no clearer now. (LADY ALICE *takes his arm.*)

BOB: This way. (*Conducts* KATE. RURAL *goes with* LADY ALICE.)

RURAL: I wish you – both – farewell.

KATE: (*going with* BOB) Alice, what will become of me?

LADY A: You will get married, dear.

KATE: Farewell.

RURAL: I wish you happy – farewell! (*Exeunt.*)

ACT V

Ghuznee Lodge. The house is a villa, with an Indian character apparently forced upon it. The lawn and shrubberies extend out as if into the auditorium. Shrubberies on either side, with a pagoda summer-house. A broad carriage-entrance leads off. A sentry-box in a bush. STRIPE is discovered, standing at the back, directing a field-glass down the avenue. A VETERAN, in Bombay cavalry uniform, walks as if keeping guard.

STRIPE: No sign of the colonel, yet his orders were for us to be in readiness to receive him at two this morning, and here's half-past eleven – I've despatched Wilcox with the old howitzer to the top of the hill, to give us a signal; hollo! whom have we here? good light cavalry figure.

    (*Enter LITTLETON down the avenue.*)

Aide-de-camp with despatches from headquarters, perhaps.

LITTLETON: I've left Bob addressing the free and independent electors of Close-borough from the hustings. (*very distant shouts*) There's another shout, elicited by his rhetoric. I believe the rascal has compromised me with every opinion on the political creed; 'twas useless arguing with him – he said, 'twas no good in losing a vote for a mere promise – so, damn the fellow if he didn't promise everything to everybody. (*distant shouts*) Whether I am whig, tory, or radical will puzzle the *Times* to discover.

    (*Enter RURAL from the house.*)

RURAL: My dear boy, I don't know what's the matter inside, but something has gone wrong; Lady Hawthorn won't hear a word from me.

LITTLETON: (*aside*) She has discovered my disguise; no matter, she will readily forgive it.

RURAL: Just now, she and Miss Rocket flew upon me, but all they could say was, 'Explain, sir, explain'.

LITTLETON: And you?

RURAL: I – I ran away, because, you see, explain was just the thing I couldn't do.

LITTLETON: (*aside*) He is in the dark still; 'twill be safer to keep him so. – My dear old friend, 'tis all a freak, a – a –

RURAL: Ah! ah! come now, you are at some of your old tricks – oh! oh! I know you are!

LITTLETON: We have planned a surprise, by which the old colonel and the earl will find that our young hearts have outmanoeuvred their old heads – but 'tis secret.

RURAL: Oh, let me into it.

LITTLETON: When the colonel arrives, and discovers Roebuck, he may storm a little.

RURAL: What for? have I not his orders that you should use his carriage?

LITTLETON: You will never mind his temper.

RURAL: Not a bit, ha! ha!

LITTLETON: The earl may possibly be annoyed –

RURAL: Annoyed! – he'll be enraged! – ha! ha! – he said he would, oho! and you – now, this is all your plot, you rogue, you know it is, isn't it?

LITTLETON: It is – but hush! here they come – leave us.

RURAL: Oh, you wild, mischievous dog – oh, just what you were, when you played me those tricks in the poultry yard; when, ha! ha! you tied a gosling to my coat tail, and when I walked off, the gander was nearly the death of me – oh! ha! ha! ha! you villain!

LITTLETON: But go, I beseech.

RURAL: (*Starts to go, and returns.*) And that fifth of November too, when –

LITTLETON: I remember, there –

RURAL: A squib in my snuff-box – oh, you little rogue, oh! bless you! oh! a squib in my snuff-box! (*Exit chuckling.*)

LITTLETON: And bless you for the simplest, kindest soul alive.

(*Enter from the house* LADY ALICE, *with a newspaper, and* KATE, *followed by* ROEBUCK.)

ROEBUCK: But hear me.

LADY A: Not a word – here's a fine catastrophe to your clever intrigues! here's an *exposée* – I shouldn't wonder if they put the whole affair into a novel, or on the stage. Fancy my follies published in penny numbers, with illustrations; or your blunders enjoying a run at the Haymarket. Bah! – I could laugh my life out at you both, if I wasn't mad with rage.

LITTLETON: But my dearest –

LADY A: No, sir, you have precluded the possibility of my ever being so –

LITTLETON: Charles, what *does* this mean?

ROEBUCK: Hang me if I know. I have only been here a few minutes, but I found them both fulminating over that *Post.*

KATE: Do you pretend ignorance, my lord?

LADY A: Listen, you precious intriguers – listen: (*Reads.*) 'Express. Elopement in high life. Enormous fortune won by a young barrister. We understand, from the best authority, that an elopement took place last night from the opera. The imprudent pair are – Mr. Littleton Coke, of *qui tam* celebrity, and the great heiress, Miss Rocket, whose fortune is said to exceed £20,000 a year.'

LITTLETON: The idiots – what could have caused –

KATE: Go on.

LADY A: 'Second edition – extraordinary express. Another elopement in high life. Last night, the young and eccentric Lady Alice Hawthorn, whose meteoric course through the fashionable world has been greeted with such admiration, eloped from Lord Pompion's house with her cousin, Lord Charles Roebuck. It is stated, one of the parties rode postillion; our authority omits to mention which.'

LITTLETON: The dolts: by what mistake could this have happened?

LADY A: By none.

ROEBUCK: How?

LADY A: 'Tis true.

---

qui tam: in law, an action brought by an informer, who sues on his own behalf as well as on behalf of the crown. Bob has evidently ascribed his own intentions to Littleton.

ROEBUCK: How!

LITTLETON: True!

KATE: Quite.

LADY A: You thought to outwit me and the old people – and thus you set about
it. (*to* LITTLETON) The lady before whom you spurred and thrashed, sir,
was Miss Rocket; (*to* ROEBUCK) and the humble individual who admired
your equitation for three hours, was your obliged servant.

LITTLETON: What! and – I – Miss – and he – you – eh!

ROEBUCK: Coke!

LITTLETON: I didn't – I – (*They look at each other, astonished.*)

ROEBUCK: Oh! but surely this mysterious blunder is not so serious – it can be
mended by –

LADY A: What, sir – when all London know that my cousin ran away with – or
rather, they don't know which of us ran away with the other – ah! you
wretch! and in the middle of the night, too – and – no – I must marry Charley
after all! (*Crosses to* ROEBUCK, *and cries.*)

KATE: And you – sir – you –

LITTLETON: I suppose I must marry you, then, after all.

LADY A: And all your cunning to outwit the governors has just effected their purposes.

ROEBUCK: But Kate – surely you will not, by marrying him to save your character, condemn yourself to eternal misery?

LITTLETON: (*crossing to him*) Eternal what, sir? let me tell you, my lord, that
this is your fault, your blunder – had I been there, I –

ROEBUCK: Mine, sir, mine!

LITTLETON: Yes, yours.

ROEBUCK: 'Tis false, sir.

LITTLETON: False! very well, my lord.

ROEBUCK: I repeat, sir, that –

LITTLETON: Enough, the word suffices; but for this presence, I feel you would
have substituted a stronger term, but – (*They speak apart as they go upstage.*)

KATE: My dear Alice, they are quarrelling.

LADY A: No!

KATE: They are. I've seen many men do it – I know it, in a minute they'll fight.

LADY A: A duel, and on our account! No more is required to complete our des-
truction. Mr. Coke – Charles – will you listen? There's nothing so like a mad
bull as a man in a rage. Charles – Mr. Coke, you shall not quarrel; you have
not the excuse of a long dinner; will you hear me?

ROEBUCK: I repeat that it was his trusting to Mr. Rural that has caused this
dreadful catastrophe – and to prove it, I will find him. (*Exit into house.*)

LITTLETON: Rural, could it – it is. Oh, my folly and weakness! Why did I entrust
so dear a confidence to him? He must exonerate me from this fatal blunder –
where shall I find him? (*Goes upstage, meets* STRIPE, *who is crossing. Speaks
in dumb show.* STRIPE *points. Exeunt.*)

KATE: Alice, dear, what's to be done?

LADY A: They must not fight, because we can't spare either of them.

KATE: But do you – do you think dear, we shall have to – to – exchange them?

LADY A: I don't know, love; but it's very likely; I never was run away with before:
but, I believe, people in such predicaments always do marry, dear, if they can.
(*a distant gun*) What's that?
> (*Enter* STRIPE.)

STRIPE: Ready, guard, the Colonel comes – that's the signal.

KATE: Oh, Alice, I dare not meet him.

LADY A: And I am ashamed!

ROCKET: (*outside*) Guard –

KATE: Here, in this pagoda. Quick! (*They enter the pagoda.*)
> (*Enter* COLONEL ROCKET, *followed by* TOM COKE, LORD
> POMPION *and* LADY POMPION.)

ROCKET: So! good! guard, turn in. (*Exeunt the men.*) Stripe!

STRIPE: Colonel!

ROCKET: (*with suppressed rage*) The reports?

STRIPE: Nothing, sir, particular, till past two this morning.

ROCKET: And then –

STRIPE: Two carriages arrived half an hour apart.

ROCKET: Whom did they contain?

STRIPE: The first, Miss Rocket and an old gentleman, in the last, only a lady.

LADY P: My niece! I knew that girl would come to some shocking end.

TOM: But she was alone.

STRIPE: Alone!

TOM: (*aside*) There's a sovereign for you.

ROCKET: Stripe – dismiss. (STRIPE *salutes and exit. They all look at each other.*)

TOM: (*aside*) I feel as if my heart was returned to my body.

LORD P: Calm yourself, my dear colonel – observe my imperturbability. Your
daughter has, unfortunately, eloped with her own groom; a buzz – three days'
amusing variations of the story, and it is forgotten. Perhaps you will be kind
enough to tell my niece that we await her here.

ROCKET: As for the rascally footboy, I'll kick him into Chodah – Kate will keep,
but let me only catch that old intriguer. Excuse me, your ladyship – till I've
found him I'm not fit to play the host. (*Goes into the house.*)

LADY P: Where can Charles be?

LORD P: I heard the shouts as we passed – perhaps they are chairing him.

LADY P: Mr. Coke, favour me with your arm – the excitement has quite unnerved
me. (TOM *and* LADY POMPION *go into the house.*)

LORD P: 'Tis done – they are wedded – I'm sure of it.
> (*Enter* ROEBUCK.)

ROEBUCK: Where can this old – my father!

LORD P: Charles, or is it a –

ROEBUCK: Of course, my lord, you have discovered all – if not, I am not in the
vein to deceive you longer.

LORD P: What do you mean?

Chodah: perhaps a corruption of *chuddar* – a large sheet worn as a shawl by women in North
India. If so, the word is being used merely because it is Indian, by Rocket – or by Boucicault.

ROEBUCK: That to achieve the hopes of my heart, I was induced to assume the disguise in which we met last night.

LORD P: Then you were –

ROEBUCK: The groom to Miss Rocket.

LORD P: And you are – are married to her?

ROEBUCK: I – I –

LORD P: Don't speak, sir – I know – I've been duped, and by my own son. Lord Charles! what excuse – what – what – Where's that meddling old fellow? This is his doing – his work – I'll find him – and let him know the consequences of thwarting a minister of state, and a peer of the realm. (*Exit into house.*)

ROEBUCK: And I, to show him how his folly has severed two young hearts for ever. (*Exit into house.*)

(*Enter* RURAL, *at the back.*)

RURAL: Bless me, what a run I've had – joy has given me youth again, and I really did have a scamper – yes – but – (*Staggers.*) Ah! these old limbs – these old limbs. (*Sits on garden chair.*)

(*Enter* LORD POMPION *from house.*)

LORD P: Oh! – at last – I have found you, sir!

(COLONEL ROCKET *rushes down from the house.*)

ROCKET: Aha! Here you are, are you?

RURAL: Yes, my dear friends, here I am.

ROCKET: Let me contain myself, and respect his age and his profession. Harkye, sir, are you not ashamed of yourself?

RURAL: (*aside*) Oh, here come the reproaches. – Yes – ha! ha! – I am – I am.

LORD P: To connive at such a scheme – a fraud.

RURAL: Ha! ha! (*aside*) He told me not to heed his anger – that he would assume it for policy – I won't. (*aloud, and in* LORD POMPION's *face*) Ha! ha! ha!

LORD P: And by what authority did you marry my son, sir?

RURAL: (*aside*) Ha! ha! ha! and he told me to do it – oh, the hypocrite. (*aloud*) Ha! ha! ha!

ROCKET: I respect your position, sir, but –

RURAL: Ha! ha! ha!

LORD P: Mr. Rural, this is indecent.

RURAL: Ha! ha! ha! ha! (*Retires upstage with* LORD POMPION.)

ROCKET: If I remain, I shall forget myself.

(*Enter* LADY ALICE, LITTLETON, KATE, *and* ROEBUCK.)

RURAL: Aha! at last they are here, my blest ones, and I am free – give me your hands. (*Crosses to* ROEBUCK.)

ROEBUCK: When you have severed our hearts for ever?

RURAL: Eh?

KATE: Oh, sir, you have destroyed the only hope of my existence.

RURAL: What!

LADY A: What could have actuated you to such a deed? or did you betray us to the earl and the colonel, and agree to compromise us into obedience?

RURAL: Bless me – Littleton –

LITTLETON: Do not look to me for help.

RURAL: I – ah – (*aside*) The rascal is keeping up the joke because the old people are here.

LADY A: Exonerate yourself, sir.

RURAL: Ha!

ROEBUCK: What excuse can you –

RURAL: Ha! ha!

KATE: You could not have mistaken –

RURAL: Ha! ha! ha!

LITTLETON: Can you not see, sir, this is reality?

RURAL: Ha! ha! – (*Chokes a laugh.*) ha!

LITTLETON: Is my ruin a subject for your mirth?

RURAL: (*in wonder, but continuing to laugh*) Ha! ha!

LADY A: It is inhuman!

RURAL: Ha! ha! ha!

LITTLETON: Or have you – yes, her suspicions are true, and you have betrayed me.

RURAL: Ha! ha! ha!

LITTLETON: And over such a deed you can laugh – farewell for ever!

> (RURAL *bursts into a paroxysm of hysterical and convulsive laughter.* LADY ALICE *runs to* RURAL *on one side,* KATE *on the other, while* ROEBUCK *and* LITTLETON *walk up and down on opposite sides.*)

LADY A: Don't weep, it was no fault of yours – you would have aided our love if our foolish young hearts had not puzzled your kind old head.

RURAL: He's gone! he's gone!

LITTLETON: No, my dear friend, (*Goes to* RURAL *and embraces him.*) pardon my cruelty to you: I have slighted your affection, (*looking at* LADY ALICE) and for what?

RURAL: Bless my heart! but I have ruined you.

LITTLETON: No!

RURAL: I have, I know I have. – I have ruined my child – my – oh, forgive me, will you, Littleton?

LITTLETON: How shall I forgive myself? Come, we will leave this place. (RURAL *gets up and clings to him.*) Lady Alice, one word, before I go.

LADY A: You shall not, till you have forgiven me.

LITTLETON: Forgiven!

KATE: Charles, I do repent my cruelty.

> (RURAL *goes upstage with* LITTLETON, ROEBUCK, *and* KATE.
> ROCKET *and* LORD POMPION *speak. Enter* TOM *from the house.*)

ROCKET: I trust, my lord, you do not suspect I had any hand in this affair?

LORD P: Let us make the best of it. I have reasons for wishing that the particulars should not be investigated.

ROCKET: (*crossing to* KATE) There, Kate, I don't forgive you for outflanking your old father; but (*Whispers.*) damme girl, you're right, he's a dashing fellow.

TOM: May I beg a moment of your ladyship's attention?

LADY A: Certainly. (*They advance. The rest retire a little.*)

TOM: A'm – a – a man of few words, and I don't think you loike me less for being honest. A've none of the ways that the gay young fellows about town cultivate to win women's hearts with – because I never in my life intended to win but one, and I meant that should be my wife's.

LADY A: I believe you.

TOM: A – ahem. (*aside*) This wants more than honesty, I find. (*Pauses – at last loud and bluntly.*) A've two estates in Yorkshire – a've twenty coal pits, and an iron hole – a've – a've four thousand honest pounds a year to spend, and a've a true English heart, very much at your ladyship's service – and a've – a've – that's all – (*pause*) Coom – don't hesitate – be honest, as I am – say yes – or – or – no.

LADY A: Honestly – I must say – no.

TOM: Well – a – that – is – at – least – honest. Yes – it is – it is – (*He is affected.*) and (*huskily*) may I ask you a straightforward question?

LADY A: Yes.

TOM: Do you love another?

LADY A: I do.

TOM: That's honest, too – oh, I loike it – and – ahem – that other –

LADY A: Is your brother.

TOM: Littleton?

LADY A: Yes.

TOM: Thank you – I – that is – thank you – (*She retires.*) wi' – my brother – wi' – very well – and – yes – I'll do't – I – will – I *oul.* (*Calls.*) Brother Littleton. (LITTLETON *advances.*) You – love – a – that lady?

LITTLETON: Yes.

TOM: Am not surprised at it – and a suppose you know that she loves you – she told me so – but would you, for her sake, quit gay London? – would you live for her only?

LITTLETON: I would, and will.

TOM: She's worthy of a prince's throne. Brother, oh give her, then, an honest heart, love her as I – as she – loves you, ahem! (*Pauses.*) I – Littleton, here is every paper you ever signed to me; 'ave never counted them, for they sickened me to look at. A brought them doon here thinking to restore them to you on my – but – no matter, turn a foolish vanity and – (*Becomes abstracted, after a pause passes his hand across his eyes.*) 'tis past – take them, Littleton, take back my father's gift – no – I'll buy no brother's birthright wi' a mess of pottage; and besides, it wouldn't do for you to go to your rich wife a beggar, and – and – Littleton, I – (*chokedly and whispering*) God bless you! (*Shakes his hand.*)

LITTLETON: Tom – brother – my friends, I –

TOM: (*seizing his hand*) Hush! – hu – (*pointing to the papers*) between ourselves, not a word, not even to minister; such things should be sacred as our mother's grave – not a word. (*They go upstage affectionately.*)

LORD P: I'll hear no more. I disapprove of the match – the young man is a pauper, and possesses no rank to entitle him.

LITTLETON: My Lord!

TOM: Not quite a pauper either, my lord, since he possesses nigh two thousand pounds a year – and is, and ever will be, my only heir to twice as much again. (*Shouts heard without. Enter* BOB.)

BOB: They're waiting to chair the member.

LORD P: Lord Charles – make haste!

BOB: Not at all. (*loud shouts outside – 'Hurrah for Coke! Coke!'*) Do you hear?

LORD P: Impossible! what's the state of the poll?

BOB: Here it is, at the close, Coke 218, Roebuck 2.

LORD P: I've been – (*aside*) stop, I may gain over the new member – (*aloud*) Mr. Coke, my hasty expression –

ROCKET: How's this, not married yet?

LORD P: Ha! Can it be possible? then I may save him yet. Colonel, things have assumed an aspect, which –

(*Enter* LADY POMPION *from house.*)

LADY P: What is all this?

BOB: (*aside to* ROEBUCK) All right, my lord, I'll settle the Earl. (*aloud*) If your lordship will allow me to explain our interview last evening to the countess.

LORD P: Not a word.

BOB: The boy, Robert –

LORD P: I beseech – my dear children, may heaven bless your felicitous union.

RURAL: May I unite 'em, may I? come here; (*Calls* LADY ALICE *and* KATE, *takes them under his arms.*) bless your young faces, your smiles fall like sunshine on my old heart; this is a delicious moment! – (*Turns round, and pushes* KATE *and* LADY ALICE *towards their wrong lovers; then turns to the audience.*) There! bless you! may heaven shower its blessings on you, as it now does on me. (ROEBUCK *and* LITTLETON *exchange* KATE *and* LADY ALICE *behind* RURAL'*s back.*) Here's a feast of joy! look at this happiness! (*Turns round to* ROEBUCK, *sees him embracing* KATE.) Hollo! bless me! (*Turns round, and sees* LITTLETON *embracing* LADY ALICE.) Good gracious me! ha! what, have I mistaken? – and – you – ah! I see – old heads and young hearts! well, no matter – bless you that way. (*to audience*) I see many young hearts before me; I hope you're all in love – I do – and that I could unite you all. Well, I bequeath you to the conduct of the old heads; and to them I would say, did you ever see a little child leading an old blind man? how can age best repay such a charity? why, by guiding the blindness of youth, which is love: this is the last debt due from an old head to a young heart.

DISPOSITION OF THE CHARACTERS AT THE FALL OF THE CURTAIN.

TOM. LADY P. LORD P. LITTLETON. LADY A. RURAL. KATE. ROEBUCK. ROCKET.
Right.   Left.

JESSIE BROWN; or, THE RELIEF OF LUCKNOW

A drama in three acts

First performed at Wallack's Theatre, New York on 22 February 1858, with the following cast:

NATIVES

THE NANA SAHIB	Mr. Boucicault
ACHMET	Mr. H. B. Phillips
REBEL SEPOYS	Mr. West and Mr. Everitt

BRITISH

RANDAL MACGREGOR	Mr. Lester
GEORDIE MACGREGOR	Mr. A. H. Davenport
REV. DAVID BLOUNT	Mr. W. R. Blake
SWEENIE	Mr. T. B. Johnston
CASSIDY	Mr. Sloan
JESSIE BROWN	Miss Agnes Robertson
MRS. CAMPBELL	Mrs. Hoey
CHARLIE and EFFIE	the Misses Reeves
ALICE	Mrs. J. H. Allen
MARY	Mrs. H. B. Phillips

Time of Representation – Two Hours and Forty Minutes.*

---

* Further evidence that the original play was longer than this acting version, probably in four acts.

II Boucicault as Nana Sahib in *Jessie Brown*

ACT I

SCENE 1. *The exterior of the Bungalow of* MRS. CAMPBELL. *Lucknow in the distance, seen over a low parapet wall at back. Table laid on right side, under a tree, with viands upon it. Native servants in attendance.*

Music. Enter left GEORDIE MACGREGOR, *with* ALICE *and* MARY, *and* ACHMET *from the house, right.*

GEORDIE: Here we are at last. What can induce Mrs. Campbell to live a mile from Lucknow?

ALICE: You are a pretty soldier – you cannot march a mile without a murmur.

GEORDIE: On my own native hills in bonnie Scotland, with my hound by my side, I have walked a dozen miles before breakfast; but under this Indian sun –

MARY: And with only a pretty girl by your side –

ALICE: Say two pretty girls. Don't be bashful, Mary – include me.

(*Enter* MRS. CAMPBELL, *right.*)

GEORDIE: Oh, Mrs. Campbell, look here! I am besieged. Delhi is nothing to the condition I shall be in if you don't relieve me.

ALICE: Mrs. Campbell, please, he won't tell us which of us he is in love with.

MRS. C: *I* will tell you, with neither. He is in love with his new uniform; he only received his commission two months ago, and every officer is for six months in love with himself.

GEORDIE: After that I'll take a glass of sangaree.

MRS. C: Where's Randal?

GEORDIE: My fiery brother, 'the MacGregor' – as Jessie will insist on calling him – is, as usual, inspecting his men.

MRS. C: Jessie is right; for your brother, Randal MacGregor, is one of the noblest men that ever breathed the Scottish air and made it purer. But tell me, what news from Delhi?

(*They sit.*)

GEORDIE: Oh, the siege continues; but it will be taken, of course – these black rascals are mere scum.

(ACHMET, *who is serving* GEORDIE, *looks round.*)

ALICE: *There* is one who disagrees with you on that point.

GEORDIE: Does he?

ACHMET: No, sahib. Allah Akbar! it is so – we *are* scum. Lady, in Hindoostan there are one hundred millions such as I am, and there are one hundred thousand such as you; yet for a century you have had your foot on our necks; we are to you a thousand to one – a thousand black necks to one white foot. Allah is great, and Mohammed is his prophet. We are *scum*!

Delhi is nothing . . . : Delhi fell to rebel sepoys in May 1857, and was not relieved until September 1857.
sangaree: a cold drink of spiced and diluted wine.
Allah Akbar: God is mighty.
Hindoostan: sometimes used to describe the area of Northern India comprising the Gangetic plain.

GEORDIE: I can't answer for the truth of your calculation, but I agree in the sentiment – you *are* scum. (*Drinks.*)

ACHMET: Sometimes the scum rises.

GEORDIE: Yes, Dusky, and when it does, the pot boils over and puts the fire out; so the scum extinguishes the element that made it rise.

ACHMET: I cannot reason with a European.

GEORDIE: No, nor fight with one; by your own calculation, it takes one thousand of you to do either one or the other.

(*Exit* ACHMET, *right.*)

MRS. C: Beware of that man, Geordie: I did not like the expression of his face as you spoke.

GEORDIE: Bah! there is virtue enough in one red coat to put a whole army of them to flight.

MRS. C: Have you ever been in battle?

GEORDIE: Never. But when I'm on parade, and hear the drums and see the uniforms, I feel like the very devil.

ALICE: There is no chance of the war coming here – is there?

GEORDIE: Not the slightest. London itself is not more peaceable than yonder city of Lucknow; the native regiments here are faithful as dogs. You need not fear danger.

MRS. C: The rebellion is still far. But when I think of the atrocities already perpetrated by the Sepoys – when I think of my two little children – oh, why do I remain here in the midst of such scenes of horror?

GEORDIE: Because you are in love with my brother Randal; the feelings of the mother urge you to go, and the feelings of the woman command you to stay.

MRS. C: (*rising*) Geordie, there is more truth than kindness in what you say.

GEORDIE: (*Holds her.*) Stay, Amy, I'm a thoughtless fool.

MRS. C: Yet you wrong me a little – I was betrothed to Randal; we quarrelled, as lovers will, and parted; – in that moment of anger I accepted the hand of Colonel Campbell.

GEORDIE: At the siege of Sebastopol, Randal became your husband's most devoted friend, and watched over him like a brother.

MRS. C: Oh, it was a noble reproof to my falsehood.

GEORDIE: And at the charge of the Highlanders, when Campbell was struck down mortally wounded, and the command devolved on my brother, Randal carried him in his arms, at the head of the regiment, into the redoubt, so that none of the glory of that day should be lost to his rival.

MRS. C: Should I not be ungrateful to my dead husband if I did not love Randal MacGregor as I do?

(JESSIE *sings off left.* GEORDIE *moves towards left.*)

MARY: Hush, listen!

Sepoys: Indian soldiers serving under British command. The English press of 1857 generally applied the word to those among the Indian soldiers who had rebelled against their English officers.

siege of Sebastopol: the reference is to the Crimean War, and the taking of Sebastopol by the allies after its eleven-month defence by the Russians in 1855.

redoubt: a small outwork in a permanent fortification.

ALICE: What is that?

GEORDIE: What is it? why it is a sprig of heather from the Highland moors. It is a
slogan on the Scotch pipes that nature has put into the prettiest throat that
ever had an arm round it. It is the pet of the regiment. – It is Jessie Brown.

MRS. C: Yes, 'tis Jessie; here she comes up the hill with her two lovers.

ALICE: Two lovers! that's extra allowance.

GEORDIE: She might have eight hundred if she liked, for that is the strength of the
78th Regiment, and there's not a man in it that would not stake his life for
a blink of her blue eye.

MRS. C: Jessie is a good girl, as honest and true as steel; she is betrothed to Sweenie
Jones, a private in the 32nd.

GEORDIE: An ugly, wiry little fellow, but a smart soldier, and as brave as a terrier.

MRS. C: But she is also followed by a soft, good-natured Irish corporal named
Cassidy, the bosom friend of Sweenie, and to see these two men so devoted
to each other, and yet so fond of the same girl, is a picture too like my own
history not to fill me with interest and emotion.

> (*Music – Scotch air – very piano.*)

GEORDIE: She belongs to our clan.

ALICE: Here she comes.

MRS. C: And here come my darling ones.

> (*Enter* SWEENIE, *carrying* CHARLIE *on his back, and* CASSIDY
> *carrying* EFFIE *on his shoulder.*)

CHARLIE: Wo, hossey! come up!

> (SWEENIE *tries to salute* GEORDIE; CASSIDY *salutes him.*)

EFFIE: (*beating* CASSIDY *with her parasol*) Go along, hossey.

CHARLIE: Oh, Sweenie, you'll have me down! hold me up, sir.

> (*Enter* JESSIE. *Music ceases.*)

JESSIE: Dinna ye hear the bairn, ye lout? – hau'd him up.

SWEENIE: How can I, when I must salute my officer?

JESSIE: Eh, sirs, it's Maister Geordie – gude day, leddies – eh, my certie, how braw
a chiel he is in his red coat and his gou'd lace. There's MacGregor in every
inch of him. Eh, why wasn't I the Queen of Scotland to make a King of him!

GEORDIE: Don't be a fool, Jessie – you talk just as you did when we were children.

JESSIE: And why shouldn't I, Geordie? In the days of 'Auld Lang Syne', when we
played together on the craigs o' Duncleuch, you aye used to kiss me when we
met and parted – you do so now when there is nane to see. Are you ashamed
of those days when we were children, Geordie? I'm not.

GEORDIE: No, Jessie; and I'll kiss you now if Sweenie does not mind.

SWEENIE: No, your honour; if Jessie says all right, so it is.

CASSIDY: We give our consint.

ALICE: (*vexed*) Jessie has three lovers instead of two, it seems.

JESSIE: Eh! (*aside*) Yon lassie loo's him, I spier it in the blink o' her e'e. She'll be
fashed wi' him for kissin' me.

GEORDIE: (*aside*) Alice is furious. (*aloud*) Come, Jessie, for 'Auld Lang Syne'.

---

slogan: here used in its original Gaelic sense of 'war-cry'.

JESSIE: (*snatching* CHARLIE *from* SWEENIE – *aside to* SWEENIE) Say ye nae like it.
SWEENIE: (*puzzled*) Eh – what! Hold, your honour, I ax your pardon, but –
JESSIE: Sweenie's jealous.
CASSIDY: We are chokin' wid it, plase your honor.
MRS. C: (*who, with* MARY, *has watched this scene, and understood* JESSIE's *motives, advances*) Go along, all of you; take your sweethearts into the kitchen. Jessie, leave the children here.
JESSIE: 'Tention, 32nd! fa' in. Reecht face – March!
> (*Exeunt* SWEENIE *and* CASSIDY, *following her word of command, right.*)
MRS. C: (*laughing*) There, girls, there's a pair of lovers reduced to discipline!
ALICE: Yet people say that nowadays the chivalry has left the officers, and is to be found in the ranks.
MRS. C: No, Alice – Jessie is beloved, because all men worship what is grave, gentle, and good; because she shrinks from hurting another's feelings, even in jest, as she did yours just now.
JESSIE: Nae, my leddy – I knaw nout o' what yer spierin' at.
MRS. C: Then take that blush away.
> (JESSIE, *running out right, stops and returns timidly to* ALICE.)
JESSIE: (*in a low voice*) Ye are nae angry wi' puir Jessie?
ALICE: (*turning and throwing her arms round her neck to kiss her*) No.
> (JESSIE *runs off, right.*)
MRS. C: Now, Geordie, you can take Jessie's kiss where she has left it, and I am sure you will hurt nobody's feelings.
ALICE: Oh, Amy.
> (GEORDIE *crosses to* ALICE.)
MRS. C: Come, girls, take Geordie in. I would be alone.
> (*Music. Exeunt* GEORDIE, ALICE, *and* MARY.)
> Randal is coming. I cannot hear his footstep, but it falls on my heart; he is beyond my senses, but love, that heavenly essence, gives me a feeling finer than sense, and I know that my lover comes; 'tis the air he breathes that conveys his presence to me, as it flutters through my heart.
> (*Enter* RANDAL MACGREGOR, *left.*)
RANDAL: Amy!
MRS. C: Ah, I knew it.
CHARLIE: Oh, dere's Randal.
EFFIE: No, Charlie, me first – kiss Effie first.
> (*They run to him.*)
RANDAL: There, that will do, run along; go, Charlie – go, Effie, you tease me.
> (*The children shrink back.*)
MRS. C: Come away, dears; you are tired, Randal.
RANDAL: No; but the sight of those children pains me.
MRS. C: They remind you that I have been unfaithful – oh, Randal, do not visit the fault of the mother upon these innocent children.
RANDAL: Amy, your repentance wounds me, and your memory of that fault is a reproach to my love. Oh, let it be buried in the grave of your noble husband.

MRS. C: Forgive me.

RANDAL: Charlie, come here – Effie, come. (*They cross – he kisses them.*) Amy, I have bad news; the rebels are at Cawnpore, not fifty miles from hence, and a report has just arrived that tells of horrors committed on our countrymen, their wives, their children, that makes my blood freeze and my heart groan.

MRS. C: Randal, Randal, are we in danger here? my children, are they safe?

RANDAL: Hush! one cry of alarm, one look of fear, and we are lost. Of our regiments in Lucknow, four will mutiny, one only will remain faithful – to-night you must leave this place.

MRS. C: Is peril so near?

> (*Enter two native servants, who remove the service.*)

RANDAL: Hush! (*Sings as he dances* CHARLIE.)

> There is nae luck aboot the hoose,
> There is nae luck awa, &c.

> > (MRS. CAMPBELL *leans, trembling, over the child at her side.*
> > *Exeunt natives. Randal lets his voice sink gradually.*)

MRS. C: They are gone.

RANDAL: Regain your courage – think of these children.

MRS. C: Randal, you exaggerate the danger; look around you – all is at peace, the people are kind and gentle – not a look of anger or of hate in any face; our servants are devoted to us.

RANDAL: Fatal security! Yonder country to you seems in repose – to me it seems like a sleeping tiger. Death is lowering in the air. You say your servants are faithful – there is one of them watching us now – we are watched – don't turn – a tall black fellow in a crimson turban. (*All this time he plays with the children.*)

MRS. C: Achmet.

RANDAL: Listen, without betraying any emotion. At midnight I shall bring down fifty men – be ready to start without delay; take nothing with you – make no preparation.

MRS. C: Why cannot we fly now – at once?

RANDAL: Because your own servants would assassinate you, and join the enemy. (*Night begins.*)

MRS. C: May they not do so ere to-night?

RANDAL: No! I gave Cassidy and Sweenie leave to come here, and sent Geordie on – that makes three, and you have only thirty servants; the natives dare not attack at such odds.

MRS. C: Does Geordie know our peril?

RANDAL: No; nor is it necessary until the hour arrives. He is young, and might lack coolness.

MRS. C: Why do you suspect my household of treachery?

Cawnpore: the Cawnpore mutiny took place in June 1857. The relief of the besieged Europeans on 17 July came too late to save the 200 women and children massacred by the followers of Nana Sahib.

There is nae luck: probably the work of Jean Adams (d. 1765), this song was printed in Herd's *Scottish Songs*, Vol. II (1776), where it is set to the tune of 'Up an' waur them a', Willie'. It is one of the finest of all domestic ballads.

RANDAL: (*drawing out a paper*) Do you know the Rajah of Bithoor?

MRS. C: Nana Sahib – I saw him at Benares, at the feast of Mohammedah, a year ago. I might not have recollected him, but he followed me with so strange a gaze that he almost terrified me.

RANDAL: Do you understand Hindoostanee?

MRS. C: No.

RANDAL: I do. (*As he reads,* ACHMET *glides on behind, and creeps to his shoulder.*) This letter was intercepted at Secunderabad, to-day. Listen as I translate: 'My faithful Achmet – to-night, at one hour after the set of moon, I shall be at the Martinier with five hundred men; when the Feringhee woman is in my zenana, to you I give a lac of rupees. Destroy the children – they are giaours. Nana Sahib.'

MRS. C: My children!

> (*Music.* ACHMET *raises a knife over* RANDAL. MRS. CAMPBELL *sees him and utters a cry.* ACHMET *drops his knife, runs up and leaps over the parapet at back.* RANDAL *turns, draws a pistol and fires at him as he disappears. The above converstion is held in a low and earnest tone, but with a light and careless manner, as if subjects of trifling importance were spoken of.*
> *Re-enter* GEORDIE, ALICE, MARY, JESSIE, SWEENIE, *and* CASSIDY.)

RANDAL: Do not be alarmed. 'Twas only – a jackal; I fired and scared him away.

CASSIDY: A jackal is it – then, be jabers, here he comes back again – and on his hind legs.

> (*Enter* BLOUNT, *with his hat smashed, left.*)

ALL: Mr. Blount!

RANDAL: The chaplain of our regiment.

CASSIDY: His riverence!

BLOUNT: Good evening, my friends. May I suggest that the next time you throw a fellow six foot high over a wall, you should intimate your intentions to peaceable persons below.

CASSIDY: A jackal, six foot high!

GEORDIE: Are you hurt, sir?

BLOUNT: No; fortunately I received the thing on my head – from whence it bounded off, and rolled down the hill-side into the jungle.

Rajah of Bithoor: a courtesy title which the tactful Europeans of Cawnpore allowed to Nana Sahib, adopted son of the last (dethroned) Peshwa of Bithur, but denied him – along with his father's huge pension – by the British authorities.

the Martinier: a school for Europeans in Lucknow, whose pupils played a prominent part in the defence of the Residency.

Feringhee: Indian term for a European.

zenana: harem. (Nana Sahib's fondness for dancing girls was notorious among shocked (and probably jealous) Europeans.)

lac of rupees: literally, 100,000 rupees. In 1978, this would have been the equivalent of £10,000 (see Christopher Hibbert, *The Great Mutiny*, London, 1978, p. 172).

giaours: there is room for doubt about whether Nana Sahib would have used this Turkish term of abuse for non-Moslems in general, and for Christians in particular. Boucicault was clearly not sure that Nana Sahib was a Hindu.

RANDAL: Return to the house, all of you. (*Exeunt all but* MRS. CAMPBELL.)
Mr. Blount, stay! one word – you are a clergyman; but once you were, I
believe, an officer in Her Majesty's Carbineers.
BLOUNT: I quitted the army from conscientious scruples.
RANDAL: Are you a coward?
BLOUNT: A coward! I think not – that is – well – no; for when I read the accounts
of these atrocities, I feel in me an emotion that is evil, very evil – a sinful
desire to smash the heads of these wretches, who butcher women and infants.
I know the feeling is horrible; I ought to forgive and pray for them. I have
bound the devil in me, but he leaks out.
RANDAL: If you saw these little ones in peril, would you fight?
BLOUNT: Fight! young man – my dear Randal – I kill human beings! a clergyman
destroy lives! what do you take me for?
RANDAL: I take you for a brave man. You were born a warrior, but your more
gentle nature refused to war against any creatures but the wicked, and you
could not shed blood except in the cause of humanity. Don't deny it; you
retired from the army and became curate of a poor Scotch village near my
home; from your lips I first learned what war was.
BLOUNT: I portrayed its horrors – its wickedness.
RANDAL: I only saw its glory; I only saw your face lighted with the animation of
the charge – you fired my soul and made me what I am.
BLOUNT: Heaven forgive me; I ruined the boy.
RANDAL: I entered the army – you followed me.
BLOUNT: Did I not promise your dying father to watch over you? – and here's
how I did it.
RANDAL: Listen, my dear old tutor. You are brave and cool, and to you alone I
can confide the defence of this house to-night.
BLOUNT: To me – good gracious!
RANDAL: You will be surrounded by Nana Sahib's troops; his design is to murder
all its inmates, except Amy, whom he destines for his zenana.
BLOUNT: The demon! May his infernal spirit roast in – what am I saying? May a
merciful Father forgive him! This is horrible.
RANDAL: At midnight summon all the household, and start for the city; I will
precede you, gather a guard, and hasten back to meet you.
MRS. C: Do you go alone?
RANDAL: My horse is at the foot of the hill, picketed in the copse; once on his
back, I am in Lucknow. Farewell!
(*Music. He embraces* MRS. CAMPBELL.)
MRS. C: Oh, Randal, shall we ever meet again?
RANDAL: We sleep to-night in yonder city, or in Heaven! (*Exit.*)
BLOUNT: Stop, Randal, my dear boy; I can't do it. He is gone – what shall I do?
Mercy on me! What arms are there in the house?
MRS. C: Two double guns, a rifle, my late husband's swords, and a brace of pistols.
BLOUNT: A clergyman – a minister of peace – what will become of me? Have you
any powder?
MRS. C: A small keg of cartridges.
BLOUNT: These poor children! I tremble in every limb. Have you any caps?

MRS. C: A box or two.

BLOUNT: The old devil is kicking in me – my blood beats hot. Get thee behind me, Satan! Oh, if I could only see these deluded murderers, to speak with them, to prepare their erring souls, before I sent them to ask for that mercy in Heaven, which, by the way, they never show on earth.

(*Music.*)

My respected and dear friend, we are engaged in a wicked deed – I feel it. Come, let us see your ammunition.

SCENE 2. *An apartment of the House, with a verandah. Night. Enter* SWEENIE *and* CASSIDY.

CASSIDY: Whist! Sweenie, come here – spake low! D'ye see that wood beyant? There's fifty black divils hidin' in it, and here's one of their raping-hooks I found in the grass.

SWEENIE: Rebels here!

CASSIDY: I was watchin' the Capting; as he hurried down they crept afther him. He has come to grief, Sweenie, for yonder is the road to Lucknow, and his horse has not passed down it yet. Oh, wurra, wurra, what will we do?

SWEENIE: Give me that sabre; stop here, Cassidy, I will creep down and see what is going on below; don't say a word to frighten the women, but if I don't come back in ten minutes, conclude I'm dead; then, in with ye, barricade the doors, and tell Master Geordie.

CASSIDY: Sweenie, avich, let *me* go. Oh, murther! you'll be killed, and Jessie will never forgive me for not goin' in your place.

SWEENIE: Cassidy, if the rebels are here in force, I shall fall; and as the savages spare neither women nor children, I'll see ye both in Heaven before morning, so I won't say good night. (*Exit left.*)

CASSIDY: Heaven speed ye, Sweenie, an' keep ye.

(*Enter* JESSIE *right.*)

JESSIE: Who is that? Cassidy!

CASSIDY: Meself, darlin'.

(*Distant shot.*)

JESSIE: What's that?

CASSIDY: (*aside.*) It's murthering the Capting they are – I dar'nt tell her. (*aloud*) That – that was Sweenie; sure he's gone down beyant, may be, that is by accident – his swoord went off on half-cock.

JESSIE: His sword!

(*Enter* GEORDIE *right.*)

GEORDIE: Jessie, come here; – eh, who's that – Cassidy?

CASSIDY: (*aside*) What'll I do at all? If he knew that Sweenie was gone to get killed for his brother!

GEORDIE: Go in, Cassidy; leave us.

CASSIDY: I'm off, your honour. (*going*) Five minutes are gone, I'll creep afther Sweenie. If I had a bagginit, or a taste of a twig itself, but I've nothin' in my hand but my fist. (*Exit left.*)

JESSIE: Did you ca' me?

---

avich: my son.   *bagginit*: bayonet.

GEORDIE: Come here, you little puss; now you shall give me that kiss I did not get this afternoon.

JESSIE: Geordie, you have been drinking.

GEORDIE: And if I have? Wine lets out the truth, Jessie; and the truth is – I love you.

JESSIE: Eh! didna ye always loov me?

GEORDIE: No, I love you as you deserve to be loved, and I can't bear to see such a pretty girl as you have grown throw yourself away on those common soldiers, like Sweenie and his comrades.

JESSIE: Oh, Geordie! Sweenie loves you – he would dee for you or for Randal.

GEORDIE: Oh, devil take Sweenie! all our mess say you are too good for him. You are the prettiest girl in Lucknow.

JESSIE: Let us gang awa in, Geordie dear.

GEORDIE: (*taking her in his arms*) No, you shan't – come, don't be foolish, Jessie. Could you not be happy with me? – don't you like an officer better than a vulgar common soldier?

JESSIE: Oh, Geordie! oh, Geordie! (*Buries her face in her hands.*)

GEORDIE: Look up, Jessie.

JESSIE: I canna, I canna.

GEORDIE: Why can't you look up into my face?

JESSIE: I'm lukin far awa – far awa, upon craigs of Duncleuch; 'tis in the days of auld lang syne, and the arm of wee Geordie MacGregor is round the waist of Jessie Brown, for he is saving her life in the sea. Na, don't tak yer arm awa, Geordie dear. I'm lukin still. Geordie is a laddie noo, and he chases the deer on the craigs of Duncleuch; beside him is poor Sweenie – poor faithful Sweenie, that follows the MacGregor like a dog; Geordie drives a stag to bay; the beastie rushes on him and throws him doon – anither minit and Geordie will na see Jessie mair – but Sweenie's dirk is quicker than that minit! the brute fell dead, but not before he gored poor Sweenie sorely. We watched by his bedside – d'ye mind the time, Geordie? your arm was round me then – na, dinna tak it awa noo.

GEORDIE: Oh, Jessie! oh, Jessie!

JESSIE: Luk up, Geordie.

GEORDIE: I cannot.

JESSIE: Why canna ye luk up into my face?

GEORDIE: Because I'm looking far away, far away into the days of auld lang syne, and they make me ashamed of what I am.

JESSIE: The blush of shame never crossed the brow of a MacGregor. Na! na! you may kiss me now; but listen, Geordie; whisper, (*sings*)

> Should auld acquaintance be forgot
> And never brought to mind,
> Should auld acquaintance be forgot
> And the days of auld lang syne.
> For auld lang syne, my dear,
> For auld lang syne,
> Then tak a kiss of kindness yet
> For auld lang syne.
> (*Exeunt right.*)

SCENE 3. *The Interior of the Bungalow; night. A room serving for a nursery – large opening at the back, with muslin curtains, discover a distant view of Lucknow, brilliant with lights.* MRS. CAMPBELL, CHARLIE, EFFIE, ALICE, *and* MARY *discovered.*

MRS. C: No, I shall not undress the children. Take Effie with you, Alice.

ALICE: Poor child, she is almost asleep now.

CHARLIE: Mamma, I want to go to bed. Where is Jessie?

> (*Enter* JESSIE *right.*)

JESSIE: Here, my precious one.

> (*Exeunt* ALICE *and* MARY, *with* EFFIE, *right.*)

MRS. C: Place him in his cot; do not remove his clothes. (*Walks up and down. – Aside*) I have calmed the agitation of the poor old chaplain, but my own overpowers me.

CHARLIE: Jessie, sing me Charley; you are not tired, are you?

JESSIE: Nae, darling; I'm never tired o' teaching ye the airs o' Scotland. (*Sings a verse of 'Charley is my Darling'. He falls asleep.*)

MRS. C: Can I entrust the secret to this girl? (*going to her*) Jessie!

JESSIE: Aweel, my lady.

MRS. C: (*in a distinct whisper – taking her arm*) There's danger near – don't start, don't cry – to-night this house is to be surrounded by the rebels – our murder is planned, but so is our escape.

JESSIE: (*rising*) It canna be! – wha tauld ye this?

MRS. C: Randal MacGregor.

JESSIE: Then it is true.

MRS. C: Hush! five hundred men will attack us.

JESSIE: Mercy on us! what will become of us?

MRS. C: Randal has promised to rescue us.

JESSIE: (*resuming her calmness*) The MacGregor has said it; dinna ye fash yersel – gin he said it he'll do it. (*Returns to the cot.*)

MRS. C: Go, Jessie, see to the fastening of all the doors, but show no fear, excite no suspicion.

JESSIE: I hae no fear. Has not the MacGregor gi'en his word to coom back? He'll tak it up, and under his claymore there can nae fear. (*Exit hastily. Music.*)

MRS. C: This girl gives me a lesson in courage – what reliance, what noble confidence she has in Randal – how calm she turned, when she heard he had given his word to secure our escape.

> (NANA SAHIB *and* ACHMET *appear at the verandah, on the balcony.* ACHMET *points to* MRS. CAMPBELL. NANA SAHIB *enters the chamber.* ACHMET *creeps along the verandah and off right.*)

What is the hour? (*looking at her watch*) It is now past eleven. Randal must have reached the city by this – it is time to prepare. (*She turns and sees* NANA SAHIB *beside her.*) Mercy!

NANA: Be silent. – You know me.

MRS. C: The Nana Sahib.

NANA: The officer who intercepted my letter to Achmet is my prisoner. My men are now surrounding your park. Escape is hopeless.

MRS. C: (*aside*) Randal taken prisoner! then we are lost.

NANA: Listen! I saw you at Benares – your soul entered through my eyes into my heart, and thrust out my own. I followed you, until like the sun you passed away where I could follow no more; I went to Bithoor, and my wives offended your soul in me. I gave them riches and sent them away – my zenana is cold! I am there alone; it awaits the form to which the soul here belongs.

MRS. C: You would murder my children and dishonour their mother.

NANA: Your children shall be mine, princes of the Mahratta; follow me, and no blood shall flow. I will withdraw my men. Lucknow shall be spared, and peace restored.

MRS. C: England would spurn the peace bought thus with the honour of one of her people. (*Goes to exit right.*)

NANA: (*approaching the cot*) This is your child?

MRS. C: My child.

NANA: (*drawing his yataghan*) No cry! or this steel is in his throat!
          (*Enter* JESSIE *left.*)

CHARLIE: Mamma, oh, dear mamma, help me.

MRS. C: Hush, Charlie, my own one, don't cry, hush. Oh, Rajah, spare my child; yes, I consent. I will follow you – spare –
          (JESSIE *snatches the yataghan from* NANA SAHIB, *and stabs him.*)

JESSIE: Drop that bairn, ye black deevil!
          (NANA SAHIB *drops the child, whom* JESSIE *catches to her breast; he staggers a moment, and falls on couch. Tableau.*)

NANA: Tehanum possess ye – mine then you shall be by force – none under this roof, but you, shall see to-morrow's sun.
          (*Distant shots. Cries within.* ACHMET *appears on the verandah.* NANA SAHIB *and* ACHMET *draw their scimitars, and leap out over the balcony. Enter* GEORDIE, ALICE, *and* MARY *right.*)

GEORDIE: What shots were those?

ALICE: What has happened?

MRS. C: The Nana Sahib, with five hundred rebels, besieges us in this house. Randal is their prisoner. Randal, who promised to rescue us.

JESSIE: Prisoner or free, the MacGregor will keep his word.

MRS. C. The impassibility of that girl drives me mad.
          (*Enter* CASSIDY, *running, left.*)

CASSIDY: He's comin', thunder and turf, he's fightin' like a cat wid tin legs and fifteen claws on aich fut.

ALICE: Who?

CASSIDY: The Captain; Sweenie is fightin' beside him. (*Shots outside.*) Hurroo! they're at it. (*Runs upstage.* GEORDIE *follows to verandah at back.*)

GEORDIE: They are in the copse.

CASSIDY: Where's a gun, oh, a gun, for the love o' heaven.

Mahratta: this warlike Hindu race had been ruled by Nana Sahib's father, Baji Rao II, until he was dethroned by the British in 1817.
yataghan: Moslem sword, often with double-curved blade.
Tehanum: Boucicault seems here to have invented a god (or devil).

JESSIE: Here is one.

> (*Shots.*)

CASSIDY: Hoo! there goes a bullet through my leg. (GEORDIE *staggers back very pale.* JESSIE *runs upstage with the gun.*) The devils see us by the light here, and they're pepperin' us handsome.

JESSIE: Look, Cassidy, look! there's a big fellow makin' for Sweenie, quick.

CASSIDY: (*firing off left*) Hoo!

JESSIE: Here they come. (*calling to them*) Quick, by this ladder.

> (*Enter* SWEENIE, *and then* RANDAL, *over the verandah.* JESSIE *comes downstage, and soothes* CHARLIE *and* EFFIE.)

RANDAL: Cast down that ladder, Cassidy, and stand to your arms.

CASSIDY: Ay, your honour.

MRS. C: Oh, Randal, you have escaped!

JESSIE: I told you the MacGregor would keep his word.

RANDAL: I was taken prisoner by about fifty men, who are posted just this side of the bridge; their main force is still beyond the river; they are led by some Rajah of rank.

MRS. C: By the Nana in person – he was here.

ALICE: Here!

MRS. C: He came by that ladder, and fled when wounded by Jessie.

JESSIE: Na! the deevil had a steel jacket on, the blow slipped awa.

RANDAL: Nana Sahib! then the whole force of the rebels is in the neighourhood – Lucknow is threatened – the garrison will be taken by surprise. Where is Geordie?

GEORDIE: (*advancing*) Here, Randal.

RANDAL: How pale you are. Are you wounded?

GEORDIE: No – it is nothing.

RANDAL: A scratch, I suppose. Geordie, a despatch must be carried to the city; I will write it, and you must bear it.

MRS. C: But can Geordie escape through the lines of the enemy who surround us? Death must be nearly certain.

RANDAL: Death *is* nearly certain, and therefore I pick my own brother for the service; besides, he is an officer, and claims the post of danger as his right. – Do you forget the name we bear? Alice, return to the interior of the house. Come, Amy, give me paper and ink. Geordie, while I am gone, see to your arms.

> (*Exeunt all but* GEORDIE *and* JESSIE, *right.*)

GEORDIE: Death – he said that death is nearly certain.

JESSIE: How pale he is! Geordie, speak – are you hurt?

GEORDIE: Oh, Jessie!

JESSIE: I saw ye flench from the shots – you came back white as snaw. You tremble – what is it, Geordie dear? – tell me.

GEORDIE: I can't, Jessie. My tongue fails me – as my limbs do – oh, Jessie – I feel I cannot face the fire.

JESSIE: What say ye?

GEORDIE: I am a coward. (*Falls on sofa.*)

JESSIE: (*running to him*) Hush, dearie; there's nae drop of coward bluid in the
MacGregor – tak' time, Geordie.

GEORDIE: I cannot help it, Jessie; the passion of fear is on me – I cannot stir.

JESSIE: Oh, my heart! oh, my heart! My Geordie, think of what Randal will say
if he sees ye so – his ain brither – his ainly one! Think, dearie, there are
women here – and bairns, puir helpless things – and if ye flench noo, they will
be killed!

GEORDIE: I know it – (*Hides his face in his hands.*) – but I am paralyzed.

JESSIE: Think of the auld mither at hame, Geordie – the proud one that nursed ye,
Geordie – the leddy that awaits her twa boys cumin' back fra' the wars –
what! will ye bring yer mither back a blighted name? Oh, hae courage for her
sake! – oh, for mine, Geordie! (*Throws her arms around him.*) Oh, why
canna' I gang beside ye, to show ye how to bleed for the auld braes of Scotland?

(*Enter* BLOUNT, *left.*)

What's there? – gang awa – oh, 'tis the minister.

BLOUNT: Is he wounded? my poor boy, is he hurt?

JESSIE: Oh, sir, help him; his heart fails – it is his first fight, and he flenches.

GEORDIE: This terrible sense of fear which paralyzes me will pass away. 'Tis a
spasm – it cannot be that my father's son, my brother's brother, can be so
miserable, so contemptible a thing as this!

BLOUNT: The boy has conscientious scruples, like me.

GEORDIE: No, no; to you – to you alone, companions of my childhood, let me
confess –

BLOUNT: No, don't you sha'n't say a word – you don't understand; I know all –
first powder smells sick; but after you see a few men fall, that goes off.

JESSIE: Yes, it clears awa'.

BLOUNT: Take your lip between your teeth and choose your man.

JESSIE: Think o' the bairns they've slaughtered in cauld bluid.

BLOUNT: Don't trust to pistols – I always preferred steel, it's more reliable, and
doesn't miss fire; use the point – it kills ten when the blade throws open your
guard, and only wounds one. Lord forgive me! I am teaching this boy how to
murder.

(*Re-enter* RANDAL, *with the order, followed by* SWEENIE.)

RANDAL: Here is the despatch. Where is my brother?

JESSIE: He is here, but stay a wee. (*aside*) Oh, what can we do?

RANDAL: How's this? what has happened?

JESSIE: Naething. (*aside*) He blenches. He canna do it. (*aloud*) Randal, I have
asked Geordie a favour, and he has granted me. That order – winna' the
soldier that bears it safe to the General get advancement?

RANDAL: My brother will win a brevet rank of Lieutenant.

JESSIE: Na: your brither is rich and can buy his rank, but my Sweenie is puir, and
Geordie has consented to let Sweenie tak' his place and win his sergeant's
stripes.

---

a brevet rank: a nominal rank, bringing no extra payment.

SWEENIE: Oh, Master Geordie! do you so? Heaven bless ye! there's not a prouder boy in the Queen's uniform to-night than I am!

GEORDIE: Jessie! Jessie!

JESSIE: Dinna' speak.

BLOUNT: (*aside*) She puts her own lover in the jaws of death! Poor girl – good girl! good girl!

RANDAL: It is better so – I have other work for Geordie. Quick then, Sweenie: at the copse, near the brook, my horse is tied to a tree. Can you ride?

SWEENIE: I can hold on.

RANDAL: This letter to the General. I will defend this house till he comes to relieve us, or we are buried under its ruins. The alarm guns which will be fired from the fort when your news is known will apprise us that you are safe in Lucknow, and have escaped. We can both see the flash and hear them from here. Away with you!

JESSIE: Heaven be wi' ye, Sweenie! Heaven be wi' ye, laddie! (*Throws her arms round him.*)

SWEENIE: I'll deserve ye this time, Jessie; ye'll be proud of me, dead or alive. (*Goes upstage.* JESSIE *falls on her knees.*)

BLOUNT: What are you about? you are not going by that road, you will be seen.

SWEENIE: I know it – they'll fire – 'tis ten to one they'll miss me; but I'll fall into the garden as if I was shot, and while they are thinking me stiff, I'll be creepin' down to the horse and off to Lucknow.

RANDAL: Well, let me see you try it.

JESSIE (*raising her hands*) Oh, my loov! 'tis for Geordie's sake.
(*RANDAL and* SWEENIE *go into the balcony.*)

MRS. C: But why should Randal go?

BLOUNT: To lead his man – habit.
(*A shot.* SWEENIE *falls over as if shot. A cry from* JESSIE.)

RANDAL: (*returning after watching*) 'Tis all right – he has escaped.

JESSIE: But he may be wounded?

RANDAL: I think not, unless there were two bullets. I have got one here. (*Takes off his cap – his temple is bleeding.*)

MRS. C: Randal!

RANDAL: Tut! we have other things to do. (*Draws out a handkerchief, presses his forehead, and replaces his cap.*) Now Amy, to work; there are but three of us here, Geordie, Cassidy, and I.

BLOUNT: You may say four! I will lay aside my conscientious scruples, and, like my namesake, David, I will smite the Philistines.

RANDAL: You have three native servants, who, I think, may be trusted. There are not more than fifty Sepoys on this side of the bridge – now if we can destroy that bridge, we shall divide our foes and hold our own for a few hours.

BLOUNT: There's a keg of powder down-stairs. I'll take it down under my arm and blow up the bridge. This enterprise is bloodless – it suits me exactly.

RANDAL: You propose, with your form, to creep down unobserved! You would be cut to pieces.

BLOUNT: But if the piece of me that held the keg got there, I might accomplish the good deed. (*aside*) I'm afraid he'll send Geordie.

RANDAL: Geordie, quick – you and I will see to this.

GEORDIE: (*rising*) I am ready.

> (RANDAL *embraces* MRS. CAMPBELL.)

JESSIE: He's ganging, look, look, he goes bravely. The MacGregor bluid is in his cheek, the dark fire is lechted.

GEORDIE: Bless you, Jessie. (*aside to her*) Sweenie has not been sacrificed in vain. I'll not belie your love, Jessie – farewell! (*Exit with* RANDAL, *left.*)

JESSIE: He's gane, he's gane, baith gane – and Sweenie – and my courage has gane, too.

> (*Enter* ALICE, MARY, *and the children.*)

ALICE: All is quiet.

BLOUNT: That's a bad sign. But let us extinguish the lights – they serve the enemy. (*He puts out the lamp – stage dark.*)

MRS. C: (*kneeling, and praying, her children grouped round her, their little hands clasped*) Oh! Heaven protect us in this dark hour of peril! preserve my poor little children!

BLOUNT: Amen! (*Goes upstage.*) They come! I see white figures in the garden.

JESSIE: My Sweenie! – have they killed my poor Sweenie? Oh, this suspense is worse than death!

BLOUNT: The house is surrounded – the whole collection is here.

MRS. C: Cassidy, fire – why don't you fire on them?

CASSIDY: (*looking in from balcony*) Plase, yer honour, ma'am, them savages is like birds – firin' frightens them away, and if we coax them here awhile, sure they won't be seeing afther the Captain Randal.

BLOUNT: Good heart, noble heart! Oh, merciful Father in Heaven, it is a pity such good people should die! Have pity on us, have pity on these weak ones and upon these little ones!

JESSIE: Oh, protect my puir Sweenie! don't let his bluid lie on my hands – and break poor Jessie's heart!

> (*A distant explosion. Music.*)

CASSIDY: D'ye hear that? It's the bridge! The devils are skelping back again to see what kind of hell is behind 'em.

> (*Sounds of conflict.*)

BLOUNT: They are coming – I hear Randal's voice.

RANDAL: (*without*) Cassidy! Cassidy!

CASSIDY: That's me! here I am, your honour. Hoo! (*Leaps over the balcony and disappears.*)

BLOUNT: The door – the door is fast inside. (*Runs out left.*)

JESSIE: No alarm guns from the city! the time is passed; no sign that he has escaped, and I sent him – I sent him. Oh, Sweenie! Sweenie!

MRS. C: They come – they are safe.

> (*Enter* RANDAL, *bearing* GEORDIE *in his arms. He places him on sofa.*)

RANDAL: See to the doors.

ALICE: He is dead!

JESSIE: Dead! wha's dead? (*Sees* GEORDIE, *and utters a scream of grief and horror.*) Geordie! what have ye done? ye have killed the bairn. Stand awa', a' o' ye. Geordie, Geordie, look to me. Oh! I did it – I killed him – only for me he wad nae have gane. Geordie! (*She kisses his face.*) Speak to me, dear! Oh, I shall go mad, Geordie, if ye dae not answer me – if ye dae not luk to me.

    (GEORDIE *raises himself at the same moment as the flash of a gun is seen from the distant city.*)

RANDAL: Ha! the alarm gun from the city.

    (*A second gun is heard – all turn upstage.*)

GEORDIE: Jessie, Jessie, do you hear those guns? Sweenie has escaped, and after a', Geordie is not a coward. (*He faints.* JESSIE *supports his head. Tableau.*)

ACT II

The interior of a mosque in Lucknow. Curtains at back centre. JESSIE *chained, left, to a pillar.* GEORDIE *is lying on a pallet, right, chained also. Rebel sepoys at the back. A divan, left. Stage sombre. Music.*

GEORDIE: (*awaking*) Where am I? Oh, these chains, those dark walls, those darker faces – I am a prisoner. Why did I awake?

JESSIE: Geordie, dear, you are better noo, the fever has left ye.

GEORDIE: Jessie, are you there? Come near me.

JESSIE: I canna, dearie, the savages have tied me like a dog to the wall.

GEORDIE: What place is this?

JESSIE: It's a church where they worship the deevil.

GEORDIE: How long have I been here?

JESSIE: For six lang weeks.

GEORDIE: Does the Residency still hold out against the rebels?

JESSIE: I dinna ken. I have been here a' the time.

GEORDIE: Were you taken prisoner when I fell into their hands?

JESSIE: Na! but when we heard that you were dying here, for want of Christian help, I cam' across to nurse ye.

GEORDIE: My poor girl! But they will murder you; they show no mercy for age or sex.

JESSIE: I ken it weel; here is the *Calcutta News*. It is fu' o' the bluidy wark the Nana made at Cawnpore.

    (*Enter* NANA SAHIB, *followed by* ACHMET, *with a paper, centre.*)
    Eh! talk o' the deevil –

NANA: Sahib, open your ears. Your countrymen are dogs. They still lie howling in the Residency – they dare not come forth – Inshallah!

GEORDIE: They look for aid.

NANA: Their hearts lie, and hope will not feed them; their food is out, they cannot live on air.

JESSIE: Ye mistak! they are living on an air noo, and it's ca'd, 'The Campbells are coomin''. And oh, could I but hear one screel of the pibroch – could I see the

---

the Residency: the Lucknow Residency held out from 30 May to 17 November 1857.
Inshallah: God willing (the usage here is inappropriate).
screel of the pibroch: Boucicault probably meant no more than 'the skirl of the bagpipe'.
'Pibroch', a series of variations for the bagpipe, has often been erroneously used to describe the instrument itself.

wavin' o' the bonnie tartan, and the braw line o' the shinin' steel, I'd na gie ye twa minits, but ye'd find the deevil before ye could say 'Cawnpore'.

NANA: Woman, be silent, read your printed words, and leave men to speak with men. (*to* GEORDIE) Your countrymen are in our hands. Beneath this mosque, even below our feet, we have a mine. It passes beneath the fort commanded by the Sahib, your brother. Behold, the powder is laid, the match is ready; we can destroy him utterly – his fort once taken, the Residency is ours. Bismillah! have I defiled my tongue with lies?

GEORDIE: The Redan fort is the key to our position.

NANA: Enough blood has been shed – let him yield – his men shall go forth unharmed; we will pour the oil of mercy on their wounds.

JESSIE: (*reading the paper*) 'And under these conditions Cawnpore was surrendered: the garrison marched out, and entered the boats provided for their safe transport.'

NANA: You say your countrymen still look for aid, but they know not that the Sahib Havelock was defeated by my troops. From Lahore to Alahabad,
·   Hindoostan is ours; you shall write these things that they may know; they will believe your word, and they will yield. Inshallah! they shall go forth safely; we will show mercy – on my head be it.

JESSIE: (*reading*) 'No sooner were the boats containing the troops, the women and children, in the midst of the stream than the enemy opened a murderous fire, and a work of slaughter began.'

NANA: What woman is that? What writing has she in her hand? Tear it away! (ACHMET *tears the paper from* JESSIE.) What says the pen there?

JESSIE: (*rising*) I'll tell ye in broad Scotch. It says that you have taught baith women and children to fecht, for you have found something that they fear more than death.

ACHMET: What's that?

JESSIE: The mercy of Nana Sahib!

NANA: Let my Ferooshees come here.
                    (ACHMET *goes to back and beckons. Enter two Hindoos, centre.*)
Take that woman and let her die.

GEORDIE: Stay, Rajah, you would not kill that poor child.
                    (*At a signal from* ACHMET *two cords descend from the roof.*)

NANA: You would have her life? Give me the letter to your brother; she herself shall bear it to the Redan fort.
                    (*They unbind* JESSIE.)

GEORDIE: That letter will not serve you. You do not know Randal MacGregor – he will die, but will never yield.

NANA: Be it so. (*rising*) Achmet, cut off the right hands of these prisoners, and let their bodies swing from the heights of this mosque.

Bismillah: in the name of God.
Redan fort: there was no Redan fort, but the Redan battery, just a few yards north of the Lucknow Residency, was crucial to the defence. It faced the only space large enough to allow the rebels to prepare a mass attack.
Ferooshees: obscure. Boucicault has invented a group-name, perhaps based on the Persian word for the act of selling.

ACHMET: On my head be it.

JESSIE: Geordie, Geordie! (*Goes to him.*)

GEORDIE: Oh, Nana, do not give me the death of a dog. Spare that poor child.

NANA: Stifle the howling of that hound.

JESSIE: Geordie, far'weel, Geordie!

GEORDIE: Hold! what would you have me do?

NANA: (*returning*) Do you see yonder ropes? They ascend to the minaret of this mosque. (*to* ACHMET) Prepare the means in yonder room to write. (*Exit* ACHMET, *right.*) Behold! write as I have said, or give your neck to the cord. Choose – I have spoken. (*Exit, right.*)

JESSIE: Ay, but you have spoken to a MacGregor!

    (*They unbind* GEORDIE. *Re-enter* ACHMET.)

GEORDIE: (*aside*) One day more – aid may come. Havelock, Outram, cannot be far.

JESSIE: (*aside*) He hesitates – if he pens that letter a' is lost again; yet if I speak the deevils will murder me.

GEORDIE: (*aside*) She shall not die. (*Exit right, followed by* ACHMET *and the Hindoos. Stage dark.*)

JESSIE: (*looking off right*) He will do't; to save my life, he will write down his ain infamy. Nae, if I bear it to the fort, I can tear it up on the way; but then they will kill him after a', and I ainly can be saved. Yonder he sits, he taks the pen – his hand shakes, but still he writes; he writes, oh, what are the words? words of infamy, that will gae hame, and fill the faces of a' the Christian world wi' shame. Oh, could I reach his heart, I would stay his hand, but that black Beelzebub is wi' him. Eh, haud a wee, I'll speak to him. (*She sings.*)

    Oh, why left I my hame, &c.

    (*after first verse*) He stops, his head fa's in his hand – tears, tears – he minds me, he minds me. (*She falls on her knees and sings the second verse.*) He knows what I mean!

    (*A portion of the floor gives way, right centre, and falls in.*)

    Ah! (*Starts back to left.*) What is that?

CASSIDY: (*putting his head through the orifice*) Pooh! what a dust. Cheu! (*Sneezes.*) That was a big pinch of snuff, anyway.

JESSIE: What's that? 'Tis Cassidy's voice.

CASSIDY: I'll call Sweenie.

    (SWEENIE'*s head appears through the orifice, beside* CASSIDY'*s.*)

JESSIE: Sweenie!

CASSIDY: Sweenie!

SWEENIE: What's the matter?

CASSIDY: Matther! Bedad, there's an echo here that spakes first – a Hindoo echo that takes the words out av yer mouth.

JESSIE: Hush, 'tis I, Jessie.

SWEENIE: Jessie!

CASSIDY: Hoo! 'Garry Owen' yer sowl! Hurroo!

Oh, why left I my hame: usually sung to the tune of 'The Lowlands of Holland'.

JESSIE: Hush! gae down quick, they are coomin'.
> (CASSIDY *and* SWEENIE *disappear.* JESSIE *draws the nusmud or Turkish carpet of the divan over the orifice. Enter* ACHMET, *with a light, right.* JESSIE *sings 'My boy Tammie' with affected unconcern.* ACHMET *examines the place, holds the light to her face, and goes out, right.* JESSIE *withdraws the carpet.*)

JESSIE: Hush, silence, whisper.
> (SWEENIE *and* CASSIDY *reappear.*)

CASSIDY: Where the divil are we at all?

JESSIE: This is a mosque, they ca' it. It is my prison and Geordie's. How did you get here?

SWEENIE: We were working in the counter mine, ordered by the captain, when we struck right into the mine prepared by the rebels to blow us up. We removed their powder, of which we were running short, and then Cassidy and I took a stroll along their mine, to see the country.

CASSIDY: The road was mighty dirty, but the view at the end of it is worth the walk.

JESSIE: Then this passage goes under ground to the fort.

CASSIDY: Bedad, Sweenie, we niver thought of that! It comes this way, but I don't know if it goes back the same.

JESSIE: D'ye see yon ropes danglin' there, they are ready for me and Geordie. Twa hours mair, and ye'd been too late. Down wi' ye noo, don't stir until I tell ye.

CASSIDY: We'll be as dumb as oysthers. (*They disappear.* JESSIE *replaces the carpet.*)
> (*Enter* NANA SAHIB *and* ACHMET, *right. Drums without. Sepoys enter, centre.*)

ACHMET: (*who has spoken with a Sepoy*) A flag of truce from the fort.
> (*Enter* RANDAL *and* BLOUNT, *centre, preceded by a native with a white flag.*)

JESSIE: The MacGregor!

RANDAL: You are the Nana?

NANA: (*seated, left*) I am he.

RANDAL: I command the Redan fort. I come to offer you an exchange of prisoners. We have taken sixty of your men.

NANA: They are in your hand, Inshallah! Death is their portion. To each man his fate.
> (*Exit* ACHMET, *right.*)

RANDAL: We fight our foes, we do not murder them.

BLOUNT: Stay, Randal, don't be so fiery. Let me speak to the Rajah. Salam, Aleikoom.

'*My boy Tammie*': first published in 1791, the tune adapted from 'Muirland Willy'.
counter mine: the defenders of the Lucknow Residency tried to counter the enemy mines by tunnelling into them. The shafts were about four feet in diameter, and between twelve and twenty feet deep.
Salam, Aleikoom: Peace be to you.

NANA: Allah, Resoul Allah! Speak! There is no God but God, and Mohammed is his prophet.

BLOUNT: There I can't agree with you, and I shall feel pleased to discuss that question at any time your leisure may permit. I am a minister of peace and a herald of mercy. Let me touch your heart. Our Heavenly Father, whom you call Allah, has given you rule and power over men. You have used it so cruelly, that all the world will shudder at your deeds of blood. This girl came here on a mission of mercy, she is not your prisoner; in every religion, and of all time, the weakness of woman protects her life, and makes her safety sacred.

NANA: The shepherds from the hills of the Himmalayah came to me and they said, 'Behold the tigers come out of the jungle and prey upon our flocks, and we fear.' Which hearing, I arose; I sought the lair of the noble beast. I found there the tigress and her cubs. I struck them, until they died; but lo, the tiger came, but did he whine and weep, saying, 'Sahib, you have done evil; my mate and my little ones are sacred, their weakness should protect them'?

BLOUNT: Are *we* tigers?

NANA: The tiger was placed here by Allah; he eats for his hunger, and kills that he may eat. Did Allah send the Briton here to make us slaves, to clutch us beneath his lion's paw, and to devour the land? Inshallah! The voiceless word of Allah has swept over the people, and it says, 'Sufferers, arise, ye shall be free!'

RANDAL: Freedom was never won by murder, for heaven never yet armed the hand of an asssassin.

NANA: What, dogs, are you to judge the ways of Allah?

(*Enter* ACHMET *with a letter, right.*)

Has the English prisoner written as I have said?

ACHMET: 'Tis done!

JESSIE: Na, it canna be!

NANA: The officer, your brother, knowing the folly of further resistance, writes here to you, Sahib, and counsels you to yield.

JESSIE: Oh, I dar' na luk at Randal.

RANDAL: (*striding up to* NANA SAHIB) You lie!

BLOUNT: Randal, forbear, perhaps Geordie has been misled, deceived?

RANDAL: Deceit can make a man a fool, but not a coward.

(*Enter* GEORDIE, *right.*)

GEORDIE: Randal!

RANDAL: Stand back, Lieutenant MacGregor! The Rajah of Bithoor declares, that in this letter to me, you have counselled us to surrender. (*a pause*) You are silent.

GEORDIE: Randal, you will forgive me when you know all, but now, and here, I dare not speak.

NANA: The proud brow of the Englishman, our tyrant, can be bowed down with shame. Achmet, read the letter.

GEORDIE: No, no, not here.

Allah, Resoul Allah: God, the prophet of God.
Mohammed is his prophet: a curious claim from a Hindu. Boucicault's researches were not profound.

ACHMET: I cannot; it's in a foreign tongue.

BLOUNT: (*looking over it*) 'Tis in Gaelic, the native tongue of Scotland; I do not understand it.

JESSIE: Eh! *I* do; let me see. There's nae words in Gaelic that would serve a coward's tongue. Let me see. (*Music. She reads silently.*) Eh, sirs, it is pure Gaelic, and rins so. (*to* NANA SAHIB) Open yer lugs, ye deevil, for here's porridge for ye, hotter than ye can sup it, may be. (*Reads.*) To Captain Randal MacGregor, Her Majesty's 78th Highlanders; 'My dearest brother, the Nana Sahib has doomed me to the death of a dog. – My execution will take place at seven o'clock; you can spare our mother that grief and me that disgrace. Jessie will point out to you the window of my prison – it looks over the Redan Fort, and is within gun-shot of our men. As the clock strikes six, I will be at the window. Draw out a firing-party, and let them send an honest volley through my heart. Heaven bless you; give my love to Alice and Mary; remember me to all the fellows of our mess – let them give me a parting cheer when I fall. Your affectionate brother, Geordie MacGregor.'

RANDAL: Geordie, my brother! my own brother!

GEORDIE: Randal! (*They embrace.*)

BLOUNT: (*bursting into an ecstasy of delight*) I can resist no longer. (*Shouts.*) God save the Queen! (*Embraces* JESSIE.)

> (NANA SAHIB *goes upstage with* ACHMET. *Artillery heard without.*)

RANDAL: What guns are those?

NANA: My artillery cover the advance of the faithful on the Redan fort. Bind these men. Your hours are numbered.

RANDAL: Traitor! we are protected by a flag of truce.

NANA: Your flag of truce shall be your winding sheet. Swing their bodies to the minaret, through the dome above. (*He points upwards, centre.*) As the hour strikes seven let it be done. (*The Sepoys seize* RANDAL, GEORDIE, *and* JESSIE.) Let the old man go, that he may bear witness over all the earth, and strike the hearts of England white with terror, when they hear the vengeance of Nana Sahib. (*Exit, left.*)

BLOUNT: Don't! Hang me too, hang me! I'll be hung, if I die for it.

ACHMET: Slaves, see the Nana's order done; on your heads be it. On the stroke of seven, draw the ropes; my duty calls me to the mine. The mine below your countrymen. In five minutes the match will be lighted, and from above, you will be able to see your soldiers blown to the skies. (*Exit, right. The Sepoys, having placed a noose round the necks of* GEORDIE *and* RANDAL, *and bound* BLOUNT *and* JESSIE, *exeunt left.*)

JESSIE: (*calling*) Sweenie, Cassidy – quick!

CASSIDY: (*throwing back the carpet*) Here I am! (*Appears in the orifice.*) I'm nearly choked wid keepin' the fight in me. (*Jumps up.*)

BLOUNT: Where do you come from?

78th Highlanders: Boucicault was either misinformed or careless. The 78th Highlanders were part of Havelock's relieving force. It was the 32nd (Cornwall) Light Infantry that bore the brunt of the siege of the Lucknow Residency.

CASSIDY: From the mine, alanna! Sweenie has run down below to look after the
naygar that's gone to blow us up; he's got a word or two to say to him.
RANDAL: Quick, cut these cords; the executioners hold the other end, outside,
and at the stroke of seven they will run us up.
(CASSIDY *cuts the cords, aided by* BLOUNT.)
GEORDIE: Free!
SWEENIE: (*below the orifice*) Come along, it's no use kicking.
RANDAL: Sweenie!
SWEENIE: All right, your honour. (*Salutes* RANDAL.) I've got a Hindoo Guy
Fawkes, matches and lantern, all complete.
CASSIDY: Come up asy, Darlint.
(SWEENIE *and* CASSIDY *pull* ACHMET, *gagged and bound, through
the orifice.*)
RANDAL: Secure that fellow, so that he may not give the alarm.
CASSIDY: Never fear, Captain.
(*Guns outside.*)
RANDAL: The attack has commenced! To the Redan, Geordie, to the Redan!
(GEORDIE *and* RANDAL *disappear down the orifice.*)
BLOUNT: Sweenie, spare that man! shed no blood, boys; do you hear me?
CASSIDY: All right, yer riverence.
BLOUNT: Bind him fast, but let him live. (*He descends.*)
SWEENIE: Here is a rope; tie him with this.
(ACHMET *struggles and tries to speak – they throw him down.*)
CASSIDY: He's as lively as a cock salmon. Hould quiet, ye divil; he's trying to
spake.
JESSIE: (*aside*) That rope – they dinna ken what it is there for.
CASSIDY: Tie him tight, and for fear he'd get the gag out and cry murdher, give the
rope a hitch round his neck.
JESSIE: Stop, release him; that cord is held by the executioners outside, and at the
stroke of seven – (*The great clock of the Mosque strikes.*) Ah! mercy.
CASSIDY: What is it?
(*The body of* ACHMET *is suddenly carried up, and disappears above
through the roof* – CASSIDY *and* SWEENIE *look amazed* – JESSIE
utters a cry and kneels, hiding her face.)

ACT III

*In this Act, the appearance of all concerned should present a marked change. The
women should seem pale and worn; the men, wan and over-fatigued, their beards
should be long and their dresses soiled and torn.*
SCENE – *The Redan, a fort commanding a certain part of the City of Lucknow,
and forming an outpost work near the Residency. A breastwork of gabions, fascines,*

---

alanna: my dear (my child).
naygar: presumably 'nigger' in an Irish accent.
gabion: cylindrical wicker basket, filled with earth to form part of a defensive wall.
fascine: cylinder of brushwood etc., used for the same purpose.

and other military appliances embraces the stage. Through embrasures four pieces of artillery are placed; one of them is dismounted as if by a cannon-ball. In the distance is seen the encampment of the rebel Sepoys, and three forts similarly constructed to the Redan, and mounted with artillery. The scene generally bears marks of a severe attack, both of musketry and cannonade. Groups of Ladies with Children, wounded Soldiers on guard, and some asleep. CASSIDY, smoking a pipe, sits beside JESSIE, who is asleep, her head resting on his knapsack, and his gray coat spread over her. SWEENIE, with his head bound and wounded, leans on his musket. MRS. CAMPBELL and her two children on the left. A gray cold light thrown over the scene indicates the dawn of day. GEORDIE at the back is looking through a field-glass, examining the position of the enemy. Music and tableau.

MRS. C: Geordie, what can you see?

GEORDIE: I can see the road to Alumbagh, from whence we expect relief, but there is no sign of troops there.

MRS. C: Day after day we hope, until hope itself dies away – for three long months we have resisted.

CHARLIE: Mamma, I am hungry.

MRS. C: Heaven help you, my poor child.

GEORDIE: (*to the men*) Lads, here's a little child starving; is there a crust among ye?

SWEENIE: (*saluting*) Not a crumb, your honour, except it's in Phil Regan's kit. He died an hour ago. There he lies. (*Points right.*)

GEORDIE: Search and see.

> (*Exit* SWEENIE, *right. Enter* RANDAL, *left.*)

RANDAL: What news of the night?

GEORDIE: Nine men dead of their wounds. Six gone into the hospital.

RANDAL: Inglis is hemmed in – can scarcely hold his own, like us, can scarcely sustain himself from hour to hour. If the columns of General Havelock's force do not appear today, we must make Lucknow our permanent residence, Geordie.

GEORDIE: You mean that you will die at this post?

> (SWEENIE *re-enters with a morsel of bread, and hands it to* MRS. CAMPBELL. *She gives it to* CHARLIE, *who is going to eat it, but hesitates, breaks it in half, and places one half of it in the hand of* EFFIE, *who still sleeps – then he eats his half.*)

MRS. C: How is Jessie?

> (GEORDIE *kneels beside* JESSIE.)

SWEENIE: She sleeps. The long weeks of suffering have worn her spirits out at last.

RANDAL: Poor Jessie, has she too lost her spirits?

CASSIDY: Lost her sperrits! Bedad, yer honor, the biggest keg of whiskey will give out at last if ye go dhrawin' at it ev'ry minit, an' afther Jessie cam' back, she

---

Alumbagh: it was from this walled park, four miles south of the Residency, that Havelock started his march through Lucknow.
Inglis: Acting Brigadier John Inglis took over command of the defence of Lucknow when Sir Henry Lawrence died on 4 July 1857.

tuk no rest, night or day, what wid nurse-tendin' the woundid men, an' comfortin' the wimmin an' childer, an' cookin', an' kaping up the sperrit of the boys at the guns. When the hunger was in her mouth, she'd always have a song in id about the ould counthry that warrum'd our hearts, or a gay word to throw us in passin', that ud fetch the tear into our eyes. Lost her sperrits, oh, ahone! them sperrits was brewed in heaven above, they nivir touched the head, but the heart of a man could get dhrunk upon 'em.

MRS. C: Poor Jessie! she has been in a state of restless excitement through all the siege, and has fallen away visibly during the last few days. A constant fever consumes her, and her mind wanders occasionally; and then recollections of home seem powerfully present to her. Overcome by fatigue, she has lain there since midnight, wrapped in her plaid. Poor child! It is strange, Randal, to see those rough men watch over her with the tenderness and grief of a mother over a sick child.

(*Enter* BLOUNT, *left.*)

BLOUNT: No news of relief?

RANDAL: None yet, but our fort here is cut off from the Residency, and Colonel Inglis may have despatches.

BLOUNT: Cheer up, lads, there's a good time coming. The old folks at home will long remember the defence of Lucknow, and every man here will be a hero in his own native village.

CASSIDY: Except me, your riverence; divil a native village I've got. I was born under a haystack; me father and mother had crossed to England for the harvest. – Me mother died of me, and me father bruk his heart wid dhrinkin', so when they sent me home to Ireland, my relations wouldn't own me, bekase I was an Englishman.

BLOUNT: My good Cassidy, hearts like yours are never without a home, while there is goodness in earth and mercy in heaven!

CASSIDY: I'm content, sir! If Jessie was not sick, and I'd an ounce of baccy, I wouldn't call the Queen me uncle. (*He draws the coat over* JESSIE.)

GEORDIE: Here's the rations for the day.

(*Enter a Sergeant with a tin vessel containing the food, left.*)

RANDAL: Now, lads, there's no bugle to call ye to breakfast, so fall in and fall to. This is the last of our food, so make it go as far as you can. (*The food is divided amongst the men – they form a group and whisper.*) As soon as the sun is up, we shall have warm work. So buckle your belts tight. (*A distant gun.*) There goes a how d'ye do from the rebels.

SWEENIE: (*advancing and saluting*) Please, your honour, the men wants to know very respectfully, sir, please if this here ration is the last of our food – what's the children and ladies a' goin' to have sarved out.

RANDAL: That is a mutinous question, sir; fall in your ranks.

SWEENIE: Ax your pardon, please, sir – the men won't eat their rations till they know. They say they wouldn't fight no how, sir, anyways comfortable, if they ain't allowed to share all fair with the women and the little 'uns.

RANDAL: Silence in the ranks! fall in, my good lads. Listen: for eighty days we have held this fort against fifty thousand rebels; from week to week our numbers have been thinned off, until few indeed remain; a few hours more, and General Havelock may arrive (*a gun*), but those few hours will be terrible.

The rebel Sepoys, grown desperate by repulse, will try to overwhelm us with their whole force. (*a gun*) To preserve the lives of these weak ones, you must have strength to repel this attack – you are starving; the food you eat is their protection.

> (*The men whisper again.*)

SWEENIE: Please, captain, the men say they'd feel worse after such a meal.

RANDAL: Do as you will. There is a Captain above who commands your hearts. Break ranks.

> (*The men hasten to the various groups of women and children, and divide their rations with them.*)

BLOUNT: The Lord is with us – his spirit is amongst us!

GEORDIE: (*to* BLOUNT) Will you not eat, sir? (*offering him food*)

BLOUNT: How can I, boy? My heart is in my mouth – I have food enough in that. (*to the groups*) Stay, my dear ones! the food is poor, but let us not forget Him who gave it. (*Each person arrests his hand at the moment of eating – raising his hat and hand.*) May He bless us, and give us strength in this dark hour of our lives.

JESSIE: (*waking*) I'm cauld – I'm verra cauld.

CASSIDY: Cowld, darlin'! sure it's September, and as hot as blazes – the Lord be praised!

MRS. C: Jessie, are you better?

JESSIE: (*looking round eagerly*) I maun get my father's breakfast; the gude man will be back soon frae the field.

CASSIDY: What is she talking about?

SWEENIE: Eat, Jessie dear; we have kept your ration till you awoke.

JESSIE: Eat, na-ah! (*Rejects the bread.*) Dinna ye see? – there's bluid upon it.

CASSIDY: Blood!

GEORDIE: Jessie!

MRS. C: Jessie! (*Crosses hastily to her.*) Jessie, you are ill! Look at me – speak to me – do you not know me? (*Kneels beside her.*)

JESSIE: Knaw ye, knaw ye! Nae, but I ken a bonnie song – a song of Scotland – it's made o' heather and bluebells, woven in a tartan, and it is so gladsome that it makes me weep.

MRS. C: Randal, Randal, her senses have gone – her mind wanders.

CHARLIE: Jessie, my own Jessie! don't look so.

JESSIE: We'll gang hame. Come to me – what's yer name?

CHARLIE: Charlie Fergus Campbell.

JESSIE: Then ye ar' Scotch – Scotch to the core of the heart. Listen. (*Sings.*)
> In winter, when the rain rained cauld, &c

SWEENIE: Jessie, Jessie, dear? Don't you know me? Sweenie.

JESSIE: Sweenie! where is he? He will be outside the byre, doon by the gates. After melking the coos, I'll coom t'ye my lad. I'll steal away to the trystin', Sweenie. Fear naught. (*Sings.*)
> Oh, whistle and I'll come to thee, my lad,

Oh, whistle and I'll come to thee, my lad: the words are by Robert Burns, and the song first appeared in George Thomson's *Original Scottish Airs*, Vol. II (1799).

   Tho' feyther and mither and aw should goe mad;
   Oh, whistle and I'll come to thee, my lad.
RANDAL: Do not weep, Amy. She is happier so – and if we fall in repulsing the
  rebels to-day, or if we are not relieved by sundown, her madness will be a
  blessing – she will be insensible to her fate.
MRS. C: Has the last hour come, Randal?
   (*Three guns are heard in quick succession.*)
RANDAL: Hark! the batteries are opening their fire. Fall in, men. Geordie, repel
  any advance by the left. I will hold the front.
CASSIDY: (*who has been looking over the back*) Plase, your honour, here come the
  black divils – they're upon us.
RANDAL: Steady, men, no hurry. Sweep them down! Forward!
   (*Music. Exit* RANDAL *right with men. Exit* GEORDIE *left with
   men. Sounds of musketry, cannon outside. Drums.*)
BLOUNT: To your knees – to your knees – and pray! This hour may be our last.
  Oh! if my scruples did not weigh so heavily upon me, I could strike for my
  country. (*Takes out a book.*)
JESSIE: (*who has been recovering her senses, as she listens to the conflict, at first
  with surprise, then with awakening comprehension*) Ah! I mind it all – I am
  awak! Where's Sweenie?
BLOUNT: Let me read aloud to you the words of peace and comfort.
   (JESSIE *turns and sees the heads of some of the Sepoys at the
   embrasures; two of them are trying to escolade the breastwork.*)
JESSIE: Look, look! they come!
   (*The women utter a cry of dismay.*)
BLOUNT: The enemy! (*Pockets the book, and seizes a gun rammer.*) In the name
  of the Lord and of Gideon!
   (BLOUNT *advances to the back. The two wounded Soldiers rise, and
   crawl to the guns.* JESSIE *runs to a bombshell that lies left, and
   finding* CASSIDY's *pipe where he has thrown it, still alight, she
   lights the fuse, and carries it with great difficulty to the breastwork,
   toppling it over.* BLOUNT, *standing on a disabled gun, deals pon-
   derous blows right and left with the rammer, and knocks over the
   Sepoys as they appear. The wounded Soldiers,* JESSIE, ALICE, *and*
   MRS. CAMPBELL *draw in the other gun, load it, and run it out
   again. The bomb is heard to explode outside, followed by cries and
   hurrahs.* MRS. CAMPBELL *applies a port fire to the gun, and fires
   it. Another shout.* JESSIE *leaps on the gun. The Children bring
   hand grenades, and roll in a cannon ball.* RANDAL *and* GEORDIE
   re-appear, right and left, leading back their men, some wounded.
   Groups are formed. The ladies tear their dresses and make bandages
   for the wounded soldiers. Tableau.*)
RANDAL: Well done, bravely done! The enemy is repulsed. It was hot work.
BLOUNT: Hot! it was terrible! I'm afraid I have killed somebody. I fear I have sent
  some sinners to their last account up there. (*Points up.*)
CASSIDY: (*taking his arm and making him point it down*) No, that's the way they
  wint. Bedad, but ye made that shillelah dance over their head – they wint
  down by dozens, it was illegant.

BLOUNT: I'll have to answer for this hereafter.

CASSIDY: Oh, make yer mind asy! Divil the question, ye'll ivir be axed about it.

GEORDIE: Who sent that bomb? It fell into their advancing column, and exploded with terrible effect.

MRS. C: 'Twas Jessie.

SWEENIE, CASSIDY, RANDAL, GEORDIE: (*together*) Jessie!

> (*They look round. JESSIE is discovered, crying bitterly, seated on the breastwork. They bring her forward.*)

MRS. C: Jessie, what ails you? Why do you weep? (*to the rest*) I never saw her cry before.

JESSIE: Na, na, but I canna help it. The clouds in my brain are pourin' oot, an' – an' – an' – (*Falls into hysteria.*)

ALICE: She is weak, poor child; hunger and fear have killed her.

BLOUNT: No! this spasm of tears relieves her overburdened brain – she will recover.

MRS C: Leave her to Alice and me.

CHARLIE: Jessie, dear, don't 'ee cry, don't cry.

> (JESSIE *embraces the children.*)

RANDAL: (*taking BLOUNT and GEORDIE aside*) We have repulsed the first attack, but the enemy is too strong for us; they will try a second and a third – we have now only twenty men left – their next attack will succeed.

BLOUNT: The Lord's will be done. Let us thank Him that we are prepared to die. Yes, it is with joyful thankfulness that I say it. There is not one human being here, that has not shown a noble, beautiful and Christian spirit, except me. I have been led away. The shepherd has killed his flock.

RANDAL: No, he has only driven the wolf away.

BLOUNT: Let us hope that it may be forgiven me. Now what shall we do?

GEORDIE: Alice, Amy, and Jessie, must they fall into the hands of these wretches? Oh, Randal, remember Cawnpore.

BLOUNT: Let *them* decide. Let them know the worst, that they may prepare to meet their fearful fate.

RANDAL: I cannot speak it. I can face the enemy, but I cannot look into the pale faces of those women and tell them that my arm is powerless to defend their honour and their lives. (*Goes up and seats himself dejectedly on a gun carriage.*)

BLOUNT: This is my mission. I will speak to them; heaven inspires me with courage! Geordie, tell me when the last moment is come. (*Sits and takes out his book.*) Let me know when our death is near.

MRS. C: Her temples throb and burn. My poor Jessie, lie down awhile and rest your head in my lap.

GEORDIE: (*near BLOUNT*) What are you reading?

BLOUNT: (*looking up*) The prayers for the dead!

> (GEORDIE *goes up, and leans on the breastwork. The men are reposing in groups.*)

ALICE: How she trembles! her hands are icy cold.

MRS. C: Jessie, are you cold?

JESSIE: (*Sings in a low voice.*)

> In winter when the rain rained cauld, &c

ALICE: Her senses wander again.

MRS. C: Jessie, my dear Jessie, try to rest your wearied brain – try to sleep.

JESSIE: Sleep! aye, let me sleep awee – but you will awak me when my feyther cooms frae the ploughin'.

MRS. C: Yes, Jessie, when the gude man comes home, I will awake you. (*aside*) Heaven help her!

JESSIE: I'm his only bairn, and he loos me weel. (*Sings slowly the first few bars of 'Robin Gray', as she falls asleep.*)

GEORDIE: (*advancing to* BLOUNT) The enemy are moving, sir. The time has come.

BLOUNT: (*closing the book*) I am ready. (*Rises.*)
    (*Distant drum is heard, very low.*)

RANDAL: The enemy! Fall in, men! (*Eight men rise and form with* SWEENIE *and* CASSIDY *at back.* RANDAL *counts them.*) Ten! ten men alone are fit for service – ten men to repulse a thousand! (*Turns aside.*)

BLOUNT: My gentle friends – to you, weak in body but so strong in soul, I speak. It is fitting that you should know that the last hour has arrived. (*Drums – a gun.*) The last earthly hope is gone – let us address ourselves to Heaven!

ALICE: Will these men desert us?

BLOUNT: In an hour not one of those men will be living.

MRS. C: But we shall be living. Oh, recollect Cawnpore! These children will be hacked to pieces before our eyes – ourselves reserved for worse than death, and then mutilated, tortured, butchered in cold blood. Randal, will you see this done – will you not preserve us from this fate? (*Kneels.* ALICE *weeps on* GEORDIE's *breast.*)

RANDAL: (*upstage centre*) Amy, my heart is broken! What can we do?

MRS. C: Kill us! Put us to a merciful death ere you fall. Oh, Randal, do not turn away from me – think of the fate reserved for her you love. Oh, death, death! a thousand times death! You are going to die – take us with you, Randal; if you leave us here, you are accessories to our dishonour and our murder.

BLOUNT: They come, they come – already they begin to ascend the hill.

ALICE: Geordie.

MRS. C: Quick, or it will be too late. Quick, Randal – oh, remember we are cowards – we are women, and we may not have the courage to kill ourselves.

RANDAL: I cannot, Amy, I cannot.

MRS. C: Lend me your dirk, then. Rather than see my children mutilated, tortured, they shall die. Our Father will forgive a mother when her children plead for her.

BLOUNT: (*at back*) They are here, Randal – they are here.

RANDAL: Murderers! they come for their prey. (*dashing down his bonnet*) Yes, I will tear them from their rage. Soldiers, one volley – your last – to free your countrywomen from the clutches of the demons. One volley to their noble and true hearts, and then give your steel to the enemy. Load.
    (*The Soldiers bite off the ends of their cartridges, and load their*

The Soldiers bite off the ends of their cartridges: the allusion is to the controversy that sparked off the whole Indian mutiny. In 1857, the British decided to introduce the new Enfield rifle to

*muskets. The women cast themselves into each other's arms, and
form a group.)*

BLOUNT: (*beginning to read the service for the dead*) In the midst of life we are
in death.

> *(A distant wail of the bagpipes is heard. JESSIE starts from her
> sleep.)*

RANDAL: Shoulder arms. Ready!

> *(Another wail of the pipes is heard.)*

JESSIE: (*uttering a cry*) Hark – hark – dinna ye hear it? – dinna ye hear it? Ay!
I'm no dreamin', it's the slogan of the Highlanders! we're saved – we're saved!
(*Throws herself on her knees.*) Oh, thank Him! whose mercy never fails the
strong in heart, and those that trust in Him.

RANDAL: Relief! – no! it is impossible.

> *(Guns outside.)*

JESSIE: I heard it! I heard it!

GEORDIE: Here comes the enemy.

JESSIE: To the guns, men – to the guns! Courage! Hark to the slogan. 'Tis the
slogan of the MacGregor, the grandest of them a'. There's help at last. Help!
d'ye hear me? Help!

RANDAL: There is no signal from the Residency, Jessie, your ears deceive you.

MRS. C: She is mad!

JESSIE: I am not daft; my Scotch ears can hear it far awa'. (*Bagpipes sound nearer.*)
There again – there – will ye believe it noo – d'ye hear – d'ye hear – d'ye
hear? – 'The Campbells are Comin''!

> *(The bagpipes swell out louder, but still distant. Distant musketry
> is heard to roll. Shouts.)*

GEORDIE: See, the flag runs up at the Residency!

> *(Cannonade.)*

RANDAL: To arms, men! One charge more, and this time drive your steel down
the throats of the murderous foe.

> *(Musketry.)*

JESSIE: Ha! they coom! they coom! yonder is the tartan. Oh! the bonnie Highland
plaid. (*She stands on a gun, and waves her tartan plaid.*) You have nae
forgotten us. (*The pipes here change the air to 'Should Auld Acquaintance
be forgot'.*) D'ye hear – d'ye hear? 'Should Auld Acquaintance be forgot'.
Noo lads, here comes the rebels. It will be yer last chance at them. (*She leaps
down.*)

RANDAL: Steady, lads!

> *(The Sepoys appear at back.)*

ALL: Hurrah!

> *(They dash up the breastwork, and after firing, club their guns and
> disappear fighting, driving the Sepoys down. Shouts and musketry
> and cannonade grow furious. The back scene is covered with a red*

---

the Indian army. Its loading required the biting or tearing of a greased cartridge. Whether the
grease was of cow or pork fat, Hindu or Moslem soldiers were unwilling to risk the breaking of
faith.

low; explosions as from mines are heard, through all of which the bagpipes continue, now very loud and near. The Sepoys appear fighting, and driven in at the back. They fall over the breastwork. GENERAL HAVELOCK *(who remains on breastwork, centre, till end) and the Highlanders, with their pipes, charge up the breastwork, and crown it in every direction, bearing down the Sepoys with the bayonet.* GEORDIE *and his men enter left.* CASSIDY *and* SWEENIE *from right, with others of the men, and face those of the Sepoys, who are driven out by the Highlanders. Grand Tableau and*

CURTAIN.)

THE OCTOROOON; or, LIFE IN LOUISIANA

A play in five acts

First performed at the Winter Garden Theatre, New York on 6 December 1859, with the following cast:

GEORGE PEYTON (Mrs. Peyton's Nephew, educated in Europe, and just returned home)	Mr. A. H. Davenport
JACOB M'CLOSKY (formerly Overseer of Terrebonne, but now Owner of one half of the Estate)	Mr. T. B. Johnston
SALEM SCUDDER (a Yankee from Massachusetts, now Overseer of Terrebonne, great on improvements and inventions, once a Photographic Operator, and been a little of everything generally)	Mr. Joseph Jefferson
PETE (an 'Ole Uncle', once the late Judge's body servant, but now 'too ole to work, sa')	Mr. George Jamieson
SUNNYSIDE (a Planter)	Mr. George Holland
LAFOUCHE (a Rich Planter)	Mr. J. H. Stoddart
PAUL (a Yellow Boy, a favourite of the late Judge's, and so allowed to do much as he likes)	Miss Ione Burke
RATTS (Captain of the Magnolia Steamer)	Mr. Harry Pearson
COLONEL POINTDEXTER (an Auctioneer)	Mr. Russell
JULES THIBODEAUX (a Young Creole Planter)	Miss H. Secor
CAILLOU (an Overseer)	Mr. Peck
JUDGE JACKSON (a Planter)	Mr. Tree
WAHNOTEE (an Indian Chief of the Lepan Tribe)	Mr. Dion Boucicault
MRS. PEYTON (Widow of the late Judge)	Mrs. W. R. Blake
ZOE (an Octoroon Girl, free)	Miss Agnes Robertson
DORA SUNNYSIDE (a Southern Belle)	Mrs. J. H. Allen
GRACE (a Yellow Girl, a Slave)	Miss Gimber
DIDO (the Cook, a Slave)	Mrs. Dunn
MINNIE (a Quadroon Slave)	Miss Walters

N.B. When Boucicault and Agnes Robertson walked out, their parts were taken over by Harry Pearson and Mrs. Allen, whose parts were, in turn, taken over by Mr. Harrison and Mrs. Stoddart.

III Joseph Jefferson as Salem Scudder in *The Octoroon*

ACT I

A view of the plantation Terrebonne, in Louisiana. A branch of the Mississippi is seen winding through the Estate. A low-built but extensive Planter's Dwelling, surrounded with a verandah and raised a few feet from the ground, occupies the left side – a table and chairs, right centre. GRACE *discovered sitting at breakfast-table with* CHILDREN. *Enter* SOLON *from house.*

SOLON: Yah! you bomn'ble fry – git out – a gen'lman can't pass for you.

GRACE: (*seizing a fly whisk*) Hee! ha – git out! (*Drives* CHILDREN *away – in escaping they tumble against and trip up* SOLON, *who falls with a tray – the* CHILDREN *steal the bananas and rolls that fall about. Enter* PETE *(he is lame) – he carries a mop and pail.*)

PETE: Hey! laws a massey! why, clar out! drop dat banana! I'll murder dis yer crowd. (*He chases* CHILDREN *about – they leap over railing at back. Exit* SOLON.) Dem little niggers is a judgment upon dis generation.
       (*Enter* GEORGE *from house.*)

GEORGE: What's the matter, Pete?

PETE: It's dem black trash, Mas'r George; dis 'ere property wants claring – dem's too numerous round; when I gets time, I'll kill some on 'em, sure!

GEORGE: They don't seem to be scared by the threat.

PETE: 'Top, you varmin! 'top till I get enough of you in one place!

GEORGE: Were they all born on this estate?

PETE: Guess they nebber was born – dem tings! what dem? – get away! Born here – dem darkies? What, on Terrebonne! Don't believe it, Mas'r George – dem black tings never was born at all; dey swarmed one morning' on a sassafras tree in the swamp – I cotched 'em, day ain't no count. Don't b'lieve dey'll turn out niggers when dere growed – dey'll come out sunthin else.

GRACE: Yes, Mas'r George, dey was born here; and old Pete is fonder on 'em dan he is of his fiddle on a Sunday.

PETE: What? dem tings – dem? – get away. (*Makes blow at the* CHILDREN.) Born here! dem darkies! What on Terrebonne? Don't b'lieve it, Mas'r George – no. One morning they swarmed on a sassafras tree in de swamp, and I cotched 'em all in a sieve – dat's how dey come on top of dis yearth – git out, you – ya, ya! (*Laughs.*)
       (*Exit* GRACE. *Enter* MRS. PEYTON, *from house.*)

MRS. P: So, Pete, you are spoiling those children as usual?

PETE: Dat's right, missus! gib it to ole Pete! he's allers in for it. Git away dere! Ya! if dey ain't all lighted like coons on dat snake fence, just out of shot. Look dar! Dem debils. Ya!

MRS. P: Pete! do you hear?

PETE: Git down dar! I'm arter you! (*Hobbles off.*)

MRS. P: You are out early this morning, George.

GEORGE: I was up before daylight. We got the horses saddled, and galloped down

---

snake fence: a fence made of roughly split rails laid zigzag.

the shell road over the Piney Patch. then, coasting the Bayou Lake, we crossed the long swamps by Paul's Path, and so came home again.

MRS. P: (*laughing*) You seem already familiar with the name of every spot on the estate.

(*Enter* PETE – *arranges breakfast etc.*)

GEORGE: Just one month ago I quitted Paris. I left that siren city as I would have left a beloved woman.

Mrs. P: No wonder! I dare say you left at least a dozen beloved women there, at the same time.

GEORGE: I feel that I departed amid universal and sincere regret. I left my loves and my creditors equally inconsolable.

MRS. P: George, you are incorrigible. Ah! you remind me so much of your uncle, the judge.

GEORGE: Bless his dear old handwriting, it's all I ever saw of him. For ten years his letters came every quarter-day with a remittance, and a word of advice in his formal cavalier style; and then a joke in the postscript that upset the dignity of the foregoing. Aunt, when he died, two years ago, I read over those letters of his, and if I didn't cry like a baby –

MRS. P: No, George; say you wept like a man. And so you really kept those foolish letters?

GEORGE: Yes; I kept the letters, and squandered the money.

MRS. P: (*embracing him*) Ah! why were you not my son – you are so like my dear husband.

(*Enter* SALEM SCUDDER.)

SCUDDER: Ain't he! Yes – when I saw him and Miss Zoe galloping through the green sugar crop, and doing ten dollars' worth of damage at every stride, says I, how like his old uncle he do make the dirt fly.

GEORGE: Oh, aunt! what a bright, gay creature she is.

SCUDDER: What, Zoe! Guess that you didn't leave anything female in Europe that can lift an eyelash beside that gal. When she goes along, she just leaves a streak of love behind her. It's a good drink to see her come into the cotton-fields – the niggers get fresh on the sight of her. If she ain't worth her weight in sunshine, you may take one of my fingers off, and choose which you like.

MRS. P: She need not keep us waiting breakfast, though. Pete, tell Miss Zoe that we are waiting.

PETE: Yes, missus. Why, Minnie, why don't you run when you hear, you lazy crittur? (MINNIE *runs off.*) Dat's de laziest nigger on dis yere property. (*Sits down.*) Don't do nuffin.

MRS. P: My dear George, you are left in your uncle's will heir to this estate.

GEORGE: Subject to your life-interest and an annuity to Zoe, is it not so?

MRS. P: I fear that the property is so involved that the strictest economy will scarcely recover it. My dear husband never kept any accounts, and we scarcely know in what condition the estate really is.

SCUDDER: Yes we do, ma'am; it's in a darned bad condition. Ten years ago the Judge took as overseer a bit of Connecticut hardware called M'Closky. The Judge didn't understand accounts – the overseer did. For a year or two all went fine. The Judge drew money like Bourbon whisky from a barrel, and never turned off the tap. But out it flew, free for everybody or anybody, to beg, borrow, or steal. So it went, till one day the Judge found the tap wouldn't run. He looked in to see what stopped it, and pulled out a big mortgage. 'Sign that,' says the overseer, 'it's only a formality.' 'All right,' says the Judge, and away went a thousand acres; so at the end of eight years, Jacob M'Closky, Esquire, finds himself proprietor of the richest half of Terrebonne –

GEORGE: But the other half is free.

SCUDDER: No, it ain't, because, just then, what does the Judge do but hire another overseer – a Yankee – a Yankee named Salem Scudder.

MRS. P: Oh, no, it was –

SCUDDER: Hold on now! I'm going to straighten this account clear out. What was this here Scudder? Well, he lived in New York by sittin' with his heels up in front of French's Hotel, and inventin' –

GEORGE: Inventing what?

SCUDDER: Improvements – anything from a staylace to a fire-engine. Well, he cut that for the photographing line. He and his apparatus arrived here, took the Judge's likeness and his fancy, who made him overseer right off. Well, sir, what does this Scudder do but introduces his inventions and improvements on this estate. His new cotton gins broke down, the steam sugar-mills burst up, until he finished off with folly what Mr. M'Closky with his knavery began.

MRS. P: Oh, Salem! how can you say so? Haven't you worked like a horse?

SCUDDER: No, ma'am, I worked like an ass – an honest one, and that's all. Now, Mr. George, between the two overseers, you and that good old lady have come to the ground; that is the state of things, just as near as I can fix it.

    (ZOE *sings without.*)

GEORGE: 'Tis Zoe.

SCUDDER: Oh! I have not spoiled that anyhow. I can't introduce any darned improvement there. Ain't that a cure for old age; it kinder lifts the heart up, don't it?

MRS. P: Poor child! what will become of her when I am gone? If you haven't spoiled her, I fear I have. She has had the education of a lady.

GEORGE: I have remarked that she is treated by the neighbours with a kind of familiar condescension that annoyed me.

SCUDDER: Do you know that she is the natural daughter of the Judge, your uncle, and that old lady thar just adored anything he cared for; and this girl, that another woman would a hated, she loves as if she'd been her own child.

GEORGE: Aunt, I am prouder and happier to be your nephew and heir to the ruins of Terrebonne than I would have been to have had half Louisiana without you.

    (*Enter* ZOE, *from house.*)

ZOE: Am I late? Ah! Mr. Scudder, good morning.

SCUDDER: Thank'ye. I'm from fair to middlin', like a bamboo cane, much the same all the year round.

---

staylace: lace used to draw together a woman's stays.
cotton gin: a machine for separating cotton from its seeds.

ZOE: No: like a sugar cane – so dry outside, one would never think there was so much sweetness within.

SCUDDER: Look here; I can't stand that gal! if I stop here, I shall hug her right off. (*Sees* PETE *who has set his pail down upstage, and goes to sleep on it.*) If that old nigger ain't asleep, I'm blamed. Hillo! (*Kicks pail from under* PETE, *and exit.*)

PETE: Hi! Debbel's in de pail! Whar's breakfass?

(*Enter* SOLON *and* DIDO *with coffee pot, dishes, etc.*)

DIDO: Bless'ee, Missey Zoe, here it be. Dere's a dish of penpans – jess taste, Mas'r George – and here's fried bananas; smell 'em, do, sa glosh.

PETE: Hole yer tongue, Dido. Whar's de coffee? (*Pours out.*) If it don't stain de cup, your wicked ole life's in danger sure! dat right! black as nigger; clar as ice. You may drink dat, Mas'r George. (*Looks off.*) Ya! here's Mas'r Sunny-side, and Missey Dora, jist drov up. Some of you niggers, run and hole de hosses; and take dis, Dido. (*Gives her coffee pot to hold, and hobbles off, followed by* SOLON *and* DIDO.)

(*Enter* SUNNYSIDE *and* DORA.)

SUNNYSIDE: Good day, ma'am. (*Shakes hands with* GEORGE.) I see we are just in time for breakfast. (*Sits.*)

DORA: Oh, none for me; I never eat. (*Sits.*)

GEORGE: (*aside*) They do not notice Zoe. (*aloud*) You don't see Zoe, Mr. Sunny-side.

SUNNYSIDE: Ah! Zoe, girl; are you there!

DORA: Take my shawl, Zoe. (ZOE *helps her.*) What a good creature she is.

SUNNYSIDE: I dare say, now, that in Europe you have never met any lady more beautiful in person, or more polished in manners, than that girl.

GEORGE: You are right, sir; though I shrank from expressing that opinion in her presence, so bluntly.

SUNNYSIDE: Why so?

GEORGE: It may be considered offensive.

SUNNYSIDE: (*astonished*) What? I say, Zoe, do you hear that?

DORA: Mr. Peyton is joking.

MRS. P: My nephew is not yet acquainted with our customs in Louisiana, but he will soon understand.

GEORGE: Never, aunt! I shall never understand how to wound the feelings of any lady; and, if that is the custom here, I shall never acquire it.

DORA: Zoe, my dear, what does he mean?

ZOE: I don't know.

GEORGE: Excuse me, I'll light a cigar. (*Goes upstage.*)

DORA: (*aside to* ZOE) Isn't he sweet? Oh, dear Zoe, is he in love with anybody?

ZOE: How can I tell?

DORA: Ask him, I want to know; don't say I told you to enquire, but find out – Minnie, fan me, it is so nice – and his clothes are French, ain't they?

ZOE: I think so; shall I ask him that too?

DORA: No, dear. I wish he would make love to me. When he speaks to one he does it so easy, so gentle, it isn't bar-room style – love lined with drinks, sighs tinged with tobacco – and they say all the women in Paris were in love with him, which I feel *I* shall be – stop fanning me – what nice boots he wears.

SUNNYSIDE: (*to* MRS. PEYTON) Yes, ma'am, I hold a mortgage over Terrebonne, mine's a ninth, and pretty near covers all the property, except the slaves. I believe Mr. M'Closky has a bill of sale on them. Oh, here he is.
    (*Enter* M'CLOSKY.)
SUNNYSIDE: Good morning, Mr. M'Closky.
M'CLOSKY: Good morning, Mr. Sunnyside, Miss Dora, your servant.
DORA: (*seated*) Fan me, Minnie. (*aside*) I don't like that man.
M'CLOSKY: (*aside*) Insolent as usual. (*aloud*) You begged me to call this morning. I hope I'm not intruding.
MRS. P: My nephew, Mr. Peyton.
M'CLOSKY: Oh, how d'ye do, sir? (*Offers hand.* GEORGE *bows coldly. Aside*) A puppy; if he brings any of his European airs here we'll fix him. (*aloud*) Zoe, tell Pete to give my mare a feed, will ye?
GEORGE: (*angrily*) Sir!
M'CLOSKY: Hillo, did I tread on ye?
MRS. P: What is the matter with George?
ZOE: (*taking fan from* MINNIE) Go, Minnie, tell Pete, run!
    (*Exit* MINNIE.)
MRS. P: Grace, attend to Mr. M'Closky.
M'CLOSKY: A julep, gal, that's my breakfast, and a bit of cheese.
GEORGE: (*aside to* MRS. PEYTON) How can you ask that vulgar ruffian to your table?
MRS. P: Hospitality in Europe is a courtesy; here, it is an obligation. We tender food to a stranger, not because he is a gentleman, but because he is hungry.
GEORGE: Aunt, I will take my rifle down to the Atchafalaya. Paul has promised me a bear and a deer or two. I see my little Nimrod yonder, with his Indian companion. Excuse me, ladies. Ho! Paul! (*Enters house.*)
PAUL: (*outside*) I'ss, Mas'r George. (*Enters with* WAHNOTEE.)
SUNNYSIDE: It's a shame to allow that young cub to run over the swamps and woods, hunting and fishing his life away instead of hoeing cane.
MRS. P: The child was a favourite of the Judge, who encouraged his gambols. I couldn't bear to see him put to work.
GEORGE: (*returning with rifle*) Come, Paul, are you ready?
PAUL: I'ss Mas'r George. Oh, golly! ain't that a pooty gun.
M'CLOSKY: See here, you imps; if I catch you and your red-skin yonder gunning in my swamps, I'll give you rats, mind – them vagabonds, when the game's about, shoot my pigs.
    (*Exit* GEORGE *into house.*)
PAUL: You gib me ratten, Mas'r Clostry, but I guess you take a berry long stick to Wahnotee; ugh, he make bacon of you.
M'CLOSKY: Make bacon of me, you young whelp. Do you mean that I'm a pig? Hold on a bit. (*Seizes whip and holds* PAUL.)
ZOE: Oh, sir! don't, pray don't.
M'CLOSKY: (*slowly lowering his whip*) Darn you, red-skin, I'll pay you off some day, both of ye. (*Returns to table and drinks.*)
SUNNYSIDE: That Indian is a nuisance. Why don't he return to his nation out west?
M'CLOSKY: He's too fond of thieving and whisky.

ZOE: No; Wahnotee is a gentle, honest creature, and remains here because he loves that boy with the tenderness of a woman. When Paul was taken down with the swamp fever the Indian sat outside the hut, and neither ate, slept, or spoke for five days, till the child could recognise and call him to his bedside. He who can love so well is honest – don't speak ill of poor Wahnotee.

MRS. P: Wahnotee, will you go back to your people?

WAHNOTEE: Sleugh.

PAUL: He don't understand; he speaks a mash up of Indian, French and Mexican. Wahnotee Patira na sepau assa wigiran.

WAHNOTEE: Weal Omenee.

PAUL: Says he'll go if I'll go with him. He calls me Omenee, the pigeon, and Miss Zoe is Ninemoosha, the sweetheart.

WAHNOTEE: (*pointing to* ZOE) Ninemoosha.

ZOE: No, Wahnotee, we can't spare Paul.

PAUL: If Omenee remain, Wahnotee will die in Terrebonne.
(*During the dialogue* WAHNOTEE *has taken George's gun; enter* GEORGE.)

GEORGE: Now I'm ready. (*Tries to regain his gun;* WAHNOTEE *refuses to give it up;* PAUL *quietly takes it from him, and remonstrates with him.*)

DORA: Zoe, he's going; I want him to stay and make love to me – that's what I came for to-day.

MRS. P: George, I can't spare Paul for an hour or two; he must run over to the landing; the steamer from New Orleans passed up the river last night, and if there's a mail they have thrown it ashore.

SUNNYSIDE: I saw the mail bags lying in the shed this morning.

MRS. P: I expect an important letter from Liverpool; away with you, Paul, bring the mail-bags here.

PAUL: I'm 'most afraid to take Wahnotee to the shed, there's rum there.

WAHNOTEE: Rum!

PAUL: Come, then, but if I catch you drinkin', oh, laws a mussey, you'll get snakes! I'll gib it you! now mind. (*Exit with* WAHNOTEE.)

GEORGE: Come, Miss Dora, let me offer you my arm.

DORA: Mr. George, I am afraid, if all we hear is true, you have led a dreadful life in Europe.

GEORGE: That's a challenge to begin a description of my feminine adventures.

DORA: You have been in love, then?

GEORGE: Two hundred and forty-nine times! let me relate you the worst cases.

DORA: No! no!

GEORGE: I'll put the naughty parts in French.

DORA: I won't hear a word! Oh, you horrible man! go on.
(*Exit* GEORGE *and* DORA *to house.*)

M'CLOSKY: Now, ma'am I'd like a little business if agreeable. I bring you news: your banker, old La Fouché, of New Orleans, is dead; the executors are winding up his affairs, and have foreclosed on all overdue mortgages, so Terrebonne is for sale. Here's the *Picayune* (*producing paper*) with the advertisement.

Picayune: the name given to the American five-cent piece, and hence to any coin of very little value. The *Picayune* was an actual Louisiana paper.

ZOE: Terrebonne for sale!

MRS. P: Terrebonne for sale, and you, sir, will doubtless become its purchaser.

M'CLOSKY: Well, ma'am I spose there's no law agin my bidding for it. The more
bidders, the better for you. You'll take care, I guess, it don't go too cheap.

MRS. P: Oh, sir, I don't value the place for its price, but for the many happy days
I've spent here; that landscape, flat and uninteresting though it may be, is
full of charm for me; those poor people, born around me, growing up about
my heart, have bounded my view of life; and now to lose that homely scene,
lose their black ungainly faces, – oh, sir, perhaps you should be as old as I am
to feel as I do when my past life is torn away from me.

M'CLOSKY: I'd be darned glad if somebody would tear my past life away from *me*.
Sorry I can't help you, but the fact is you're in such an all-fired mess that you
couldn't be pulled out without a derrick.

MRS. P: Yes, there is a hope left yet, and I cling to it. The house of Mason Brothers,
of Liverpool, failed some twenty years ago in my husband's debt.

M'CLOSKY: They owed him over 50,000 dollars.

MRS. P: I cannot find the entry in my husband's accounts, but you, Mr. M'Closky,
can doubtless detect it. Zoe, bring here the Judge's old desk; it is in the
library.

                  (*Exit* ZOE *to house.*)

M'CLOSKY: You don't expect to recover any of this old debt, do you?

MRS. P: Yes, the firm has recovered itself, and I received a notice two months ago
that some settlement might be anticipated.

SUNNYSIDE: Why, with principal and interest this debt has been more than
doubled in twenty years.

MRS. P: But it may be years yet before it will be paid off, if ever.

SUNNYSIDE: If there's a chance of it, there's not a planter round here who
wouldn't lend you the whole cash, to keep your name and blood amongst us.
Come, cheer up, old firend.

MRS. P: Ah! Sunnyside, how good you are – so like my poor Peyton.

                (*Exit* MRS. PEYTON *and* SUNNYSIDE *to house.*)

M'CLOSKY: Curse their old families – they cut me – a bilious, conceited, thin lot
of dried up aristocracy. I hate 'em. Just because my grandfather wasn't some
broken-down Virginia transplant, or a stingy old Creole, I ain't fit to sit down
to the same meat with them – it makes my blood so hot I feel my heart hiss.
I'll sweep these Peytons from this section of the country. Their presence
keeps alive the reproach against me, that I ruined them; yet, if this money
should come. Bah! There's no chance of it. Then, if they go they'll take Zoe
– she'll follow them. Darn that girl, she makes me quiver when I think of her;
she's took me for all I'm worth.

                (*Enter* ZOE *from house, with the desk.*)

Oh, here! do you know what the annuity the old Judge left you is worth
to-day? not a picayune.

ZOE: It's surely worth the love that dictated it; here are the papers and accounts.
       (*putting it on the table*)

Creole: a person born or naturalised in the Americas, though of European or African Negro
race. The name has no colour-connotation.

M'CLOSKY: Stop, Zoe; come here! How would you like to rule the house of the richest planter on Atchapalaga – eh? or say the word, and I'll buy this old barrack, and you shall be mistress of Terrebonne.

ZOE: Oh, sir, do not speak so to me!

M'CLOSKY: Why not? Look here, these Peytons are bust, cut 'em; I am rich, jine me; I'll set you up grand, and we'll give these first families here our dust, until you'll see their white skins shrivel up with hate and rage; what d'ye say?

ZOE: Let me pass! Oh, pray, let me go!

M'CLOSKY: What, you won't, won't ye? If young George Peyton was to make you the same offer, you'd jump at it pretty darned quick, I guess. Come, Zoe, don't be a fool, I'd marry you if I could, but you know I can't, so just say what you want. Here, then, I'll put back these Peytons in Terrebonne, and they shall know you done it; yes, they'll have you to thank for saving them from ruin.

ZOE: Do you think they would live here on such terms?

M'CLOSKY: Why not? We'll hire out our slaves, and live on their wages.

ZOE: But I'm not a slave.

M'CLOSKY: No, if you were I'd buy you, if you cost all I'm worth.

ZOE: Let me pass!

M'CLOSKY: Stop!

(*Enter* SCUDDER.)

SCUDDER: Let her pass!

M'CLOSKY: Eh?

SCUDDER: Let her pass! (*Takes out his knife. Exit* ZOE *to house.*)

M'CLOSKY: Is that you, Mr. Overseer? (*Examines paper.*)

SCUDDER: Yes, I'm here somewhere, interferin'.

M'CLOSKY: (*sitting*) A pretty mess you've got this estate in –

SCUDDER: Yes – me and Co. – we done it; but, as you were senior partner in the concern, I reckon you got the big lick.

M'CLOSKY: What d'ye mean?

SCUDDER: Let me proceed by illustration. (*Sits.*) Look thar! (*Points with his knife off.*) D'ye see that tree? It's called a live oak, and is a native here; beside it grows a creeper; year after year that creeper twines its long arms round and round the tree – sucking the earth dry all about its roots – living on its life – over-running its branches, until at last the live oak withers and dies out. Do you know what the niggers round here call that sight? They call it the Yankee hugging the Creole. (*Sits.*)

M'CLOSKY: Mr. Scudder, I've listened to a great many of your insinuations, and now I'd like to come to an understanding what they mean. If you want a quarrel –

SCUDDER: No, I'm the skurriest crittur at a fight you ever see; my legs have been too well brought up to stand and see my body abused; I take good care of myself, I can tell you.

M'CLOSKY: Because I heard that you had traduced my character.

I'd marry you if I could: there were still statutes against miscegenation in most southern states.

SCUDDER: Traduced! Whoever said so lied. I always said you were the darndest thief that ever escaped a white jail to misrepresent the North to the South.

M'CLOSKY: (*raising hand to back of his neck*) What!

SCUDDER: Take your hand down – take it down. (M'CLOSKY *lowers his hand.*) Whenever I gets into company like yours, I always start with the advantage on my side.

M'CLOSKY: What d'ye mean?

SCUDDER: I mean that before you could draw that bowie-knife you wear down your back, I'd cut you into shingles. Keep quiet, and let's talk sense. You wanted to come to an understanding, and I'm coming thar as quick as I can. Now, Jacob M'Closky, you despise me because you think I'm a fool; I despise you because I know you to be a knave. Between us we've ruined these Peytons; you fired the Judge, and I finished off the widow. Now, I feel bad about my share in the business. I'd give half the balance of my life to wipe out my part of the work. Many a night I've laid awake and thought how to pull them through, till I've cried like a child over the sum I couldn't do; and you know how darned hard 'tis to make a Yankee cry.

M'CLOSKY: Well, what's that to me?

SCUDDER: Hold on, Jacob, I'm coming to that; I tell ye, I'm such a fool – I can't bear the feeling, it keeps at me like a skin complaint, and if this family is sold up –

M'CLOSKY: What then?

SCUDDER: (*rising*) I'd cut my throat – or yours – yours I'd prefer.

M'CLOSKY: Would you now? Why don't you do it?

SCUDDER: 'Cos I's skeered to try! I never killed a man in my life – and civilization is so strong in me I guess I couldn't do it – I'd like to, though!

M'CLOSKY: And all for the sake of that old woman and that young puppy, eh? No other cause to hate – to envy me – to be jealous of me – eh?

SCUDDER: Jealous! what for?

M'CLOSKY: Ask the colour in your face; d'ye think I can't read you like a book? With your New England hypocrisy, you would persuade yourself it was this family alone you cared for: it ain't – you know it ain't – 'tis the 'Octoroon', and you love her as I do, and you hate me because I'm your rival. That's where the tears come from, Salem Scudder, if you ever shed any – that's where the shoe pinches.

SCUDDER: Wal, I do like the gal; she's a –

M'CLOSKY: She's in love with young Peyton; it made me curse – whar it made you cry, as it does now. I see the tears on your cheeks now.

SCUDDER: Look at 'em, Jacob, for they are honest water from the well of truth. I ain't ashamed of it – I do love the gal; but I ain't jealous of you, because I believe the only sincere feeling about you is your love for Zoe, and it does your heart good to have her image thar; but I believe you put it thar to spile. By fair means I don't think you can get her, and don't you try foul with her,

---

Octoroon: a person with one-eighth negro blood. Zoe is the daughter of Judge Peyton by an unnamed quadroon slave.

'cause if you do, Jacob, civilization be darned, I'm on you like a painter, and
when I'm drawed out I'm pizin. (*Exit to house.*)

M'CLOSKY: Fair or foul, I'll have her – take that home with you! (*Opens desk.*)
What's here? Judgments? Yes, plenty of 'em; bill of costs; account with
Citizen's Bank. What's this? 'Judgment 40,000, Thibodeaux against Peyton';
surely that is the judgment under which this estate is now advertised for sale.
(*Takes up paper and examines it.*) Yes, 'Thibodeaux against Peyton, 1838'.
Hold on! whew! this is worth taking to. In this desk the Judge used to keep
one paper I want – this should be it. (*Reads.*) 'The free papers of my daughter,
Zoe, registered February 4th, 1841'. Why, Judge, wasn't you lawyer enough
to know that while a judgment stood against you, it was a lien on your slaves?
Zoe is your child by a quadroon slave, and you didn't free her. Blood! if this
is so, she's mine! This old Liverpool debt – that may cross me. If it only arrive
too late – if it don't come by this mail. Hold on! this letter the old lady
expects – that's it: let me only head off that letter, and Terrebonne will be
sold before they can recover it. That boy and the Indian have gone down to
the landing for the post-bags; they'll idle on the way as usual; my mare will
take me across the swamp, and before they can reach the shed, I'll have
purified them bags. Ne'er a letter shall show this mail. Ha, ha! (*Calls.*) Pete,
you old turkey-buzzard, saddle my mare. Then, if I sink every dollar I'm
worth in her purchase, I'll own that Octoroon. (*Stands with his hand exten-
ded toward the house, and tableau.*)

ACT II

The Wharf – goods, boxes, and bales scattered about – a camera on stand. SCUD-
DER, DORA, GEORGE, *and* PAUL *discovered;* DORA *being photographed by*
SCUDDER, *who is arranging photographic apparatus;* GEORGE *and* PAUL *look-
ing on at back.*

SCUDDER: Just turn your face a leetle this way – fix your – let's see – look here.

DORA: So?

SCUDDER: That's right. (*Puts his head under the darkening apron.*) It's such a
long time since I did this sort of thing, and this old machine has got so dirty
and stiff, I'm afraid it won't operate. That's about right. Now don't stir.

PAUL: Ugh! she look as though she war gwine to have a tooth drawed!

SCUDDER: I've got four plates ready, in case we miss the first shot. One of them is
prepared with a self-developing liquid that I've invented. I hope it will turn
out better than most of my notions. Now fix yourself. Are you ready?

DORA: Ready!

SCUDDER: Fire! – one, two, three. (*Takes out watch.*)

PAUL: Now it's cooking. Laws mussey, I feel it all inside, as if I was at a lottery.

SCUDDER: So! (*Throws down apron.*) That's enough. (*Withdraws slide, turns and*

---

painter: American panther, or cougar.
a lien on your slaves: the legal right of the creditor to retain property pending settlement of a
debt means that Zoe was not Judge Peyton's legal property at the time when he 'freed' her. She
is still a slave.

sees PAUL.) What! what are you doing there, you young varmint? Ain't you
took them bags to the house yet?

PAUL: Now, it ain't no use trying to get mad, Mas'r Scudder. I'm gwine! I only
come back to find Wahnotee; whar is dat ign'ant Ingiun?

SCUDDER: You'll find him scenting round the rum store, hitched up by the nose.
(*Exit into room.*)

PAUL: (*calling at door*) Say, Mas'r Scudder, take me in dat telescope?

SCUDDER: (*inside room*) Get out, you cub! clar out!

PAUL: You got four ob dem dishes ready. Gosh, wouldn't I like to hav myself
took! What's de charge, Mas'r Scudder? (*Runs off.*)

SCUDDER: (*entering from room*) Job had none of them critters on his plantation,
else he'd never ha' stood through so many chapters. Well, that has come out
clear, ain't it? (*Shows plate.*)

DORA: Oh, beautiful! Look, Mr. Peyton.

GEORGE: (*looking*) Yes, very fine!

SCUDDER: The apparatus can't mistake. When I travelled round with this machine,
the homely folks used to sing out, 'Hillo, mister this ain't like me!' 'Ma'am,'
says I, 'the apparatus can't mistake.' 'But, mister, that ain't my nose.' 'Ma'am,
your nose drawed it. The machine can't err – you may mistake your phiz,
but the apparatus don't.' 'But, sir, it ain't agreeable.' 'No, ma'am, the truth
seldom is.'

(*Enter* PETE, *puffing.*)

PETE: Mas'r Scudder! Mas'r Scudder!

SCUDDER: Hillo! what are you blowing about like a steamboat with one wheel
for?

PETE: You blow, Massa Scudder, when I tole you; dere's a man from Noo Aleens
just arriv' at de house, and he's stuck up two papers on de gates; 'For sale –
dis yer property', and a heap of oder tings – and he seen missus, and arter he
shown some papers she burst out crying – I yelled; den de corious of little
niggers dey set up, den de hull plantation children – de live stock reared up
and created a purpiration of lamentation as did de ole heart good to har.

DORA: What's the matter?

SCUDDER: He's come.

PETE: Dass it – I saw'm!

SCUDDER: The sheriff from New Orleans has taken possession – Terrebonne is in
the hands of the law.

(*Enter* ZOE.)

ZOE: Oh, Mr. Scudder! Dora! Mr. Peyton! come home – there are strangers in
the house.

DORA: Stay, Mr. Peyton; Zoe, a word! (*Leads her forward – aside.*) Zoe, the more
I see of George Peyton the better I like him; but he is too modest – that is a
very impertinent virtue in a man.

ZOE: I'm no judge, dear.

DORA: Of course not, you little fool; no one ever made love to you, and you can't
understand. I mean that George knows I am an heiress; my fortune would
release this estate from debt.

ZOE: Oh, I see!

DORA: If he would only propose to marry me I would accept him, but he don't know that, and he will go on fooling in his slow European way until it is too late.

ZOE: What's to be done?

DORA: You tell him.

ZOE: What? that he isn't to go on fooling in his slow –

DORA: No, you goose! twit him on his silence and abstraction – I'm sure it's plain enough, for he has not spoken two words to me all the day; then joke round the subject, and at last speak out.

SCUDDER: Pete, as you came here did you pass Paul and the Indian with the letter bags?

PETE: No, sar; but dem vagabonds neber take de 'specable straight road, dey goes by de swamp. (*Exit up path.*)

SCUDDER: Come, sir!

DORA: (*to* ZOE) Now's your time. (*aloud*) Mr. Scudder, take us with you – Mr. Peyton is so slow, there's no getting him on.

(*Exit* DORA *and* SCUDDER.)

ZOE: They are gone! (*glancing at* GEORGE) Poor fellow, he has lost all.

GEORGE: Poor child! how sad she looks now she has no resource.

ZOE: How shall I ask him to stay?

GEORGE: Zoe, will you remain here? I wish to speak to you.

ZOE: (*aside*) Well, that saves trouble.

GEORGE: By our ruin, you lose all.

ZOE: Oh, I'm nothing; think of yourself.

GEORGE: I can think of nothing but the image that remains face to face with me: so beautiful, so simple, so confiding – that I dare not express the feelings that have grown up so rapidly in my heart.

ZOE: (*aside*) He means Dora.

GEORGE: If I dared to speak!

ZOE: That's just what you must do, and do it at once, or it will be too late.

GEORGE: Has my love been divined?

ZOE: It has been more than suspected.

GEORGE: Zoe, listen to me then – I shall see this estate pass from me without a sigh, for it possesses no charm for me; the wealth I covet is the love of those around me – eyes that are rich in fond looks – lips that breathe endearing words; the only estate I value is the heart of one true woman, and the slaves I'd have are her thoughts.

ZOE: George, George, your words take away my breath!

GEORGE: The world, Zoe, the free struggle of minds and hands is before me; the education bestowed on me by my dear uncle is a noble heritage which no sheriff can seize; with that I can build up a fortune, spread a roof over the heads I love, and place before them the food I have earned; I will work –

ZOE: Work! I thought none but coloured people worked.

GEORGE: Work, Zoe, is the salt that gives flavour to life.

ZOE: Dora said you were slow – if she could hear you now –

GEORGE: Zoe, you are young; your mirror must have told you that you are beautiful. Is your heart free?

ZOE: Free? Of course it is!

GEORGE: We have known each other but a few days, but to me those days have
been worth all the rest of my life. Zoe, you have suspected the feeling that
now commands an utterance – you have seen that I love you.

ZOE: Me! you love *me*?

GEORGE: As my wife – the sharer of my hopes, my ambitions, and my sorrows;
under the shelter of your love I could watch the storms of fortune pass un-
heeded by.

ZOE: *My* love! *My* love? George, you know not what you say. *I* the sharer of your
sorrows – your wife. Do you know what I am?

GEORGE: Your birth – I know it. Has not my dear aunt forgotten it – she who had
the most right to remember it? You are illegitimate, but love knows no prejudice.

ZOE: (*aside*) Alas! he does not know, he does not know! and will despise me, spurn
me, loathe me, when he learns who, what he has so loved. (*aloud*) George,
oh! forgive me! Yes, I love you – I did not know it until your words showed
me what has been in my heart; each of them awoke a new sense, and now I
know how unhappy – how very unhappy I am.

GEORGE: Zoe, what have I said to wound you?

ZOE: Nothing; but you must learn what I thought you already knew. George, you
cannot marry me, the laws forbid it!

GEORGE: Forbid it?

ZOE: There is a gulf between us, as wide as your love – as deep as my despair; but,
oh, tell me, say you will pity me! that you will pity me! that you will not
throw me from you like a poisoned thing!

GEORGE: Zoe, explain yourself – your language fills me with shapeless fears.

ZOE: And what shall I say? I – my mother was – no, no – not her! Why should I
refer the blame to her? George, do you see that hand you hold; look at these
fingers, do you see the nails are of a blueish tinge?

GEORGE: Yes, near the quick there is a faint blue mark.

ZOE: Look in my eyes; is not the same colour in the white?

GEORGE: It is their beauty.

ZOE: Could you see the roots of my hair you would see the same dark fatal mark.
Do you know what that is?

GEORGE: No.

ZOE: That – that is the ineffacable curse of Cain. Of the blood that feeds my heart,
one drop in eight is black – bright red as the rest may be, that one drop
poisons all the flood. Those seven bright drops give me love like yours, hope
like yours – ambition like yours – life hung with passions like dew-drops on
the morning flowers; but the one black drop gives me despair, for I'm an unclean thing – forbidden by the laws – I'm an Octoroon!

GEORGE: Zoe, I love you none the less; this knowledge brings no revolt to my
heart, and I can overcome the obstacle.

ZOE: But *I* cannot.

GEORGE: We can leave this country and go far away where none can know.

ZOE: And our mother, she, who from infancy treated me with such fondness, she
who, as you said, had most reason to spurn me, can she forget what I am?

Will she gladly see you wedded to the child of her husband's slave? No! she
would revolt from it, as all but you would; and if I consented to hear the
cries of my heart, if I did not crush out my infant love, what would she say
to the poor girl on whom she had bestowed so much? No, no!

GEORGE: Zoe, must we immolate our lives on her prejudice?

ZOE: Yes, for I'd rather be black than ungrateful! Ah, George, our race has at least
one virtue – it knows how to suffer.

GEORGE: Each word you utter makes my love sink deeper into my heart.

ZOE: And I remained here to induce you to offer that heart to Dora!

GEORGE: If you bid me do so I will obey you –

ZOE: No, no! if you cannot be mine, oh, let me not blush when I think of you.

GEORGE: Dearest Zoe!

(*Exeunt. As they exit* M'CLOSKY *rises from behind rock, and looks
after them.*)

M'CLOSKY: She loves him! I felt it – and how she can love! (*Advances.*) That one
drop of black blood burns in her veins, and lights up her heart like a foggy
sun. Oh, how I lapped up her words like a thirsty bloodhound! I'll have her if
it costs me my life! Yonder the boy still lurks with those mail bags; the devil
still keeps him here to tempt me, darn his yellow skin – I arrived just too late,
he had grabbed the prize as I came up. Hillo! he's coming this way, fighting
with his Ingiun. (*Conceals himself.*)

(*Enter* PAUL, *wrestling with* WAHNOTEE.)

PAUL: It ain't no use now, you got to gib it up!

WAHNOTEE: Ugh!

PAUL: It won't do! you got dat bottle of rum hid under your blanket – gib it up
now, you – Yar! (*Wrenches it from him.*) You nasty, lying, Ingiun! It no use
you putting on airs; I ain't gwine to sit up wid you all night, and you drunk.
Hillo! war's the crowd gone? And dar's de 'paratus – oh gosh! if I could take
a likeness of dis child! Uh, uh, let's have a peep. (*Looks through camera.*)
Oh, golly! yah, you Wahnotee! you stan' dah, I see you. Ta demine usti.
(*Looks at* WAHNOTEE *through the camera;* WAHNOTEE *springs back with
an expression of alarm.*)

WAHNOTEE: No tue Wahnotee.

PAUL: Ha, ha! tinks it's a gun; you ign'ant Ingiun, it can't hurt you! Stop, here's
dem dishes – plates – dat's what he call 'em, all fix; I see Mas'r Scudder do it
often – tink I can take likeness – stay dere, Wahnotee.

WAHNOTEE: No, carabine tue.

PAUL: I must operate and take my own likeness too – how debbel I do dat? Can't
be ober dar an' here too – I ain't twins. Ugh! ach! 'Top, you look, you
Wahnotee, you see dis rag, eh? Well, when I say go, den lift dis rag like dis,
see! den run to dat pine tree up dar (*points*), and back agin, and den pull
down de rag, so, d'ye see?

WAHNOTEE: Hugh!

PAUL: Den you hab glass ob rum.

WAHNOTEE: Rum!

PAUL: Dat wakes him up. Coute Wahnotee in Omenee dit, go, Wahnotee, poina la
fa, comb a pine tree, la revient sala, la fa.

Act II

WAHNOTEE: Firewater!

PAUL: Yes, den a glass ob fire water, now den. (*Throws mail-bags down, and sit.
    on them.*) Pret, now den, go.

        (WAHNOTEE *raises apron, and runs off.* PAUL *sits for his picture* –
        M'CLOSKY *appears.*)

M'CLOSKY: Where are they? Ah, yonder goes the Indian!

PAUL: De time he gone just about enough to cook dat dish plate.

M'CLOSKY: Yonder is the boy – now is my time! What's he doing? Is he asleep?
    (*Advances.*) He is sitting on my prize! Darn his carcase! I'll clear him off
    there – he'll never know what stunned him. (*Takes* WAHNOTEE*'s tomahawk
    and steals to* PAUL.)

PAUL: Dam dat Injun! is dat him creeping dar? I daren't move fear to spile myself.
    (M'CLOSKY *strikes him on the head; he falls dead.*)

M'CLOSKY: Hooraw! the bags are mine – now for it! (*Opens mail-bags.*) What's
    here? Sunnyside, Pointdexter, Jackson, Peyton; here it is – the Liverpool
    post-mark, sure enough! (*Opens letter – reads.*) 'Madam, we are instructed
    by the firm of Mason and Co. to inform you that a dividend of forty per cent
    is payable on the 1st proximo, this amount in consideration of position, they
    send herewith, and you will find enclosed by draft to your order on the bank
    of Louisiana, which please acknowledge – the balance will be paid in full, with
    interest, in three, six, and nine months – your drafts on Mason Brothers, at
    those dates, will be accepted by La Pelisse and Compagnie, N.O., so that you
    may command immediate use of the whole amount at once if required.
    Yours, &c., James Brown.' What a find! this infernal letter would have saved
    all. (*During the reading of letter he remains nearly motionless under the
    focus of camera.*) But now I guess it will arrive too late – these darned U.S.
    mails are to blame. The Injun! he must not see me. (*Exit rapidly.*)

        (WAHNOTEE *runs on, pulls down apron – sees* PAUL *lying on
        ground – speaks to him – thinks he is shamming sleep – gesticulates
        and jabbers – goes to him, moves him with feet, then kneels down
        to rouse him – to his horror finds him dead – expresses great grief –
        raises his eyes – they fall upon the camera – rises with savage growl,
        seizes tomahawk, and smashes camera to pieces, then goes to* PAUL
        *– expresses grief, sorrow, and fondness, and takes him in his arms to
        carry him away – Tableau.*)

    ACT III

A Room in MRS. PEYTON*'s house. An auction bill stuck up.* SOLON *and* GRACE
discovered.

PETE: (*outside*) Dis way – dis way.

        (*Enter* PETE, POINTDEXTER, JACKSON, LAFOUCHE, *and*
        CAILLOU.)

PETE: Dis way, gen'lmen; now Solon – Grace – dey's hot and tirsty – sangaree,
    brandy, rum.

JACKSON: Well, what d'ye say, Lafouche – d'ye smile?

        (*Enter* THIBODEAUX *and* SUNNYSIDE.)

THIB: I hope we don't intrude on the family.

PETE: You see dat hole in dar, sar? (*pointing to door*) I was raised on dis yar plantation – neber see no door in it – always open, sar, for stranger to walk in.

SUNNYSIDE: And for substance to walk out.

(*Enter* RATTS.)

RATTS: Fine southern style that, eh?

LAFOUCHE: (*reading bill*) 'A fine, well-built old family mansion, replete with every comfort.'

RATTS: There's one name on the list of slaves scratched, I see.

LAFOUCHE: Yes; No. 49, Paul, a quadroon boy, aged thirteen.

SUNNYSIDE: He's missing.

POINT: Run away, I suppose.

PETE: (*indignantly*) No, sar; nigger nebber cut stick on Terrebonne; dat boy's dead, sure.

RATTS: What, Picayune Paul, as we called him, that used to come aboard my boat? – poor little darkey, I hope not; many a picayune he picked up for his dance and nigger songs, and he supplied our table with fish and game from the Bayous.

PETE: Nebber supply no more, sar – nebber dance again. Massa Ratts, you h'ard him sing about de place where de good niggers go de last time?

RATTS: Well?

PETE: Well, he gone dar hisself; why I tink so – 'cause we missed Paul for some days, but nebber tout nothin', till one night dat ingiun Wahnotee suddenly stood right dare 'mongst us – was in his war paint, and mighty cold and grave – he sit down by de fire. 'Whar's Paul?' I say – he smoke and smoke, but nebber look out ob de fire; well knowing dem critters, I wait a long time – den he say, 'Wahnotee great chief'; den I say nothing – smoke anoder time – at last, rising to go, he turned round at door, and say berry low – oh, like a woman's voice – he say, 'Omenee Pangeuk' – dat is, Paul is dead – nebber see him since.

RATTS: That redskin killed him.

SUNNYSIDE: So we believe; and so mad are the folks around, that if they catch the redskin they'll lynch him, sure.

RATTS: Lynch him! Darn his copper carcass, I've got a set of Irish deck-hands aboard that just loved that child; and after I tell them this, let them get a sight of the redskin, I believe they would eat him, tomahawk and all. Poor little Paul!

THIB: What was he worth?

RATTS: Well, near on 500 dollars.

PETE: (*scandalised*) What, sar! You p'tend to be sorry for Paul, and prize him like dat – 500 dollars! Tousand dollars, Massa Thibodeaux.

(*Enter* SCUDDER.)

SCUDDER: Gentlemen, the sale takes place at three. (*to* POINTDEXTER) Good morning, Colonel. It's near that now, and there's still the sugar-houses to be

---

Bayous: streams with little current. The word is peculiar to the southern states of the U.S.A.

inspected. Good day, Mr. Thibodeaux – shall we drive down that way? Mr. Lafouche, why, how do you do, sir? you're looking well.

LAFOUCHE: Sorry I can't return the compliment.

RATTS: Salem's looking kinder hollowed out.

SCUDDER: What Mr. Ratts, are you going to invest in swamps?

RATTS: No; I want a nigger.

SCUDDER: Hush.

PETE: Eh? wass dat?

SCUDDER: Mr. Sunnyside, I can't do this job of showin' round the folks; my stomach goes agin it. I want Pete here a minute.

SUNNYSIDE: I'll accompany them, certainly.

SCUDDER: (*eagerly*) Will ye? Thank ye! thank ye!

SUNNYSIDE: We must excuse Scudder, friends. I'll see you round the estate.
    (*Enter* GEORGE *and* MRS. PEYTON.)

LAFOUCHE: Good morning, Mrs. Peyton. (*All salute.*)

SUNNYSIDE: This way, gentlemen.

RATTS: (*aside to* SUNNYSIDE) I say, I'd like to say summit soft to the old woman; perhaps it wouldn't go well, would it?

THIB: No; leave it alone.

RATTS: Darn it, when I see a woman in trouble, I feel like selling the skin off my back.
    (*Exit* THIBODEAUX, SUNNYSIDE, RATTS, POINTDEXTER, GRACE, JACKSON, LAFOUCHE, CAILLOU, SOLON.)

SCUDDER: (*aside to* PETE) Go outside there; listen to what you hear, then go down to the quarters and tell the boys, for I can't do it. Oh, get out.

PETE: He said, I want a nigger; laws! mussey! what am going to cum ob us! (*Exit slowly, as if concealing himself.*)

GEORGE: My dear aunt, why do you not move from this painful scene? Go with Dora to Sunnyside.

MRS. P: No, George, your uncle said to me with his dying breath, 'Nellie, never leave Terrebonne,' and I never *will* leave it, till the law compels me.

SCUDDER: Mr. George – I'm going to say somethin' that has been chokin' me for some time. I know you'll excuse it – that's Miss Dora – that girl's in love with you; yes, sir, her eyes are startin' out of her head with it; now her fortune would redeem a good part of this estate.

MRS. P: Why, George, I never suspected this!

GEORGE: I did, aunt, I confess, but –

MRS. P: And you hesitated, from motives of delicacy?

SCUDDER: No, ma'am, here's the plan of it; Mr. George is in love with Zoe.

GEORGE: Scudder!

MRS. P: George!

SCUDDER: Hold on now! things have got so jammed in on top of us, we ain't got time to put kid gloves on to handle them. He loves Zoe, and has found out that she loves him. (*sighing*) Well, that's all right, but as he can't marry her, and as Miss Dora would jump at him –

MRS. P: Why didn't you mention this before?

SCUDDER: Why, because *I* love Zoe too, and I couldn't take that young feller from her, and she jist living on the sight of him, as I saw her do, and they so happy in spite of this yere misery around them, and they reproachin' themselves with not feeling as they ought. I've seen it, I tell you, and darn it, ma'am, can't you see that's what's been a hollowing me out so – I beg your pardon.

MRS. P: Oh, George – my son, let me call you – I do not speak for my own sake, nor for the loss of the estate, but for the poor people here; they will be sold, divided, and taken away – they have been born here. Heaven has denied me children, so all the strings of my heart have grown around and amongst them like the fibres and roots of an old tree in its native earth. Oh, let all go, but save them! with them around us, if we have not wealth, we shall at least have the home that they alone can make –

GEORGE: My dear mother – Mr. Scudder – you teach me what I ought to do; if Miss Sunnyside will accept me as I am, Terrebonne shall be saved; I will sell myself, but the slaves shall be protected.

MRS. P: *Sell* yourself, George! is not Dora worth any man's –

SCUDDER: Don't say that, ma'am; don't say that to a man that loves another gal; he's going to do a heroic act, don't spile it.

MRS. P: But Zoe is only an Octoroon!

SCUDDER: She's won this race agin the white anyhow; it's too late now to start her pedigree. (*as* DORA *enters*) Come, Mrs. Peyton, take my arm; hush! here's the other one; she is a little too thoroughbred – too much of the greyhound, but the heart's there, I believe. (*Exit with* MRS. PEYTON.)

DORA: Poor Mrs. Peyton.

GEORGE: Miss Sunnyside, permit me a word; a feeling of delicacy has suspended on my lips an avowal, which –

DORA: (*aside*) Oh dear, has he suddenly come to his senses?

(*Enter* ZOE. *She stops at back.*)

GEORGE: In a word – I have seen and admired you!

DORA: (*aside*) He has a strange way of showing it – European, I suppose.

GEORGE: If you would pardon the abruptness of the question, I would ask you – Do you think the sincere devotion of my life to make yours happy would succeed?

DORA: (*aside*) Well, he has the oddest way of making love.

GEORGE: You are silent?

DORA: Mr. Peyton, I presume you have hesitated to make this avowal, because you feared in the present condition of affairs here, your object might be misconstrued, and that your attention was rather to my fortune than myself. (*a pause*) Why don't he speak? – I mean, you feared I might not give you credit for sincere and pure feelings. Well, you wrong me. I don't think you capable of anything else than –

GEORGE: No, I hesitated because an attachment I had formed before I had the pleasure of seeing you had not altogether died out.

DORA: (*smiling*) Some of those sirens of Paris, I presume. (*pause*) I shall endeavour not to be jealous of the past; perhaps I have no right to be. (*pause*) But now that vagrant love is – eh, faded – is it not? Why don't you speak, sir?

GEORGE: Because, Miss Sunnyside, I have not learned to lie.

DORA: Good gracious – who wants you to?

GEORGE: I do, but I can't do it. No, the love I speak of is not such as you suppose – it is a passion that has grown up here, since I arrived; but it is a hopeless, mad, wild feeling, that must perish.

DORA: Here! since you arrived! Impossible; you have seen no one; whom can you mean?

ZOE: (*advancing*) Me.

GEORGE: Zoe!

DORA: You!

ZOE: Forgive him, Dora, for he knew no better until I told him. Dora, you are right; he is incapable of any but sincere and pure feelings – so are you. He loves me – what of that? you know you can't be jealous of a poor creature like me. If he caught the fever, were stung by a snake, or possessed of any other poisonous or unclean thing, you could pity, tend, love him through it, and for your gentle care he would love you in return. Well, is he not thus afflicted now? I am his love – he loves an Octoroon.

GEORGE: Oh, Zoe, you break my heart!

DORA: At college they said I was a fool – I must be. At New Orleans they said, 'She's pretty, very pretty, but no brains.' I'm afraid they must be right; I can't understand a word of all this.

ZOE: Dear Dora, try to understand it with your heart. You love George, you love him dearly, I know it, and you deserve to be loved by him. He will love you – he must; his love for me will pass away – it shall. You heard him say it was hopeless. Oh, forgive him and me!

DORA: (*weeping*) Oh, why did he speak to me at all, then? You've made me cry, then, and I hate you both! (*Exit through room.*)

> (*Enter* MRS. PEYTON *and* SCUDDER, M'CLOSKY *and* POINT-
> DEXTER.)

M'CLOSKY: I'm sorry to intrude, but the business I came upon will excuse me.

MRS. P: Here is my nephew, sir.

ZOE: Perhaps I had better go.

M'CLOSKY: Wal, as it consarns you, perhaps you better had.

SCUDDER: Consarns Zoe?

M'CLOSKY: I don't know, she may as well hear the hull of it. Go on, Colonel Pointdexter. Ma'am – the mortgagee, auctioneer, and general agent.

POINT: Pardon me, madam, but do you know these papers? (*Hands papers to* MRS. PEYTON.)

MRS. P: (*taking them*) Yes, sir, they were the free-papers of the girl Zoe; but they were in my husband's secretaire – how came they in your possession?

M'CLOSKY: I – I found them.

GEORGE: And you purloined them?

M'CLOSKY: Hold on, you'll see. Go on, Colonel.

POINT: The list of your slaves is incomplete – it wants one.

SCUDDER: The boy Paul – we know it.

POINT: No sir, you have omitted the Octoroon girl, Zoe.

MRS. P: ⎫ Zoe!
ZOE: ⎭ Me!

POINT: At the time the Judge executed those free-papers to his infant slave, a judgment stood recorded against him; while that was on record he had no right to make away with his property. That judgment still exists – under it and others this estate is sold today. Those free-papers ain't worth the sand that's on 'em.

MRS. P: Zoe a slave! It is impossible!

POINT: It is certain, madam; the Judge was negligent, and, doubtless, forgot this small formality.

SCUDDER: But the creditors will not claim the gal?

M'CLOSKY: Excuse me; one of the principal mortgagees has made the demand. (*Exit with* POINTDEXTER.)

SCUDDER: Hold on yere, George Peyton, you sit down there; you're trembling so, you'll fall down directly – this blow has staggered me some.

MRS. P.: Oh, Zoe, my child! don't think too hardly of your poor father.

ZOE: I shall do so if you weep – see, I'm calm.

SCUDDER: Calm as a tombstone, and with about as much life – I see it in your face.

GEORGE: It cannot be! It shall not be!

SCUDDER: Hold your tongue – it must; be calm – darn the things! the proceeds of this sale won't cover the debts of the estate. Consarn those Liverpool English fellers, why couldn't they send something by the last mail? Even a letter promising something – such is the feeling round amongst the planters – darn me if I couldn't raise thirty thousand on the envelope alone, and ten thousand more on the post-mark.

GEORGE: Zoe, they shall not take you from us while I live.

SCUDDER: Don't be a fool; they'd kill you, and then take her, just as soon as – stop, old Sunnyside, he'll buy her! that'll save her.

ZOE: No, it won't; we have confessed to Dora that we love each other. How can she then ask her father to free me?

SCUDDER: What in thunder made you do that?

ZOE: Because it was the truth, and I had rather be a slave with a free soul than remain free with a slavish, deceitful heart. My father gives me freedom – at least he thought so – may heaven bless him for the thought, bless him for the happiness he spread around my life. You say the proceeds of the sale will not cover his debts – let me be sold then, that I may free his name – I give him back the liberty he bestowed upon me, for I can never repay him the love he bore his poor Octoroon child, on whose breast his last sigh was drawn, into whose eyes he looked with the last gaze of affection.

MRS. P: Oh! my husband! I thank heaven you have not lived to see this day.

ZOE: George, leave me. I would be alone a little while.

GEORGE: Zoe! (*Turns away overpowered.*)

ZOE: Do not weep, George – dear George, you now see what a miserable thing I am.

GEORGE: Zoe!

SCUDDER: I wish they could sell *me*! I brought half this ruin on this family, with my all-fired improvements; I deserve to be a nigger this day – I feel like one inside. (*Exit.*)

ZOE: Go now, George – leave me – take her with you. (*Exit* MRS. PEYTON *and* GEORGE.) A slave! a slave! Is this a dream – for my brain reels with the blow? He said so. What! then I shall be sold! – sold! and my master – oh! (*Falls on her knees with her face in her hands.*) No – no master but one. George – George! Hush, they come! save me! No, (*Looks off.*) 'tis Pete and the servants – they come this way. (*Enters inner room.*)

(*Enter* PETE, GRACE, MINNIE, SOLON, DIDO, *and all Niggers.*)

PETE: Cum yer now – stand round, 'cause I've got to talk to you darkies – keep dem children quiet – don't make no noise, de missus up dar har us.

SOLON: Go on, Pete.

PETE: Gen'l'men, my coloured frens and ladies, dar's mighty bad news gone round. Dis yer prop'ty to be sold – old Terrebonne whar we all been raised, is gwine – dey's gwine to take it away – can't stop here no how.

OMNES: Oo! – Oo!

PETE: Hold quiet, you trash o' niggers! tink anybody wants you to cry? Who's you to set up screeching? – be quiet! But dis ain't all. Now, my culled brethren, gird up your lines, and listen – hold on your bret – it's a-comin' – we taught dat de niggers would belong to de old missus, and if she lost Terrebonne, we must live dere allers, and we would hire out, and bring our wages to ole Missus Peyton.

OMNES: Ya! ha! Well –

PETE: Hush! I tell ye, taint so – we can't do it – we've got to be sold –

OMNES: Sold!

PETE: Will you hush? she will hear you. Yes! I listen dar jess now – dar was ole lady cryin' – Massa George – ah! you seen dem big tears in his eyes. Oh, Massa Scudder, he didn't cry zackly; both ob his eye and cheek look like de bad Bayou in low season – so dry dat I cry for him. (*raising his voice*) Den say de missus, 'Taint for de land I keer, but for dem poor niggers – dey'll be sold – dat wot stagger me.' 'No,' say Massa George, 'I'd rather sell myself fuss; but they shan't suffer no how – I see 'em dam fuss.'

OMNES: Oh, bless um! Bless Mas'r George.

PETE: Hole yer tongues. Yes, for you, for me, for dem little ones, dem folks cried. Now den, if Grace dere wid her chil'n were all sold, she'll begin screetchin' like a cat. She didn't mind how kind old Judge was to her; and Solon, too, he'll holler, and break de ole lady's heart.

GRACE: No, Pete; no, I won't. I'll bear it.

PETE: I don't tink you will any more, but dis here will, 'cause de family spile Dido, day has. She nebber was worth much 'a dat nigger.

DIDO: How dar you say dat? you black nigger, you. I fetch as much as any odder cook in Louisiana.

PETE: What's de use of your takin' it kind, and comfortin' de missus heart, if Minnie dere, and Louise, and Marie, and Julia is to spile it?

MINNIE: We won't, Pete; we won't.

PETE: (*to the men*) Dar, do ye hear dat, ye mis'able darkeys; dem gals is worth a boatload of kinder men, dem is. Cum, for de pride of de family, let every darkey look his best for de Judge's sake – dat ole man so good to us, and dat ole woman – so dem strangers from New Orleans shall say, dem's happy darkies, dem's a fine set of niggers; every one say when he's sold, 'Lor' bless dis yer family I'm gwine out of and send me as good a home.'

OMNES: We'll do it , Pete; we'll do it.

PETE: Hush! hark! I tell ye dar's somebody in dar. Who is it?

GRACE: It's Missy Zoe. See! see!

PETE: Come along; she har what we say, and she's crying 'fore us. None o' ye ig'rant niggers could cry for yerselves like dat. Come here quite; now quite. (*Exit* PETE *and all the Negroes, slowly.*)

(*Enter* ZOE, *supposed to have overheard the last scene.*)

ZOE: Oh! must I learn from these poor wretches how much I owe, and how I ought to pay the debt? Have I slept upon the benefits I received, and never saw, never felt, never knew that I was forgetful and ungrateful? Oh, my father! my dear, dear father! forgive your poor child; you made her life too happy, and now these tears will flow; let me hide them till I teach my heart. Oh, my – my heart! (*Exit with a low wailing suffocating cry.*)

(*Enter* M'CLOSKY, LAFOUCHE, JACKSON, SUNNYSIDE *and* POINTDEXTER.)

POINT: (*looking at watch*) Come, the hour is past. I think we may begin business. Where is Mr. Scudder?

JACKSON: I want to get to Ophelensis to-night.

(*Enter* DORA.)

DORA: Father, come here.

SUNNYSIDE: Why, Dora, what's the matter? your eyes are red.

DORA: Are they? thank you. I don't care, they were blue this morning, but it don't signify now.

SUNNYSIDE: My darling! who has been teasing you?

DORA: Never mind. I want you to buy Terrebonne.

SUNNYSIDE: Buy Terrebonne! What for?

DORA: No matter – buy it!

SUNNYSIDE: It will cost me all I'm worth – this is folly, Dora.

DORA: Is my plantation at Comptableau worth this?

SUNNYSIDE: Nearly – perhaps.

DORA: Sell it, then, and buy this.

SUNNYSIDE: Are you mad, my love?

DORA: Do you want *me* to stop here and *bid* for it?

SUNNYSIDE: Good gracious! no.

DORA: Then I'll do it, if you don't.

SUNNYSIDE: I will! I will! But for heaven's sake go – here comes the crowd. (*Exit* DORA.) What on earth does that child mean or want?

(*Enter* SCUDDER, GEORGE, RATTS, CAILLOU, PETE, GRACE, MINNIE *and all the negroes. A large table is in the centre at back.* POINTDEXTER *mounts the table with his hammer – his* CLERK *sits at his feet. A* NEGRO *mounts the table from behind. The company sit.*)

POINT: Now, gentlemen, we shall proceed to business. It ain't necessary for me to dilate, describe, or enumerate; Terrebonne is known to you as one of the richest bits of sile in Louisiana, and its condition reflects credit on them as had to keep it. I'll trouble you for that piece of baccy, Judge – thank you – so, gentlemen, as life is short, we'll start right off. The first lot on here is the estate in block, with its sugar-houses, stock machines, implements, good dwelling-houses and furniture; if there is no bid for the estate and stuff we'll sell it in smaller lots. Come, Mr. Thibodeaux, a man has a chance once in his life – here's yours.

THIB: Go on. What's the reserve bid?

POINT: The first mortgagee bids forty thousand dollars.

THIB: Forty-five thousand.

SUNNYSIDE: Fifty thousand.

POINT: When you have done joking, gentlemen, you'll say one hundred and twenty thousand; it carried that easy on mortgage.

LAFOUCHE: Then why don't you buy it yourself, Colonel?

POINT: I'm waiting on your fifty thousand bid.

CAILLOU: Eighty thousand.

POINT: Don't be afraid, it ain't going for that, Judge.

SUNNYSIDE: Ninety thousand.

POINT: We're getting on.

THIB: One hundred –

POINT: One hundred thousand bid for this mag –

CAILLOU: One hundred and ten thousand –

POINT: Good again – one hundred and –

SUNNYSIDE: Twenty.

POINT: And twenty thousand bid. Squire Sunnyside is going to sell this at fifty thousand advance to-morrow. (*Looks round.*) Where's that man from Mobile that wanted to give one hundred and eighty thousand?

THIB: I guess he ain't left home yet, Colonel.

POINT: I shall knock it down to the Squire – going – gone – for 120,000 dollars. (*Raises hammer.*) Judge, you can raise the hull on mortgage – going for half its value. (*Knocks.*) Squire Sunnyside, you've got a pretty bit o' land, squire. Hillo, darkey, hand me a smash dar.

SUNNYSIDE: I got more than I can work now.

POINT: Then buy the hands along with the property. Now, gentlemen, I'm proud to submit to you the finest lot of field hands and house servants that were ever offered for competition; they speak for themselves, and do credit to their owners. (*Reads.*) 'No. 1, Solon, a guest boy and good waiter.'

PETE: That's my son – buy him, Mass'r Ratts, he's sure to serve you well.

POINT: Hold your tongue!

RATTS: Let the darkey alone – 800 for that boy.

CAILLOU: Nine.

RATTS: A thousand.

SOLON: Thank you, Massa Ratts, I die for you, sar; hold up for me, sar.

---

smash: mint-flavoured drink composed of a spirit, ice, water and sugar.
guest boy: the text in Dicks' Standard Plays has *guess boy*.

RATTS: Look here, the boy knows and likes me, Judge; let him come my way.

CAILLOU: Go on, I'm dumb.

POINT: One thousand bid. (*Knocks.*) He's yours, Captain Ratts, Magnolia steamer. (SOLON *goes and stands behind* RATTS.) 'No. 2, the yellow girl, Grace, with two children – Saul, aged 4, and Victoria, 5.' (*They get on table.*)

SCUDDER: That's Solon's wife and children, Judge.

GRACE: (*to* RATTS) Buy me, Massa Ratts, do buy me, sar.

RATTS: What in thunder should I do with you and those devils on board my boat.

GRACE: Wash, sar – cook, sar – anything.

RATTS: Eight hundred agin, then – I'll go it.

JACKSON: Nine.

RATTS: I'm broke, Solon – I can't stop the Judge.

THIB: What's the matter, Ratts? I'll lend you all you want. Go in, if you've a mind to.

RATTS: Eleven.

JACKSON: Twelve.

SUNNYSIDE: Oh, oh!

SCUDDER: (*to* JACKSON) Judge, my friend. The Judge is a little deaf. Hello! (*speaking in his ear-trumpet*) This gal and them children belong to that boy Solon there. You're bidding to separate them, Judge.

JACKSON: The devil I am! (*Rises.*) I'll take back my bid, Colonel.

POINT: All right, Judge; I thought there was a mistake. I must keep you, Captain, to the eleven hundred.

RATTS: Go it.

POINT: Eleven hundred – going – going – sold! 'No. 3, Pete, a house-servant.'

PETE: Dat's me – yer, I'm comin' – stand around dar. (*Tumbles upon the table.*)

POINT: Aged seventy-two.

PETE: What's dat? a mistake, sar – forty-six.

POINT: Lame.

PETE: But don't mount to nuffin – kin work cannel. Come, Judge! pick up – now's your time, sar.

JACKSON: One hundred dollars.

PETE: What, sar? me! for me – look ye here. (*Dances.*)

GEORGE: Five hundred.

PETE: Massa George – ah no, sar – don't buy me – keep your money for some udder dat is to be sold. I ain't no count, sar.

POINT: Five hundred bid – it's a good price. (*Knocks.*) He's yours, Mr. George Peyton. (PETE *goes down.*) 'No. 4, the Octoroon girl, Zoe.'

(*Enter* ZOE, *very pale, and stands on table – hitherto* M'CLOSKY *has taken no interest in the sale, now turns his chair.*)

SUNNYSIDE: (*rising*) Gentlemen, we are all acquainted with the circumstances of this girl's position, and I feel sure that no one here will oppose the family who desires to redeem the child of our esteemed and noble friend, the late Judge Peyton.

OMNES: Hear! bravo! hear!

---

cannel (= canel): cinnamon.

IV The slave auction in Act III of *The Octoroon*: M'Closky draws his knife to defend himself from George Peyton's attack, while Zoe watches from the table (drawn from the London performance at the Adelphi for the *Illustrated London News*, 30 November 1861)

POINT: While the proceeds of this sale promises to realize less than the debts upon it, it is my duty to prevent any collusion for the depreciation of the property.

RATTS: Darn ye! you're a man as well as an auctioneer, ain't ye?

POINT: What is offered for this slave?

SUNNYSIDE: One thousand dollars.

M'CLOSKY: Two thousand.

SUNNYSIDE: Three thousand.

M'CLOSKY: Five thousand.

GEORGE: Demon!

SUNNYSIDE: I bid seven thousand, which is the last dollar this family possesses.

M'CLOSKY: Eight.

THIB: Nine.

OMNES: Bravo!

M'CLOSKY: Ten. It's no use, Squire.

SCUDDER: Jacob M'Closky, you shan't have that girl. Now, take care what you do. Twelve thousand.

M'CLOSKY: Shan't I? Fifteen thousand. Beat that any of ye.

POINT: Fifteen thousand bid for the Octoroon.

(*Enter* DORA.)

DORA: Twenty thousand.

OMNES: Bravo!

M'CLOSKY: Twenty-five thousand.

OMNES: (*Groan.*) Oh! oh!

GEORGE: Yelping hound – take that! (*Rushes on* M'CLOSKY, *who draws his knife.*)

SCUDDER: (*darting between them*) Hold on, George Peyton – stand back. This is your own house; we are under your uncle's roof; recollect yourself. And, strangers, ain't we forgittin' there's a lady present. (*The knives disappear.*) If we can't behave like Christians, let's try and act like gentlemen. Go on, Colonel.

LAFOUCHE: He didn't ought to bid against a lady.

M'CLOSKY: Oh, that's it, is it? then I'd like to hire a lady to go to auction to buy my hands.

POINT: Gentlemen, I believe none of us have two feelings about the conduct of that man; but he has the law on his side – we may regret, but we must respect it. Mr. M'Closky has bid twenty-five thousand dollars for the Octoroon. Is there any other bid? For the first time, twenty-five thousand – last time! (*Brings hammer down.*) To Jacob M'Closky, the Octoroon girl Zoe, twenty-five thousand dollars.

(*Tableau.*)

ACT IV

The Wharf. The Steamer 'Magnolia' alongside. A bluff rock upstage right. RATTS *discovered, supervising the loading of ship. Enter* LAFOUCHE *and* JACKSON.

JACKSON: How long before we start, captain?

RATTS: Just as soon as we put this cotton on board.

(*Enter* PETE, *with lantern, and* SCUDDER, *with note-book.*)

SCUDDER: One hundred and forty-nine bales. Can you take any more?

RATTS: Not a bale. I've got engaged eight hundred bales at the next landing, and one hundred hogsheads of sugar at Patten's Slide – that'll take my guards under – hurry up thar!

VOICE: (*outside*) Wood's aboard.

RATTS: All aboard then.

(*Enter* M'CLOSKY.)

SCUDDER: Sign the receipt, captain, and save me going up to the clerk.

M'CLOSKY: See here – there's a small freight of turpentine in the fore-hold there, and one of the barrels leaks; a spark from your engines might set the ship on fire, and you'd go with it.

RATTS: You be darned! Go and try it if you've a mind to.

LAFOUCHE: Captain, you've loaded up here until the boat is sunk so deep in the mud she won't float.

RATTS: (*calling off*) Wood up thar, you Pollo – hang on to the safety valve – guess she'll crawl off on her paddles.

(*Shouts heard.*)

JACKSON: What's the matter?

(*Enter* SOLON.)

SOLON: We got him!

SCUDDER: Who?

SOLON: The Inginn!

SCUDDER: Wahnotee? where is he? d'ye call running away from a fellow catching him?

RATTS: Here he comes.

OMNES: Where? where?

(*Enter* WAHNOTEE; *they are all about to rush on him.*)

SCUDDER: Hold on! stan' round thar! no violence – the critter don't know what we mean.

JACKSON: Let him answer for the boy, then.

M'CLOSKY: Down with him – lynch him.

OMNES: Lynch him!

(*Exit* LAFOUCHE.)

SCUDDER: Stan' back, I say! I'll nip the first that lays a finger on him. Pete, speak to the red-skin.

PETE: Whar's Paul, Wahnotee? What's come ob de child?

WAHNOTEE: Paul wunce – Paul pangeuk.

PETE: Pangeuk – dead.

WAHNOTEE: Mort!

M'CLOSKY: And you killed him?

(*They approach again.*)

SCUDDER: Hold on!

PETE: Um, Paul reste?

WAHNOTEE: Hugh vieu – (*going left*) Paul reste ci!

---

guards: lateral extensions of steamboat's deck.

SCUDDER: Here, stay! (*Examines the ground.*) The earth has been stirred here lately.

WAHNOTEE: Weenee Paul. (*Points down and shows by pantomime how he buried PAUL.*)

SCUDDER: The Inginn means that he buried him there! Stop, here's a bit of leather. (*Draws out mail-bags.*) The mail-bags that were lost! (*Sees tomahawk in WAHNOTEE's belt – draws it out and examines it.*) Look! here are marks of blood – look thar, red-skin, what's that?

WAHNOTEE: Paul! (*Makes sign that PAUL was killed by a blow on the head.*)

M'CLOSKY: He confesses it; the Indian got drunk, quarrelled with him, and killed him.

(*Re-enter LAFOUCHE, with smashed apparatus.*)

LAFOUCHE: Here are evidences of the crime, this rum bottle half emptied – this photographic apparatus smashed – and there are marks of blood and footsteps around the shed.

M'CLOSKY: What more d'ye want – ain't that proof enough? Lynch him!

OMNES: Lynch him! Lynch him!

SCUDDER: Stan' back, boys! he's an Inginn – fair play.

JACKSON: Try him, then – try him on the spot of his crime.

OMNES: Try him! try him!

LAFOUCHE: Don't let him escape!

RATTS: I'll see to that. (*Draws revolver.*) If he stirs, I'll put a bullet through his skull, mighty quick.

M'CLOSKY: Come – form a court, then; choose a jury – we'll fix this varmin.

(*Enter THIBODEAUX and CAILLOU.*)

THIB: What's the matter?

LAFOUCHE: We've caught this murdering Inginn, and are going to try him.

(*WAHNOTEE sits, rolled in blanket.*)

PETE: Poor little Paul – poor little nigger!

SCUDDER: This business goes agin me, Ratts – 'taint right.

LAFOUCHE: We're ready; the jury empanelled – go ahead – who'll be accuser?

RATTS: M'Closky.

M'CLOSKY: Me!

RATTS: Yes; you was the first to hail Judge Lynch.

M'CLOSKY: Well, what's the use of argument, whar guilt sticks out so plain? The boy and Inginn were alone when last seen.

SCUDDER: Who says that?

M'CLOSKY: Everybody – that is, I heard so.

SCUDDER: Say what you know – not what you heard.

M'CLOSKY: I know, then, that the boy was killed with that tomahawk – the redskin owns it – the signs of violence are all round the shed – this apparatus smashed – ain't it plain that in a drunken fit he slew the boy, and when sober concealed the body yonder?

OMNES: That's it – that's it.

RATTS: Who defends the Indian?

SCUDDER: I will; for it's agin my natur' to b'lieve him guilty; and if he be, this ain't the place, nor you the authority to try him. How are we sure the boy is dead at all? There are no witnesses but a rum bottle and an old machine. Is it on such evidence you'd hang a human being?

RATTS: His own confession.

SCUDDER: I appeal against your usurped authority; this Lynch law is a wild and lawless proceeding. Here's a pictur' for a civilized community to afford; yonder, a poor ignorant savage, and round him a circle of hearts, white with revenge and hate, thirsting for his blood; you call yourselves judges – you ain't – you're a jury of executioners. It is such scenes as these that bring disgrace upon our Western life.

M'CLOSKY: Evidence! Evidence! Give us evidence, we've had talk enough; now for proof.

OMNES: Yes, yes! Proof, proof!

SCUDDER: Where am I to get it? the proof is here, in my heart!

PETE: (*who has been looking about the camera*) 'Top sar! 'top a bit! Oh, laws-a-mussey, see dis, here's a pictur' I found sticking in that yar telescope machine, sar! look, sar!

SCUDDER: A photographic plate. (PETE *holds lantern up.*) What's this, eh? two forms! the child – 'tis he! dead – and above him – Ah! ah! Jacob M'Closky – 'twas you murdered that boy!

M'CLOSKY: Me?

SCUDDER: You! You slew him with that tomahawk, and as you stood over his body with the letter in your hand, you thought that no witness saw the deed, that no eye was on you; but there was, Jacob M'Closky, there was – the eye of the Eternal was on you – the blessed sun in heaven, that, looking down, struck upon this plate the image of the deed. Here you are, in the very attitude of your crime!

M'CLOSKY: 'Tis false!

SCUDDER: 'Tis true! the apparatus can't lie. Look there, jurymen – (*showing plate to jury*) – look there. Oh, you wanted evidence – you called for proof – Heaven has answered and convicted you.

M'CLOSKY: What court of law would receive such evidence? (*going*)

RATTS: Stop! *this* would – you called it yourself; you wanted to make us murder that Inginn, and since we've got our hands in for justice, we'll try it on *you*. What say ye? shall we have one law for the redskin and another for the white?

OMNES: Try him! try him!

RATTS: Who'll be accuser?

SCUDDER: I will! Fellow citizens, you are convened and assembled here under a higher power than the law. What's the law? When the ship's abroad on the ocean – when the army is before the enemy – where in thunder's the law? It is in the hearts of brave men who can tell right from wrong, and from whom justice can't be bought. So it is here, in the wilds of the West, where our hatred of crime is measured by the speed of our executions – where necessity is law! I say, then, air you honest men? air you true? put your hands on your naked breasts, and let every man as don't feel a real American heart there, bustin' up with freedom, truth, and right, let that man step out. That's the oath I put to ye – and then say, darn ye, go it!

OMNES: Go on! Go on!

SCUDDER: No! I won't go on; that man's down – I won't strike him even with
   words. Jacob, your accuser is that picter of the crime – let that speak – defend
   yourself.
M'CLOSKY: (*drawing knife*) I will, quicker than lightning.
RATTS: Seize him, then! (*They rush on* M'CLOSKY *and disarm him.*) He can fight,
   though – he's a painter, claws all over.
SCUDDER: Stop! Search him; we may find more evidence.
M'CLOSKY: Would you rob me first, and murder me afterwards?
RATTS: (*searching him*) That's his programme – here's a pocket-book.
SCUDDER: (*opening it*) What's here? Letters! Hello! To 'Mrs. Peyton, Terrebonne,
   Louisiana, United States'. Liverpool post-mark. Ho! I've got hold of the tail
   of a rat – come out. (*Reads.*) What's this? – a draft for 85,000 dollars, and
   credit on Palisse and Co., of New Orleans, for the balance. Hi! the rat's out –
   you killed the boy to steal this letter from the mail-bag – you stole this letter
   that the money should not arrive in time to save the Octoroon; had it done
   so, the lien on the estate would have ceased, and Zoe be free.
OMNES: Lynch him! – lynch him! – down with him!
SCUDDER: Silence in the court – stand back; let the gentlemen of the jury retire,
   consult, and return their verdict.
RATTS: I'm responsible for the crittur – go on.
PETE: (*to* WAHNOTEE) See, Inginn, look far. (*Shows him plate.*) See dat innocent,
   look, dare's the murderer of poor Paul.
WAHNOTEE: Ugh! (*Examines plate.*)
PETE: Ya! as he? Closky tue Paul – kill de child with your tomahawk dar; 'twasn't
   you, no – ole Pete allus say so. Poor Inginn lub our little Paul.
         (WAHNOTEE *rises and looks at* M'CLOSKY – *he is in his war paint
         and fully armed.*)
SCUDDER: What say ye, gentlemen? Is the prisoner guilty, or is he not guilty?
OMNES: Guilty!
SCUDDER: And what is to be his punishment?
OMNES: Death! (*All advance.*)
WAHNOTEE: (*crossing to* M'CLOSKY) Ugh!
SCUDDER: *No, Inginn; we deal out justice here, not revenge. 'Tain't you he's
   injured, 'tis the white man, whose laws he has offended.
RATTS: Away with him – put him down the aft hatch, till we rig his funeral.
M'CLOSKY: Fifty against one! Oh, if I had you one by one alone in the swamp,
   I'd rip ye all. (*He is borne off in boat, struggling.*)
SCUDDER: Now, then, to business.
PETE: (*re-entering from boat*) O, law, sir, dat debil Closky, he tore hisself from de
   gen'lam, knock me down, take my light, and trows it on de turpentine bar-
   rels, and de shed's all afire! (*Fire seen.*)
JACKSON: (*re-entering*) We are catching fire forward; quick, cut free from the
   shore.
RATTS: All hands aboard there – cut the starn ropes – give her headway!

---

* For the English version, which differs from the American version after this point, see Appendix C.

ALL: Ay, ay!
> (*Cry of 'Fire' heard – engine bells heard – steam whistle noise.*)

RATTS: Cut all away forard – overboard with every bale afire.
> (*The Steamer moves off – fire still blazing.* M'CLOSKY *re-enters, swimming.*)

M'CLOSKY: Ha! have I fixed ye? Burn! burn! that's right. You thought you had cornered me, did ye? As I swam down, I thought I heard something in the water, as if pursuing me – one of them darned alligators, I suppose – they swarm hereabout – may they crunch every limb of ye. (*Exit.*)
> (WAHNOTEE *is seen swimming. He finds trail and follows* M'CLOSKY. *The Steamer floats on at back, burning.*)

ACT V

SCENE 1. *Negroes' Quarters. Enter* ZOE.

ZOE: It wants an hour yet to daylight – here is Pete's hut – (*Knocks.*) He sleeps – no; I see a light.

DIDO: (*entering from hut*) Who dat?

ZOE: Hush, aunty! 'Tis I – Zoe.

DIDO: Missy Zoe! Why you out in de swamp dis time ob night; you catch de fever sure – you is all wet.

ZOE: Where's Pete?

DIDO: He gone down to de landing last night wid Mas'r Scudder; not come back since – kint make it out.

ZOE: Aunty, there is sickness up at the house; I have been up all night beside one who suffers, and I remembered that when I had the fever you gave me a drink, a bitter drink that made me sleep – do you remember it?

DIDO: Didn't I? Dem doctors ain't no 'count; dey don't know nuffin.

ZOE: No; but you, Aunty, you are wise – you know every plant, don't you, and what it is good for?

DIDO: Dat you drink is fust rate for red fever. Is de folks' head bad?

ZOE: Very bad, Aunty; and the heart aches worse, so they can get no rest.

DIDO: Hold on a bit, I get you de bottle. (*Exit.*)

ZOE: In a few hours that man, my master, will come for me: he has paid my price, and he only consented to let me remain here this one night, because Mrs. Peyton promised to give me up to him to-day.

DIDO: (*re-entering with phial*) Here 'tis – now you give one timble-full – dat's nuff.

ZOE: All there is there would kill one, wouldn't it?

DIDO: Guess it kill a dozen – nebber try.

ZOE: It's not a painful death, Aunty, is it? You told me it produced a long, long sleep.

DIDO: Why you tremble so? why you speak so wild? what you's gwine to do, missey?

ZOE: Give me the drink.

DIDO: No. Who dat sick at de house?

ZOE: Give it to me.

DIDO: No, you want to hurt yourself. Oh, Miss Zoe, why you ask old Dido for dis pizen?

ZOE: Listen to me. I love one who is here, and he loves me – George. I sat outside his door all night – I heard his sighs – his agony – torn from him by my coming fate; and he said, 'I'd rather see her dead than his!'

DIDO: Dead!

ZOE: He said so – then I rose up, and stole from the house, and ran down to the bayou; but its cold, black, silent stream terrified me – drowning must be so horrible a death. I could not do it. Then, as I knelt there, weeping for courage, a snake rattled beside me. I shrunk from it and fled. Death was there beside me, and I dared not take it. Oh! I'm afraid to die; yet I am more afraid to live.

DIDO: Die!

ZOE: So I came here to you; to you, my own dear nurse; to you, who so often hushed me to sleep when I was a child; who dried my eyes and put your little Zoe to rest. Ah! give me the rest that no master but One can disturb – the sleep from which I shall awake free! You can protect me from that man – do let me die without pain.

DIDO: No, no – life is good for young ting like you.

ZOE: Oh! good, good nurse: you will, you will.

DIDO: No – g'way.

ZOE: Then I shall never leave Terrebonne – the drink, nurse; the drink; that I may never leave my home – my dear, dear home. You will not give me to that man? Your own Zoe, that loves you, Aunty, so much, so much. (*Gets phial.*) Ah! I have it.

DIDO: No, missey. Oh! no – don't.

ZOE: Hush! (*Runs off.*)

DIDO: Here, Solon, Minnie, Grace! (*They enter.*)

ALL: Was de matter?

DIDO Miss Zoe got de pizen. (*Exit.*)

ALL: Oh! oh! (*Exeunt.*)

SCENE 2. *Cane-brake Bayou: Bank, Triangle Fire – Canoe.* M'CLOSKY *discovered asleep.*

M'CLOSKY: Burn, burn! blaze away! How the flames crack. I'm not guilty; would ye murder me? Cut, cut the rope – I choke – choke! – Ah! (*Wakes.*) Hello! where am I? Why, I was dreaming – curse it! I can never sleep now without dreaming. Hush! I thought I heard the sound of a paddle in the water. All night, as I fled through the cane-brake, I heard footsteps behind me. I lost them in the cedar swamp – again they haunted my path down the bayou, moving as I moved, resting when I rested – hush! there again! – no; it was only the wind over the canes. The sun is rising. I must launch my dug-out, and put for the bay, and in a few hours I shall be safe from pursuit on board one of the coasting schooners that run from Galveston to Matagorda. In a little time this darned business will blow over, and I can show again! If it was the ghost of that murdered boy haunting me! Well – I didn't mean to kill him, did I? Well, then, what has my all-cowardly heart got to skeer me so for?

(Gets in canoe and rows off. WAHNOTEE *paddles canoe on, gets out and finds trail – paddles off after him.)*

SCENE 3. *Cedar swamp. Enter* SCUDDER *and* PETE.
SCUDDER: Come on, Pete, we shan't reach the house before midday.
PETE: Nebber mind, sa, we bring good news – it won't spile for de keeping.
SCUDDER: Ten miles we've had to walk, because some blamed varmin onhitched our dug-out. I left it last night all safe.
PETE: P'r'aps it floated away itself.
SCUDDER: No; the hitching line was cut with a knife.
PETE: Say, Mas'r Scudder, s'pose we go in round by de quarters and raise de darkies, den dey cum long wid us, and we 'proach dat ole house like Gin'ral Jackson when he took London out dar.
SCUDDER: Hello, Pete, I never heard of that affair.
PETE: I tell you, sa – hush!
SCUDDER: What?
PETE: Was dat? – a cry out dar in the swamp – dar again!
SCUDDER: So it is. Something forcing its way through the undergrowth – it comes this way – it's either a bear or a runaway nigger. *(Draws pistol.* M'CLOSKY *rushes on and falls at* SCUDDER*'s feet.)* Stand off – what are ye?
PETE: Mas'r Closky.
M'CLOSKY: Save me – save me! I can go no farther. I heard voices.
SCUDDER: Who's after you?
M'CLOSKY: I don't know, but I feel it's death! In some form, human, or wild beast, or ghost, it has tracked me through the night. I fled; it followed. Hark! there it comes – it comes – don't you hear a footstep on the dry leaves?
SCUDDER: Your crime has driven you mad.
M'CLOSKY: D'ye hear it – nearer – nearer – ah!
                    (WAHNOTEE rushes on, and at M'CLOSKY*.)*
SCUDDER: The Inginn! by thunder.
PETE: You'se a dead man, Mas'r Closky – you got to b'lieve dat.
M'CLOSKY: No – no. If I must die, give me up to the law; but save me from the tomahawk. You are a white man; you'll not leave one of your own blood to be butchered by the redskin?
SCUDDER: Hold on now, Jacob; we've got to figure on that – let us look straight at the thing. Here we are on the selvage of civilization. It ain't our sile, I believe, rightly; but Nature has said that where the white man sets his foot, the red man and the black man shall up sticks and stand around. But what do we pay for that possession? In cash? No – in kind – that is, in protection, forbearance, gentleness, in all them goods that show the critters the difference between the Christian and the savage. Now, what have you done to show them the distinction? for, darn me if I can find out.
M'CLOSKY: For what I have done, let me be tried.
SCUDDER: You have been tried – honestly tried and convicted. Providence has chosen your executioner. I shan't interfere.
PETE: Oh, no; Mas'r Scudder, don't leave Mas'r Closky like dat – don't sa – 'tain't what good Christian should do.

SCUDDER: D'ye hear that, Jacob? This old nigger, the grandfather of the boy you murdered, speaks for you – don't that go through you? D'ye feel it? Go on, Pete, you've waked up the Christian here, and the old hoss responds. (*Throws bowie-knife to* M'CLOSKY.) Take that, and defend yourself.

> (*Exit* SCUDDER *and* PETE – WAHNOTEE *faces* M'CLOSKY – *Fight.* M'CLOSKY *runs off* – WAHNOTEE *follows him* – *Screams outside.*)

SCENE 4. *Parlour at Terrebonne. Enter* ZOE. *Music.*

ZOE: My home, my home! I must see you no more. Those little flowers can live, but I cannot. To-morrow they'll bloom the same – all will be here as now, and I shall be cold. Oh! my life, my happy life; why has it been so bright?

> (*Enter* MRS. PEYTON *and* DORA.)

DORA: Zoe, where have you been?

MRS. P: We felt quite uneasy about you.

ZOE: I've been to the negro quarters. I suppose I shall go before long, and I wished to visit all the places, once again, to see the poor people.

MRS. P: Zoe, dear, I'm glad to see you more calm this morning.

DORA: But how pale she looks, and she trembles so.

ZOE: Do I? (*Enter* GEORGE.) Ah! he is here.

DORA: George, here she is.

ZOE: I have come to say good-bye, sir; two hard words – so hard they might break many a heart, mightn't they?

GEORGE: Oh, Zoe! can you smile at this moment?

ZOE: You see how easily I have become reconciled to my fate – so it will be with you. You will not forget poor Zoe! but her image will pass away like a little cloud that obscured your happiness a while – you will love each other; you are both too good not to join your hearts. Brightness will return amongst you. Dora, I once made you weep; those were the only tears I caused anybody. Will you forgive me?

DORA: Forgive you – (*Kisses her.*)

ZOE: I feel you do, George.

GEORGE: Zoe, you are pale. Zoe! – she faints!

ZOE: No; a weakness, that's all – a little water. (DORA *gets water.*) I have a restorative here – will you pour it in the glass? (DORA *attempts to take it.*) No; not you – George. (GEORGE *pours contents of phial in glass.*) Now, give it to me. George, dear George, do you love me?

GEORGE: Do you doubt it, Zoe?

ZOE: No! (*Drinks.*)

DORA: Zoe, if all I possess would buy your freedom, I would gladly give it.

ZOE: I am free! I had but one Master on earth, and he has given me my freedom!

DORA: Alas! but the deed that freed you was not lawful.

ZOE: Not lawful – no – but I am going to where there is no law – where there is only justice.

GEORGE: Zoe, you are suffering – your lips are white – your cheeks are flushed.

ZOE: I must be going – it is late. Farewell, Dora. (*retiring*)

PETE: (*outside*) Whar's Missus – whar's Mas'r George?

GEORGE: They come.
    (*Enter* SCUDDER.)
SCUDDER: Stand around and let me pass – room thar! I feel so big with joy,
  creation ain't wide enough to hold me. Mrs. Peyton, George Peyton,
  Terrebonne is yours. It was that rascal M'Closky – but he got rats, I swow –
  he killed the boy, Paul, to rob this letter from the mail-bags – the letter from
  Liverpool you know – he set fire to the shed – that was how the steamboat
  got burned up.
MRS. P: What d'ye mean?
SCUDDER: Read – read that. (*Gives letter.*)
GEORGE: Explain yourself.
    (*Enter* SUNNYSIDE.)
SUNNYSIDE: Is it true?
SCUDDER: Every word of it, Squire. Here, you tell it, since you know it. If I was
  to try I'd bust.
MRS. P: Read, George. Terrebonne is yours.
    (*Enter* PETE, DIDO, SOLON, MINNIE *and* GRACE.)
PETE: Whar is she – whar is Miss Zoe?
SCUDDER: What's the matter?
PETE: Don't ax me. Whar's de gal? I say.
SCUDDER: Here she is – Zoe! – water – she faints.
PETE: No – no. 'Tain't no faint – she's a dying, sa; she got pizon from old Dido
  here, this mornin'.
GEORGE: Zoe!
SCUDDER: Zoe! is this true? – no, it ain't – darn it, say it ain't. Look here, you're
  free, you know; nary a master to hurt you now; you will stop here as long as
  you've a mind to, only don't look so.
DORA: Her eyes have changed colour.
PETE: Dat's what her soul's gwine to do. It's going up dar, whar dere's no line
  atween folks.
GEORGE: She revives.
ZOE: (*on sofa*) George – where – where –
GEORGE: Oh, Zoe! what have you done?
ZOE: Last night I overheard you weeping in your room, and you said, 'I'd rather
  see her dead than so!'
GEORGE: Have I then prompted you to this?
ZOE: No; but I loved you so, I could not bear my fate; and then I stood between
  your heart and hers. When I am dead she will not be jealous of your love for
  me, no laws will stand between us. Lift me; so – (GEORGE *raises her head.*) –
  let me look at you, that your face may be the last I see of this world. Oh!
  George, you may, without a blush, confess your love for the Octoroon. (*Dies.*
  GEORGE *lowers her head gently. Kneels. Others form picture.*)
    (*Darken front of house and stage. Light fires. – Draw flats and dis-*
    cover PAUL's *grave.* – M'CLOSKY *dead on it.* – WAHNOTEE
    standing triumphantly over him.)

THE SHAUGHRAUN

An original Irish drama in three acts

First performed at Wallack's Theatre, New York on 14 November 1874, with the following cast:

CAPTAIN MOLINEUX (a young English officer commanding a detachment at Ballyragget)	Mr. H. J. Montague
ROBERT FFOLLIOTT (a young Irish gentleman, under sentence as a Fenian, in love with Arte O'Neal)	Mr. J. B. Polk
FATHER DOLAN (the parish priest of Suil-a-beg, his tutor and guardian)	Mr. John Gilbert
CORRY KINCHELA (a squireen)	Mr. Edward Arnott
HARVEY DUFF (a police agent in disguise of a peasant)	Mr. Harry Beckett
CONN (the shaughraun, the soul of every fair, the life of every funeral, the first fiddle at all weddings and patterns)	Mr. Dion Boucicault
SERGEANT JONES (of the 41st)	Mr. W. J. Leonard
MANGAN	Mr. J. F. Josephs
REILLY	Mr. E. M. Holland
SULLIVAN	Mr. C. E. Edwin
DOYLE	Mr. J. Peck
DONOVAN	Mr. G. Atkins
ARTE O'NEAL (in love with Robert)	Miss Jeffreys Lewis
CLAIRE FFOLLIOTT (a Sligo lady)	Miss Ada Dyas
MOYA (Father Dolan's niece, in love with Conn)	Mrs. Ione Burke
MRS. O'KELLY (Conn's mother)	Mme. Ponisi
BRIDGET MADIGAN (a keener)	Mrs. J. Sefton
NANCY MALONE (a keener)	Miss E. Blaisdell

The cast for the first London performance (Drury Lane, 4 September 1875) included Agnes Robertson as Moya, William Terriss as Captain Molineux, Henry Sinclair as Kinchela, Shiel Barry as Harvey Duff, Marie Dalton as Arte, and Rose Leclercq as Claire.

V The interior of the Adelphi Theatre, London, after its rebuilding by T. H. Wyatt in 1858

ACT I

SCENE 1. *Suil-a-beg. The cottage of* ARTE O'NEAL. *The stage is a yard in the rear of the cottage. The dairy window is seen facing the audience. Door in return of cottage. The ruins of Suil-a-more Castle cover a bold detached headland in the half distance. The Atlantic bounds the picture. Sunset.* CLAIRE FFOLLIOTT *is at work at a churn.*

CLAIRE: Phoo! how my arms ache! (*Sings.*)
      'Where are you going, my pretty maid?
      I'm going a milking, sir, she said.'
          (*Enter* MRS. O'KELLY *with large pan of milk; she places it in the dairy as she speaks.*)
MRS. O'K: Sure, Miss, that is too hard work entirely for the likes of you.
CLAIRE: Go on, now, Mrs. O'Kelly, and mind your own business. D'ye think I'm not equal to making the butter come?
MRS. O'K: It's yourself can make the butter come. You have only got to look at the milk and the butter will rise. But oh! Miss, who's this coming up the cliff? It can't be a visitor.
CLAIRE: 'Tis one of the officers from Ballyragget.
MRS. O'K: Run in quick before he sees you, and I'll take the churn.
CLAIRE: Not I; I'll stop where I am. If he was the Lord Lieutenant himself I'd not stir, or take a tuck out of my gown. Go tell the mistress.
MRS. O'K: And is that the way you will recave the quality? (*Exit.*)
CLAIRE: (*Sings, working.*)
      'Then what is your fortune, my pretty maid?'
      He is stopping to reconnoitre.
      'What is your fortune, my pretty maid?'
      Here he comes.
      'My face is my fortune, sir, she said.'
      There's no lie in that anyway, and a mighty small income I've got.
          (*Enter* MOLINEUX, *looking about.*)
MOLINEUX: My good girl.
CLAIRE: Sir to you. (*aside*) He takes me for the dairy maid.
MOLINEUX: Is this place called Swillabeg?
CLAIRE: No. It is called Shoolabeg.
MOLINEUX: Beg pardon; your Irish names are so unpronounceable. You see I am an Englishman.
CLAIRE: I remarked your misfortune; poor crature, you couldn't help it.
MOLINEUX: I do not regard it as a misfortune.
CLAIRE: Got accustomed to it, I suppose. Were you born so?
MOLINEUX: Is your mistress at home?
CLAIRE: My mistress? Oh! 'tis Miss O'Neal you mane!
MOLINEUX: Delicious brogue – quite delicious! Will you take her my card?
CLAIRE: I'm afeard the butther would spoil if I lave it now.
MOLINEUX: What is your pretty name?

---

return: wing or side of a building.

CLAIRE: Claire. What's yours?

MOLINEUX: Molineux – Captain Molineux. Now, Claire, I'll give you a crown if you will carry my name to your mistress.

CLAIRE: Will you take my place at the churn while I go?

MOLINEUX: How do you work the infernal thing?

CLAIRE: Take hould beside me, an' I'll show you. (*He takes the handle of the churn beside her; they work together.*) There, so – that's it – beautiful – you were intended for a dairy-maid.

MOLINEUX: I know a dairy-maid that was intended for me.

CLAIRE: That speech only wanted a taste of the brogue to be worthy of an Irishman.

MOLINEUX: (*kissing her*) Now I'm perfect.

CLAIRE: (*starting away*) What are you doing?

MOLINEUX: Testing the brogue! Stop, my dear; you forget the crown I promised you – here it is. Don't hide your blushes. They become you.

CLAIRE: Never fear I'll be even wid yer honor yet. Don't let the butther spoil, now, while I'm gone. (*going*) What's your name again? (*looking at card*) Mulligrubs?

MOLINEUX: No! Molineux.

CLAIRE: I ax your pardon! You see I'm Irish, and them English names are so unpronounceable! (*Exit.*)

MOLINEUX: (*churning gravely*) She is as fresh and fragrant as one of her own pats of butter. If the mistress be as sweet as the maid, I shall not regret being stationed in the wilderness. Deuced hard work this milk pump! There is a strange refinement about that Irish girl. When I say strange, I am no judge; for I have never done the agricultural shows; I have never graduated in milkmaids; but this one must be the cream of the dairy. Confound this piston-rod. I feel like a Chinese toy.

(*Enter* ARTE O'NEAL, *following* CLAIRE.)

ARTE: What can he want? Why, Claire! what is he doing?

CLAIRE: I have not the slightest idea. (*Crosses to behind.*)

ARTE: (*advancing*) Captain Molineux.

MOLINEUX: (*confused*) Oh, a thousand pardons! I just was a–amusing myself. I am – a – very fond of machinery, and so – (*Bows.*) Miss O'Neal, I presume.

ARTE: (*introducing* CLAIRE) My cousin, Miss Claire Ffolliott.

MOLINEUX: Miss Ffolliott! really, I took her for a – (*aside*) Oh, Lord! what have I done?

ARTE: (*aside*) Claire has been at some mischief here.

CLAIRE: (*at churn, aside to* MOLINEUX) Don't hide your blushes, Captain, they become you.

MOLINEUX: (*aside*) Spare me!

ARTE: I hope you come to tell me how I can be of some service to you.

MOLINEUX: I have just arrived with a detachment of our regiment at Ballyragget. The government received information that a schooner carrying a distinguished Fenian hero was hovering around the coast, intending to land her passengers

---

Fenian: the Fenian brotherhood, a revolutionary secret society active against the British in Ireland in the 1860s, had its escape route and its emotional headquarters in the U.S.A.

in this neighbourhood; so a gunboat has been sent round to these waters, and we are under orders to co-operate with her. Deuced bore, not to say ridiculous. There is no foundation for the scare; but we find ourselves quartered here without any resources.

ARTE: I regret I cannot extend to you the hospitalities of Suil-a-beg; an unmarried girl is unable to play the hostess.

CLAIRE: Even two unmarried girls couldn't play the hostess.

MOLINEUX: But you own the finest shooting in the west of Ireland – the mountains are full of grouse, and the streams about are alive with salmon.

CLAIRE: The Captain would beg leave to sport over your domain. Shall I spare you the humiliation of confessing that you are not mistress in your own house, much less lady of your own manor? Do you see that ruin yonder? Oh, 'tis the admiration of the traveller, and the favourite study of painters, who come from far and near to copy it. It was the home of my forefathers once, when they kept open house for the friend, the poor, or the stranger. The mortgagee has put up a gate now, so visitors pay sixpence a head to admire the place, and their guide points across to this cabin where the remains of the 'ould family', two lonely girls, live, God knows how! You ask her leave to kill game on Suil-a-more and Keim-an-Eigh. (*crossing to dairy window*) Do you see that salmon? It was snared last night in the Pool-a-Brikein, by Conn the Shaughraun. He killed those grouse at daylight on the side of Maumturk. That's our daily food, and we owe it to a poacher.

MOLINEUX: You have to suffer bitterly, indeed, for ages of family imprudence, and the Irish extravagance of your ancestors.

ARTE: Yes, sir; the extravagance of their love for their country, and the imprudence of their fidelity to their faith.

MOLINEUX: But surely you cannot be without some relatives?

CLAIRE: I have a brother, the heir to this estate.

MOLINEUX: Is he abroad?

CLAIRE: Yes; he is a convict, working out his sentence in Australia.

MOLINEUX: Oh, I beg pardon. I did not know. (*to* ARTE) Have you no relatives?

ARTE: Yes, I am the affianced wife of her brother.

MOLINEUX: (*confused*) Really, ladies, I have to offer you a thousand apologies.

ARTE: I do not accept one; it carries insult to the man I love.

MOLINEUX: At least you will permit me to regret having aroused such distressing memories.

CLAIRE: Do you think they ever sleep?

MOLINEUX: No, naturally, of course not. I meant – (*aside*) I am astray on an Irish bog here, and every step I take gets me deeper in the mire.

CLAIRE: (*aside*) How confused he is! That's a good fellow, although he is an Englishman.

ARTE: I am very sorry we have not the power to grant you a privilege which you see we do not enjoy.

KINCHELA: (*outside*) Holloo! – is there nobody at home?

ARTE: Here comes a gentleman who can oblige you.

KINCHELA: (*outside*) Holloo – one of you! Don't ye hear me? Bridget, Conn, come and hould my pony.

MOLINEUX: Who is this stentorian gentleman?

CLAIRE: Mr. Corry Kinchela – one who has trimmed his fortunes with prudence, and his conscience with economy.

(*Enter* CORRY KINCHELA.)

KINCHELA: Where the divil is everybody; Oh, there yur are! I had to stable my own horse! Oh! my sarvice to you, sir – I believe I've the honour of addressing Captain Molineux. I'm just back from Dublin, and thought I'd stop on my road to tell you that the court has decreed the sale of this estate, undher foreclosure, and in two months you will have to turn out.

ARTE: In two months, then, even this poor shelter will be taken from us!

KINCHELA: I'm afeard the rightful owner will want to see the worth of his money! But, never fear, two handsome girls like yourselves will not be long wanting a shelter or a welcome. Eh, Captain – ho! ho! It will be pick and choose for them anywhere, I'm thinking.

MOLINEUX: (*aside*) This fellow is awfully offensive to me.

KINCHELA: I've been away for the last few weeks, so I've not been able to pay my respects to your officers, and to invite you all to sport over this property – you are right welcome, Captain. My name is Kinchela – Mr. Corry Kinchela – of Ballyragget House, where I'll be proud to see my table cloth undher your chin. I don't know why one of these girls did not introduce me.

MOLINEUX: They paid me the compliment of presuming I had no desire to form your acquaintance.

KINCHELA: What! Do you know, sir, you are talking to a person of position and character.

MOLINEUX: (*back turned to* KINCHELA) I don't care a straw for your position, and I don't like your character.

KINCHELA: Do you mane to insult me, sir?

MOLINEUX: (*turning to him*) I am incapable of it.

KINCHELA: Ah!

MOLINEUX: In the presence of ladies; but I believe I should be entitled to do so, for you insulted them in mine. (*turning to* CLAIRE) I ask your pardon for the liberty I took with you when I presented myself.

CLAIRE: (*offering her hand*) The liberty you took with him when he presented himself clears the account.

KINCHELA: We'll meet again, sir.

MOLINEUX: I hope not. (*to* ARTE, *shaking hands*) Good evening.

ARTE: I would detain you, Captain, but you have a long walk across the mountain, and the darkness is falling; the road is treacherous.

(MOLINEUX *shakes hands with* CLAIRE *again, and exits.*)

KINCHELA: The divil guide him to pass the night in a bog-hole up to his neck. Listen hither, you two. Sure, I don't want to be too hard upon you. To be sure, the sale of this place will never cover my mortgage on it. It will come to me, every acre of it. (*Turns to* ARTE.) Bedad, the law ought to throw your own sweet self in as a make-weight to square my account. (*She turns away; he turns to* CLAIRE.) See now, there's your brother, Robert Ffolliott, goin' to rot over there in Australia; and here, in a few weeks, you both will be without a roof itself over your heads. Now, isn't it a cruel thing entirely to let this go on; when, if that girl would only say the word, I'd make her Mrs. Kinchela?

(CLAIRE *starts away, making a circle of the stage; stops at lower pillar of porch, leaning against it;* KINCHELA *follows and speaks to her over her shoulder.*) And I've got a hoult of the ear of our country member; shure, he'll get Robert the run o' the colony – as free as a fish in a pond he'll be over there. And stop now, (*to* ARTE) you shall send him a thousand pounds that I'll give you on our wedding day.

ARTE: I'd rather starve with Robert Ffolliott in a jail than I'd own the County Sligo, if I'd to carry you as a mortgage on it.

KINCHELA: D'ye think the boy cares what becomes of you, or who owns you? Not a hapoth! How many letters have you had from him the last year past?

ARTE: Alas! not one.

KINCHELA: Not one! (*aside*) I knew that, for I have them all safe under lock and kay at home. (*aloud*) See that! not one thought – not a sign from him! And here am I every day in the week like a dog at your door. It is too hard on me entirely – I've some sacret foe schaming behind my back to ruin me in your heart. (*Enter* FATHER DOLAN.) I know it is the same that is sending over to Robert Ffolliott the money, without which he'd starve outright beyant there! I'd like to find out who it is.

DOLAN: I am the man, Mr. Kinchela.

KINCHELA: Father Dolan. And may I ask, sir, on what grounds you dar to impache me in the good opinion of these girls?

DOLAN: Certainly. (*Turns to* ARTE.) Miss O'Neal – Claire, my dear – will you leave me awhile alone with Mr. Kinchela; he wants to know the truth about himself. (*Music.*)

CLAIRE: And you can't insult him in the presence of ladies!

> (ARTE *crosses to door, turns, curtseys to* KINCHELA, *and exit.* CLAIRE *follows, with a look at him.*)

DOLAN: The father of young Ffolliott bequeathed to you and to me the care of his infant son. Heaven forgive me if I grew so fond of my darling charge I kept no watch over you, my partner in the trust. Year after year you dipped the estate, with your sham improvements and false accounts. You reduced the rents to impoverish the income, so it might not suffice to pay the interest on the mortgages.

KINCHELA: Go on, sir; this is mighty fine – go on. I wish I had a witness by, I'd make you pay for this – is there any more?

DOLAN: There is. You hope to buy the lad's inheritance for an old song when it is sold. Thus you fulfil the trust confided to you by your benefactor, his poor father, whose hand you held when he expired in my arms. Thus you have kept your oath to the dead.

KINCHELA: Would not every acre of it have escheated to the Crown as the estate of a convicted felon – only I saved it for his family by getting young Ffolliott to make it over before the sentence was pronounced upon him?

DOLAN: Yes, to make it over to you in trust for these two girls, his sister and his betrothed.

---

hapoth: i.e. a halfpenceworth.

KINCHELA: To be sure, wasn't you by, and helped to persuade him? More betoken, you were a witness to the deed.

DOLAN: I was. I helped you to defraud the orphan boy, and since then I've been the witness to how you have robbed these helpless women. Oh beware, Kinchela. When these lands were torn from Owen Roe O'Neal in the old times, he laid his curse on the spoilers, for Suil-a-more was the dowry of his bride, Grace Ffolliott. Since then many a strange family has tried to hold possession of the place; but every year one of that family would die; the land seemed to swallow them one by one – till the O'Neals and Ffolliotts returned, none other thrived upon it.

KINCHELA: Sure, that's the rason I want Arte O'Neal for my wife; won't that kape the ould blood to the fore? Ah, sir, why wouldn't you put in the good word for me to the girl? Do I ask betther than to give back all I have to the family? Sure, there's nothing, sir, done that can't be mended that way.

DOLAN: I'd rather rade the service over her grave and hear the sods falling on her coffin than spake the holy words to make her your wife. Corry Kinchela, I know you, 'twas by your manes, and to serve this end, my darling boy, her lover – was denounced and convicted.

KINCHELA: 'Tis false!

DOLAN: It is true; but that truth is locked in my soul, and Heaven keeps the key.

KINCHELA: (*aside*) Some white-hearted cur has confessed agin me. (*aloud*) Very well, sir – then out of the house these girls shall turn homeless; and beggars.

DOLAN: Not homeless while I have a roof over me; not beggars, I thank God, who gives me the crust to share with them. (*Exit.*)

KINCHELA: How could he know I had any hand in bringing young Ffolliott to the dock? Who could have turned tail on me?

(*Enter* HARVEY DUFF.)

DUFF: Whisht, sir.

KINCHELA: Who's there – Harvey Duff?

DUFF: Yes, sir; I saw your coppaleen beyant under the shed, and I knew yourself was in it; I've great news entirely for you, news enough to burst a budget!

KINCHELA: You are always findin' a mare's nest.

DUFF: I've found one now wid a divil's egg in it.

KINCHELA: Well, out with it.

DUFF: There was a fire on Rathgarron Head last night; you know what that manes?

KINCHELA: A signal to some smuggler at sea that the coast is clear and to run in to land his cargo.

DUFF: Divil a keg was landed from that ship, barrin' only one man that was put ashore; not a boy was on the strand to meet the boat, nor a car, nor a skip to hurry off the things; only one crature and that was Conn the Shaughraun; 'twas himself that lighted the signal; 'twas him that stud up to his middle in the salt to lift the man ashore. I seen it all as I lay flat on the edge of the cliff and looked down upon the pair of them below.

KINCHELA: Well, what's all this to me?

DUFF: Wait; sure I'm hatchin' the egg for you! Who's that, ses I to meself, that

---

coppaleen: pony.

Conn would carry ashore in his two arrams as tindher as a mother would hould a child? Who's that stranger, ses I; he is capering round for all the world like a dog that's just onloosed. Who's that he's houlding by the two hands of him, as if 'twas Moya Dolan herself he'd got before him instead of a ragged sailor boy?

KINCHELA: Well, did you find out who it was?

DUFF: Maybe I didn't get snug in behind the bushes beside the pathway up the cliff. They passed close to me, talkin' low; but I heard his voice and I saw the man as plain as I see you now.

KINCHELA: Saw whom?

DUFF: Robert Ffolliott.

KINCHELA: Robert Ffolliott!

DUFF: 'Twas himself, I tell ye.

KINCHELA: You are sure?

DUFF: Am I sure? D'ye think I can mistake the face that turned upon me in the coort when they sentenced him on my evidence, or the voice that said: 'If there's justice in Heaven, you and I will meet again on this side of the grave; then,' ses he, 'have yer sowl ready.' And the look he fixed on me shrivelled up me sowl inside like a boiled cockle that ye might pick out with a pin. Am I sure? I wish I was as sure of Heaven!

KINCHELA: He has escaped from the penal settlement – ay, that's it – and where would he go to straight, but here into the trap baited wid the girl he loves?

DUFF: There'll be a price offered for him, sir, and your honour will put it my way to airn an honest penny. Wouldn't they hang him this time? Egorra! I'd be peaceable if he was only out o' the way for good.

KINCHELA: Listen to me. D'ye know what took me to Dublin? I heard that the Queen had resolved to release the Fenian prisoners under sentence.

DUFF: Murdher alive! I'm a corpse.

KINCHELA: I saw the Chief Secretary. He mistook my fear for hope. It is true, ses he, I'm expecting every day to get the despatch. I wish you joy.

DUFF: Be jabers, but I'd like to have seen your face when you got that polthogue in the gob.

KINCHELA: Robert Ffolliott returned! – a free man. He will throw the estate into Chancery.

DUFF: Where will he throw me?

KINCHELA: He is a fugitive convict still; can't we deal with him?

DUFF: If his own people round here get to know he's among them, why, a live coal in a keg of gunpowdher would not give you an idaya of the County Sligo.

KINCHELA: I know it. High and low they love him as much as they hate me – bad cess to them!

DUFF: Oh, niver fear; he will keep in the dark for his own sake.

KINCHELA: Keep watch on the Shaughraun; (*music*) find out where the pair of them lie in hidin'. Bring me the news to Ballyragget House. Meanwhile, I'll think what's best to be done. Be off, quick! (*Exit* DUFF.) Robert Ffolliott here – tare an' ages, I'm ruined, horse and foot. I'll have all Connaught and

---

polthogue: punch or slap.   *tare an' ages*: derived from 'tears and aches' (of Christ).

the Coort o' Chancery on me back. Duff is right – 'tis life or death with me and him. Well, it shall be life with you, Arte O'Neal, and death to him that parts us. (*Exit.*)

SCENE 2. *The Devil's Jowl. A cleft on the rocks in the sea coast. Enter* ROBERT FFOLLIOTT.

ROBERT: It must be past the hour when Conn promised to return. How often he and I have climbed these rocks together in search of the sea-birds' eggs, and waded for cockles in the strand below. Dear, faithful, ragged playfellow – many a cuff I've had for playing truant to ramble with you – how many a lecture from my dear old tutor, Father Dolan, who told me I ought to be ashamed of my love for the Shaughraun. Ah! my heart was not so much to blame, after all.

MOLINEUX: (*outside*) Hillo!

ROBERT: That is not his voice.

MOLINEUX: (*outside*) Hillo!

ROBERT: Why, 'tis a man in the uniform of an officer – he has seen me. (*Calls.*) Take care, sir, don't take that path – turn to the right – round that boulder – that's the road! Egad! another step and he would have gone over the cliff. He is some stranger who has lost his way.

(*Enter* MOLINEUX.)

MOLINEUX: What an infernal country! First I was nearly smothered in a bog, and then, thanks to you, my good fellow, I escaped breaking my neck. Do you know the way to Ballyragget? How far is it to the barracks?

ROBERT: Two miles.

MOLINEUX: Irish miles, of course.

ROBERT: I shall be happy to show you the road, but regret I cannot be your guide. The safest for a stranger is by the cliff to Suil-a-beg.

MOLINEUX: But I have just come from there.

ROBERT: From Suil-a-beg?

MOLINEUX: I shall not regret to revisit the place; charming spot. I have just passed there the sweetest hour of my life.

ROBERT: You saw the lady of the house, I presume.

MOLINEUX: Pardon me, sir; I mistook your yachting costume. I thought at first you were a common sailor. Perhaps you are acquainted with Miss Ffolliott?

ROBERT: Yes, but we have not met for some time. I thought you referred to Arte – I mean Miss O'Neal.

MOLINEUX: Oh! she is charming of course, but Miss Ffolliott is an angel. She has so occupied my thoughts that I lost my way; in fact, instead of going straight home, I have evidently been revolving in an orbit round that house, by a kind of centrifugal attraction of which she is the centre.

ROBERT: But surely you admired Miss O'Neal?

MOLINEUX: Oh, she is well enough; bright little thing! but beside Claire Ffolliott –

ROBERT: I prefer the beauty of Miss O'Neal.

MOLINEUX: I don't admire your taste.

ROBERT: Well, let us drink to each of them.

MOLINEUX: With pleasure, if you can supply the opportunity. (ROBERT *pulls out his flask, and fills the cup.*) Ah! I see you are provided. Allow me to present myself, Captain Molineux of the Forty-first. Here's to Miss Claire Ffolliott.

ROBERT: Here's to Miss Arte O'Neal. (*They drink.*)

MOLINEUX: I beg pardon; I did not catch your name.

ROBERT: I did not mention it – (*pause*)

MOLINEUX: This liquor is American whisky, I perceive.

ROBERT: Do you find anything wrong about it?

MOLINEUX: Nothing whatever. (*He offers his cup to be filled again.*) But it reminds me of a duty I have to perform. We have orders to capture a very dangerous person who will be or has been landed on this coast lately, and as these rocks are just the place where he might find refuge –

ROBERT: Not at all unlikely. I'll keep a look out for him.

MOLINEUX: I propose to revisit this spot with a file of men tonight. Here's your health.

ROBERT: Sir, accept my regards. Here's good luck to you.

MOLINEUX: Good night. (*Music; a whistle heard outside.*) What is that?

ROBERT: It is a ring at the bell. (*aside*) 'Tis Conn. A friend of mine is waiting for me on the cliff above us.

MOLINEUX: Oh. I beg pardon. Farewell. (*going*)

ROBERT: Stop. You might not fare well if you ascended that path alone.

MOLINEUX: Why not?

ROBERT: Because my friend is at the top of it, and if he saw you coming out alone – (*aside*) He would think I had been caught, and, egad, the Shaughraun might poach the Captain.

MOLINEUX: Well, if he met me, what then?

ROBERT: You see, the poor fellow is mad on one point. He can't bear the sight of one colour, and that's red. His mother was frightened by a mad bull, and the minute Conn sees a bit of scarlet, such, for example, as your coat there, the bull breaks out in him, and he might toss you over the cliff; so, by your leave –

MOLINEUX: This is the most extraordinary country I was ever in. (*Exeunt arm-in-arm.*)

SCENE 3. *The exterior of* FATHER DOLAN's *cottage. Night. Lighted window.*
Enter MOYA *with pail, which she puts down.*

MOYA: There! Now I have spancelled the cow and fed the pig, my uncle will be ready for his tay. Not a sign of Conn for the past three nights. What's come to him?

(*Enter* MRS. O'KELLY.)

MRS. O'K: Is that yourself Moya? I've come to see if that vagabond of mine has been round this way.

MOYA: Why would he be here? Hasn't he got a home of his own?

MRS. O'K: The shebeen is his home when he's not in jail. His father died o' dhrink, an' Conn will go the same way.

---

spancelled: hobbled.   *shebeen*: an unlicensed alehouse for the illegal sale of spirits.

MOYA: I thought your husband was drowned at sea.

MRS. O'K: And bless him, so he was.

MOYA: (*aside*) Well! that's a quare way of dying o' drink.

MRS. O'K: The best of men he was when he was sober. A betther never dhrawed the breath o' life.

MOYA: But you say he never was sober.

MRS. O'K: Never; and Conn takes afther him.

MOYA: Mother!

MRS. O'K: Well?

MOYA: I'm afeard I'll take afther Conn.

MRS. O'K: Heaven forbid and protect you agin him, for you are a good, dacent girl, and desarve the best of husbands.

MOYA: Them's the ones that get the worst. More betoken yourself, Mrs. O'Kelly.

MRS. O'K: Conn never did an honest day's work in his life, but dhrinkin', and fishin', and shootin', and spoortin', and love makin'.

MOYA: Sure, that's how the quality pass their lives.

MRS. O'K: That's it. A poor man that sports the soul of a gentleman is called a blackguard.

CONN: (*entering*) Somebody is spakin' about me.

MOYA: (*running to embrace him*) Conn!

CONN: My darlin', was the mother makin' little of me. Don't believe a word that comes out of her. She's jealous, divil a haperth else. She's chokin' wid it this minute, just bekase she sees my arms about ye. She's as proud of me as an ould hen that's got a duck for a chicken. Hould yer whisht now, wipe your mouth, and gi' me a kiss.

MRS. O'K: (*embracing him*) Oh, Conn, what have you been afther? The polis were in my cabin to-day about you. They say you stole Squire Foley's horse.

CONN: Stole his horse! Sure the baste is safe and sound in his paddock this minute!

MOYA: But he says you stole it for the day to go huntin'.

CONN: Well, now, here's a purty thing, for a horse to run away a man's caracther like this! Oh, wurra! may I never die in sin but here was the way of it. I was standing by ould Foley's gate, when I heard the cry of the hounds comin' across the tail end of the bog, and there they wor, my dear, spread out like the tail of a paycock, and the finest dog fox ye ever seen was sailin' ahead o' them up the boreen and right across the church-yard. It was enough to rise the inhabitants. Well, as I looked, who should come up and put his head over the gate beside me but the Squire's brown mare? Small blame to her. Divil a thing I said to her, nor she to me, for the hounds had lost the scent, we knew by their yelp and whine, as they hunted among the gravestones, when – whish! – the fox went by us. I lept on the gate an' gave a shriek of a view halloo to the whip. In a minute the pack caught the scent agin, and the whole field came roarin' past. The mare lost her head and tore at the gate. Stop, ses I, ye divil, and I slipped a taste of a rope over her head and into her mouth. Now, mind the cunnin' of the baste; she was quiet in a minute. Come home asy now, ses I, and I threw my leg across her. Be jabers! no sooner was I on her bare back than whoo! holy rocket! she was over the gate and tearin' like

---

boreen: narrow road.

mad afther the hounds. Yoicks! ses I, come back the thief o' the world, where are you takin' me to? as she went through the huntin' field, and laid me beside the masther o' the hounds, Squire Foley himself. He turned the colour of his leather breeches. Mother o' Moses! ses he, is that Conn the Shaughraun on my brown mare? Bad luck to me, ses I, it's no one else. You stole my horse, ses the Squire. That's a lie, ses I, it was your horse stole me! (MRS. O'KELLY *turns away to conceal her laughter.*)

MOYA: What did he say to that?

CONN: I couldn't stop to hear – for just then we took a stone wall and a double ditch together, and he stopped behind to keep an engagement he had in the ditch.

MRS. O'K: You'll get a month in jail for this.

CONN: Well! it was worth it.

MRS. O'K: And what brings you here? Don't you know Father Dolan has forbidden you the house?

CONN: The Lord bless him – I know it well – but I've brought something wid me to-night that will get me absolution. I've left it wid the ladies at Suil-a-beg, but they will bring it up here to share fair wid his reverence.

MRS. O'K: What is it at all?

CONN: Go down, mother, and see, and when you see it, kape your tongue betune your teeth, if one o' your sex can.

MRS. O'K: Well, but you're the quare mortil. (*Exit.*)

MOYA: Oh, Conn, I'm afeard my uncle won't see you. (FATHER DOLAN, *inside, calls 'Moya'.*) There, he's calling to me.

CONN: Go in, and tell him I'm sthravagin' outside till he's soft; now, put on your sweetest lip, darlin'.

MOYA: Never fear; sure, he does be always tellin' me my heart is too near my mouth.

CONN: Ah! I hope nobody will ever measure the distance but me, my jewel. (*Kisses her. Music.*)

MOYA: Ah! Conn, do you see these flowers? I picked them by the wayside as I came along, and I put them in my breast. They are dead already; the life and fragrance have gone out of them, killed by the heat of my heart. So it may be with you if I pick you and put you there. (*pause*) Won't the life go out of your love? Hadn't I better lave you where you are?

CONN: For another girl to make a posy of me? Ah, but my darling Moya, sure if I were one of these flowers, and you were to pass me by like that, I do believe that I'd pluck myself and walk after you on my stalk. (*Exit MOYA. CONN sings a song.*)

SCENE 4. *A room in the house of* FATHER DOLAN. *Fireplace with a lighted fire. Window at back door. Lamp on table.* FATHER DOLAN *is seated by the fire in arm chair, reading, face to fire.*

---

sthravagin': loitering.

sings a song: that Conn was originally intended to sing a song here is clearly indicated in the Wallack's prompt copy, as well as by Father Dolan's reference in Scene 4. But the song is not named, and may have been omitted in performance.

DOLAN: What keeps Moya so long outside? Moya!
> (*Enter* MOYA *with tea-things.*)

MOYA: Yes, uncle; here's your tay. I was waiting for the kettle to boil.

DOLAN: I thought I heard voices outside.

MOYA: It was the pig. (*Gives* FATHER DOLAN *cup of tea, then to fire with kettle.*)

DOLAN: And I heard somebody singing.

MOYA: It was the kettle, uncle.

DOLAN: Go tell that pig not to come here till he's cured, and if I hear any strange kettles singin' round here, my kettle will boil over.

MOYA: Sure, darlin' uncle, I never knew that happen but you put your own fire out. (*kneeling at fire*)

DOLAN: See now, Moya, that ragamuffin Conn will be your ruin – what makes you so fond of the rogue?

MOYA: All the batins I got for him when I was a child, an' the hard words you gave me since.

DOLAN: Has he one good quality undher Heaven? if he has, I'll forgive him.

MOYA: He has one.

DOLAN: What is it?

MOYA: He loves me.

DOLAN: Love! Oh, that word covers more sins than charity. I think I hear it rainin', Moya, and I would not keep a dog out in such a night.

MOYA: Oh! (*She laughs behind his back.*)

DOLAN: You may let him stand out o' the wet; (MOYA *beckons. Enter* CONN.) but don't let him open his mouth. Gi' me another cup o' tay, Moya; I hope it will be stronger than the last.

MOYA: Oh, what'll I do? Sure, he wants his tay stronger, and I've no more tay in the house.
> (*Pause.* CONN *pours whisky into teapot.* MOYA *gives cup to* FATHER DOLAN.)

DOLAN: Well, haven't you a word to say for yourself?

CONN: Divil a one, your reverence.

DOLAN: You are goin' to ruin.

CONN: I am; bad luck to me.

DOLAN: And you want to take a dacent girl along with you.

CONN: I'm a vagabone entirely!

DOLAN: What sort of life do you lead? What is your occupation? Stealing the salmon out of the river of a night!

CONN: No, sir; I'm not so bad as that, but I'll confess to a couple o' throut – sure the salmon is out o' sayson. (*Pulls out two trout from his bag, and gives them to* MOYA.)

DOLAN: And don't you go poaching the grouse on the hillside?

CONN: I do – divil a lie in it. (*Pulls out two grouse.*)

DOLAN: D'ye know where all this leads to?

CONN: Well, along wid the grouse, I'll go to pot. (MOYA *laughs and removes the game and fish.*)

DOLAN: Bless me, Moya, this tay is very strong, and has a curious taste.

CONN: Maybe the wather is to blame in regard o' bein' smoked.

DOLAN: And it smells of whisky!

CONN: It's not the tay ye smell, sir; it's me.

DOLAN: That reminds me; didn't you give me a promise last Aister – a blessed promise made on your two knees that you would lave off drink?

CONN: I did, barrin' only one thimbleful a day, just to take the cruelty out o' the wather.

DOLAN: One thimbleful! I allowed you that concession – no more.

CONN: God bless you, you did; and I kep me word.

DOLAN: Kept your word! How dare you say that? Didn't I find you ten days afther, stretched out as drunk as a fiddler at Tim O'Maley's wake?

CONN: Ye did – bad luck to me!

DOLAN: And you took only one thimbleful?

CONN: Divil a dhrop more, see this. Ah, will you listen to me, sir? I'll tell you how it was. When they axed me to the wake, I wint. Oh, I wouldn't decaive you – I wint. There was the Mulcaheys and the Malones and the –

DOLAN: I don't want to hear about that. Come to the drink.

CONN: Av coorse, egorra; I came to that soon enough. Well, sir, when, afther blessing the keeners and the rest o' them, I couldn't despise a dhrink out o' respect for the corpse – long life to it. But boys, ses I, I'm on a pinance, ses I. Is there a thimble in the house? ses I, for divil a dhrop more than the full av it will pass my lips this blessed day.

DOLAN: Ah!

CONN: Well, as the divil's luck would have it, there was only one thimble in the place, and that was a tailor's thimble, and they couldn't get it full; (FATHER DOLAN, *unable to conceal his laughter, goes to fire and pokes it* – MOYA *up to dresser with plate to her face.*) egorra, but they got me full first.

DOLAN: Ah, Conn, I'm afeard liquor is not the worst of your doings. We lost sight of you lately for more than six months. In what jail did you pass that time?

CONN: I was on me thravels.

DOLAN: On your travels? Where?

CONN: Round the world. See, sir, afther Masther Robert was tuck and they sint him away, the heart seemed to go out o' me intirely. I'd stand by the say and look over it an' see the ships sailin' away to where he may be, till the longing grew too big for my body, an' one night I jumped into the coast-guard boat, stuck up the sail, and went to say.

DOLAN: Bless the boy! You didn't think you could get to Australia in a skiff?

CONN: I didn't think at all – I wint. All night I tossed about, and next day, and that night, till at daylight I came across a big ship. Stop, ses I, and put me ashore, for the love of Heaven! I'm out o' my coorse. They whipped me on deck. Where d'ye come from? ses the Captain. Suil-a-beg, ses I. I'll be obleeged to you to lave me anywhere handy by there. You'll have to go to Melbourne first, ses he. Is that anywhere in the County Sligo? ses I, lookin' like a lamb. If ye'd heern the shout of laffin' I got for that. Why, ye omadhaun, ses he, ye'll never see home for six months. Then I set up a wierasthru.

---

omadhaun: fool.
wierasthru: a contraction of an exclamation of lament, meaning 'Oh, Mary, what sorrow'.

Poor divil, ses the Captain, I'm sorry for you; but you must cross the say.
What sort o' work can you do best? I can play on the fiddle, ses I. Take him
forrad and good care of him, ses he, and so they did. That's how I got my
passage to Australia.

DOLAN: You rogue, you boarded that ship on purpose.

MOYA: Ay, to get nearer the young Masther – and did you find him, Conn?

CONN: I did; an' oh, sir, when he laid eyes on me, he put his two arums about me
neck, an' sobbed an' clung to me like when we war childre together. What
brings you here? ses he. To bring you back wid me, ses I. That's impossible,
ses he, I'm watched. So is the salmon in Glenamoy, ses I, but I get 'em out.
So's the grouse on Keim-an-Eigh, but I poach them; and now I've come to
poach you, ses I; and I did it.

    (*Music. Enter* ROBERT FFOLLIOTT, *with* CLAIRE *and* ARTE.)

DOLAN: Is this the truth you are telling me? You found him!

CONN: (*seizing* MOYA *and stopping her mouth as she was about to utter a cry on
seeing* ROBERT) Safe, and in fine condition.

DOLAN: Escaped and free; tell me –

CONN: Oh, egorra! he must speak for himself now.

ROBERT: Father Dolan. (*Throws off disguise and embraces him.*)

DOLAN: Robert! my darling boy. Oh, blessed day! do I hold you to my heart
again? (*Embraces him.*)

CONN: (*aside to* MOYA) There's nobody lookin'. (*Kisses her.*)

MOYA: Conn! behave!

ARTE: He has been hiding on the sea-shore among the rocks for a whole day and
two nights.

CLAIRE: All alone, with sea-weed for his bed.

MOYA: Oh! if I'd only known that.

CONN: And nothing to eat but a piece of tobacco and a cockle.

ARTE: And he would not stop at Suil-a-beg to taste a morsel until he would come
over here to see you.

DOLAN: Come near the fire. Moya, hurry now, and put food on the table. Sit ye
down. Let me see you all around me once again. (MOYA *brings in food, then
fetches tumblers.*) And to think I cannot offer you a glass of wine, nor warm
your welcome with a glass of liquor. I have not got a bottle in the house.
(CONN *pulls out his bottle and puts it on table.*) The rogue! (*They form a
group round the fire.*)

ROBERT: We may thank poor Conn, who contrived my escape. I made my way to
America.

ARTE: What became of Conn?

ROBERT: I left him in my place.

CLAIRE: But how did you escape, Conn?

CONN: Oh! asy enough, miss – they turned me out.

ARTE: Turned you out?

CONN: As if I wor a stray cat. Very well, ses I, Ballymulligan is my parish; I'm a
pauper; send me or gi' me board wages where I am. No, ses they, we've Irish
enough here already. Then send me back to Sligo, ses I – and they did.

CLAIRE: They might well take you for a cat, for you seem always to fall on your
legs.

DOLAN: I can't get over my surprise, to see my blessed child sitting there by my side. Now we'll all drink his health. (*Music.*)

CONN: Which thimble am I to drink out of?

DOLAN: The tailor's, you reprobate. Are you ready, girls? Now, then, (*The face of* HARVEY DUFF *appears at the window.*) here's his health, and long life to him – may Heaven keep watch over –

ROBERT: (*rising, glass in hand, and pointing to window*) Look! look there! (DUFF *disappears before they turn.*)

CLAIRE: What was it?

ARTE: How pale you are.

ROBERT: The face – I saw the face – there, at the window – the same I saw when I was in the dock.

CLAIRE: Ah, Robert, you dream!

ROBERT: The police spy – Harvey Duff – the man that denounced me. 'Twas his white face pressed against the glass, yonder – glaring at me. (*Exit* CONN.) Oh, can it be a vision?

ARTE: It was! you are weak, dear. Eat – recover your strength.

MOYA: It wasn't a face, but an empty stomach.

ROBERT: It gave my heart a turn. You must be right. It was a weakness – the disorder of my brain – it must have been so.

DOLAN: The night is very dark. (*Closes curtains. Re-enter* CONN.) Well?

CONN: Nothing.

DOLAN: I thought so. Come now – refresh yourself.

CONN: (*aside*) Moya, there was somebody there!

MOYA: How d'ye know? Did you see him?

CONN: No, but I left Tatthers outside.

MOYA: Your dog! why didn't he bark?

CONN: He couldn't! I found this in his mouth.

MOYA: What's that?

CONN: The sate of a man's breeches; whisht, he's growling now; he never talks till he wants me to help him. (*Exit.*)

ROBERT: (*eating*) My visit here must be a very short one. The vessel that landed me is now standing off and on the coast awaiting my signal to send in a boat ashore to take me away again.

ARTE: I am afraid your arrival was expected by the authorities; they are on the watch.

ROBERT: I know they are! I have had a chat with them on the subject – and a very nice fellow the authority seemed to be, and a great admirer of my rebel sister there!

CLAIRE: Captain Molineux.

ROBERT: He and I met this evening at the Coot's Nest.

CLAIRE: How dare the fellow talk about me!

ROBERT: Look at her! She's all ablaze! Her face is the colour of his coat.

CLAIRE: I never saw the creature but once.

ROBERT: Then you made good use of your time; I never saw a man in such a condition. He's not a man – he's a trophy! (*Music.*)

CLAIRE: Bob, you are worse than he is.

DOLAN: I could listen to him all night.

ARTE: So could I.

CONN: (*dashing window open*) Sir – quick – away wid yees! Hide – the redcoats are on us. (*Leaps in.*)

ARTE: Oh, Robert! fly!

MOYA: This way – by the kitchen, through the garden.

CONN: No, the back dure is watched – by a couple of them. Is it locked?

MOYA: Fast.

CONN: Give me your coat and hat; I'll make a dash out. Tatthers will attend to one, I'll stretch the other, and the rest will give me chase, thinking it is yourself; then you can slip off onbeknonst. (*three knocks at the door*)

DOLAN: It is too late.

MOYA: Hide yourself in the ould clock-case in the kitchen! There's just room for him in it.

ARTE: Quick, Robert, quick! Oh, save yourself if you can! (*Exeunt.*)

CLAIRE: Oh! I wish I was a man; I would not give him up without a fight. (*Exit.*)

CONN: Egorra, the blood o' the ould stock is in her. (*standing at door with bottle in his hand*) I'll stretch 'em as they come. (*two knocks at door*)

DOLAN: Conn, put that down and open the door.

> (MOYA *takes bottle from* CONN. *He opens door.* SERGEANT *and two* SOLDIERS *enter.* SOLDIERS *stand each side of door.* SERGEANT *draws window-curtains and discovers two* SOLDIERS – *who remain there.* MOLINEUX *passes window. As he enters,* SERGEANT *salutes and exit.*)

MOLINEUX: I deeply regret to disturb your household at such an hour, but my duty sir, is imperative; a convict, escaped from penal servitude, has landed on this coast, and I am charged with his capture. (*Enter CLAIRE and ARTE.*) Miss Ffolliott, I am sorry to be obliged to perform so painful a duty in your presence – and in yours, Miss O'Neal.

CLAIRE: Especially, sir, when the man you seek is my brother.

ARTE: And my affianced husband.

MOLINEUX: Believe me, I would exchange places with him if I could.

> (*Enter SERGEANT.*)

SERGEANT: (*saluting*) Please, sir, there's a mad dog, sir, a-sittin' at the back door as has bit four of the men awful.

CONN: Tatthers was obliged to perform a painful juty.

CLAIRE: Call off your dog, Conn; open the back door, Moya.

> (*Exit CONN and MOYA.*)

MOLINEUX: Your assurance gives me hope that we have been misled.

ARTE: The house is very small, sir. Here is a bedroom; let your men search it.

> (*Re-enter MOYA, CONN and two SOLDIERS.*)

MOYA: I suppose you have seen there's never a human bein' in my kitchen barrin' the cat; my bedroom is up them stairs, maybe you'd like to search that.

MOLINEUX: I shall be obliged, sir, to visit every room, sound every piece of furniture, from the roof to the cellar; but the indignity of the proceedings is more offensive to my feelings than it can be to yours. I will accept your simple assurance that the person we are in search of is not in your house. Give me that, and I will withdraw my men.

CLAIRE: (*offering her hand to* MOLINEUX) Thank you.

ARTE: (*aside to* FATHER DOLAN) Save him, sir, oh save him!

DOLAN: (*aside*) Oh, God, help me in this great temptation.

ARTE: (*aside*) You will not betray him! Speak; oh say he is not here.

MOLINEUX: I await your reply.

CONN: (*aside*) I wish he would take my word.

DOLAN: The lad – the – person you seek – my poor boy – oh, sir, for mercy's sake, don't ask me! – he has been here – but –

MOLINEUX: He is gone? – he went before we arrived?

ARTE: Yes – yes!

CONN: Yes, sir; he wint away before he came at all.

MOLINEUX: Have I your word as a priest, sir, that Robert Ffolliott is not under this roof?

> (FATHER DOLAN, *after a passionate struggle with himself, turns from* MOLINEUX, *and buries his face in his hands. Enter* ROBERT.)

ROBERT: No, sir. Robert Ffolliott is here!

> (ARTE, *with a suppressed cry, throws herself into* CLAIRE'*s arms.*)

MOLINEUX: I am very sorry for it. (ROBERT *embraces* FATHER DOLAN.) Secure your prisoner!

> (SERGEANT *advances;* ROBERT *meets him, is handcuffed;* SERGEANT *retires two or three paces;* FATHER DOLAN *totters across and falls on his knees;* ROBERT *raises him and puts him in chair;* SERGEANT *touches* ROBERT *on shoulder, then moves to door;* ROBERT *is going when* ARTE *throws her arms round his neck.*)

DOLAN: Oh Robert, Robert, forgive me! what have I done?

CONN: Be asy, Father, sure he'd rather have the iron on his hands, than you the sin upon your sowl.

> (*Tableau. Slow act drop.*)

ACT II

SCENE 1. *A room in Ballyragget House. Music. Enter* KINCHELA *and* HARVEY DUFF.

KINCHELA: Come in – how pale you are – did he resist?

DUFF: Gi' me a glass of sperrets!

KINCHELA: Recover yourself. Is he wounded?

DUFF: Divil a scratch, but I am!

KINCHELA: Where?

DUFF: Never mind.

KINCHELA: Come and sit down.

DUFF: No! I'm asier on my feet.

KINCHELA: How did it happen?

DUFF: While I was peepin' through the key-hole of the kitchen door.

KINCHELA: I mean how was he taken?

DUFF: I did not stop to see, for when he caught sight of my face agin the windy, his own turned as white as your shirt. I believe he knew me.

KINCHELA: Impossible! that black wig disguises you completely. You have shaved off your great red whiskers. Your own mother wouldn't know you.

DUFF: No, she wouldn't; the last time I went home she pelted me out wid the poker. But if the people round here suspected I was Harvey Duff, they would tear me to rags. There wouldn't survive a piece of me as big as the one I left in the mouth of that divil of a dog.

KINCHELA: Don't be afraid, my good fellow. I'll take care of you. (*Gets glass and bottle.* DUFF *drinks.*)

DUFF: And it is yourself you will be taking care of at the same time. There's a pair of us, Misther Kinchela, mind me now. We are harnessed to the same pole, and as I'm dhruv you must thravel!

KINCHELA: What do you mean?

DUFF: I mane that I have been your partner in this game to chate young Ffolliott – out of his liberty first, then out of his estate, and now out of his wife! Where's my share?

KINCHELA: Your share! of what?

DUFF: Oh, not of the wife. Take her and welcome, but where's my share of the money?

KINCHELA: Were you not handsomely paid at the time for doing your duty?

DUFF: My jooty! was it my jooty to come down here amongst the people disguised as a Fenian delegate, and pass meself aff for a head centre so that I could swear them in and then denounce them? Who gave me the offis how to trap young Ffolliott? Who was it picked out Andy Donovan an' sent him in irons across the say, laving his young wife in a madhouse?

KINCHELA: Hush, not so loud!

DUFF: D'ye remember the curse of Bridget Madigan, when her only boy was found guilty on my evidence? Take your share of that! and give me some of what I've airned!

KINCHELA: You want a share of my fortune!

DUFF: A share of our fortune.

KINCHELA: Every penny I possess is invested in this estate. If Robert Ffolliott returns home a free man, I could not hold more of it than would stick to my brogues when I was kicked out. Listen to this letter that I found here tonight waiting for me. It is from London. (*Reads.*) 'On Her Majesty's Service. The Home Office. In reply to your enquiries concerning Robert Ffolliott, undergoing penal servitude, I am directed by his Lordship to inform you that Her Majesty has been pleased to extend a full pardon to the Fenian prisoners.'

DUFF: Pardoned! I'm a corpse!

KINCHELA: (*Reads.*) 'But as Robert Ffolliott has effected his escape, the pardon will not extend to him, unless he should reconstitute himself a prisoner.'

DUFF: Oh Lord! sure that is exactly what he has done. He gave himself up.

KINCHELA: Was he not captured?

DUFF: No! bad luck to it! Our schame to catch him has only qualified him for that pardon.

KINCHELA: What! has an infernal fate played such a trick upon me?

DUFF: The divil will have his joke.

KINCHELA: His freedom and his return here is your death-warrant and my ruin.
DUFF: I'll take the next ship to furrin parts.
KINCHELLA: Stay – This news is only known to ourselves.
DUFF: In a couple of days it will be all over Ireland, and they will let him out! Tare alive, what'll I do at all? Where'll I go? I'll swear an information agin meself and get sent to jail – for purtection.
KINCHELA: Listen – I've a plan! Can I rely on your help?
DUFF: I'll do anything short o' murther – but I'll get somebody to do that for me. What's to be done?
KINCHELA: I'll visit him in prison, and offer him the means to escape. Now what more likely than he should be killed while making the attempt?
DUFF: Oh! Whew! The soldiers will not dhraw a trigger on him, barrin' a magistrate is by to give the ordher.
KINCHELA: But the police will. You will go at once to the police barracks at Sligo – pick your men, tell them we apprehend an attempt at rescue. The late attack on the police van at Manchester, and the explosion at Clerkenwell prison in London, will warrant extreme measures.
DUFF: The police won't fire if he doesn't defend himself.
KINCHELA: But he will.
DUFF: Where will he get the arms?
KINCHELA: I'll provide them for him.
DUFF: Corry Kinchela – the devil must be proud of you.
KINCHELA: We must get some of our own people to help, and if the police hesitate – sure it's the duty of every loyal subject to kill a fugitive convict. What men could we depend on at a pinch?
DUFF: There's Sullivan, and Doyle, and Mangan, and all their smugglin' crew.
KINCHELA: Where can you find them?
DUFF: At the Coot's Nest. They expect the lugger in at every tide.
KINCHELA: Have them ready and sober to-night. Come to me for instructions at midday. (*going – stops*) Ah! that will do – that will do – he will fall into that trap; (*Rubs his hands.*) it can't fail. (*Exit. Music.*)
DUFF: Harvey Duff, take a frind's advice, get out o' this place as quick as you can; take your little pickin's and your passage across the say, find some place where a rogue can live peaceable; have some show and a chance of makin' an honorable livin'. (*Exit.*)

SCENE 2. *The parlour at* FATHER DOLAN*'s, as before.* ARTE *and* FATHER DOLAN *at the fireside;* CLAIRE *looking out of window.*
DOLAN: There, my darling, do not sob so bitterly; sure, that will do no good, and only spoil your blue eyes.
ARTE: What's the good of my eyes if I can't see him. Let me cry. God help me, what else can I do? Oh if I could only see him, speak to him for one minute. Do you think they would let me in?
DOLAN: I have sent a letter to the Captain; Moya has carried it to the barracks.

Manchester and Clerkenwell: the reference is to two actual Fenian raids – both ill-starred – which took place in 1867.

ARTE: If Claire had gone instead of Moya: had she pleaded for us, he would not refuse her.

CLAIRE: But I could not go.

DOLAN: Why not?

CLAIRE: I could not ask that Englishman a favour.

DOLAN: You speak unkindly, and unjustly. He acted with a gentle forbearance and a respect for my character and our sorrow I cannot forget.

CLAIRE: Nor can I.

DOLAN: It made a deep impression on my heart.

CLAIRE: Yes! A bitter curse on the day I ever laid eyes on him!

ARTE: Oh, Claire, you wrong him! Surely I have no cause to regard him as a friend, but you did not see the tears in his eyes when I appealed to his mercy.

CLAIRE: Didn't I?

DOLAN: Poor fellow, he suffered for what he was obliged to do; you should not hate the man.

CLAIRE: I don't; and that's what ails me.

ARTE: Are you mad?

CLAIRE: I am. I've tried to hate him and I can't. D'ye think I was blind to all you saw? I tried to shut my eyes, but I only shut him in; I could not shut him out. I hate his country and his people.

DOLAN: You were never there.

CLAIRE: Never; and I wish they had never been here; particularly this fellow, who has the impudence to upset all my principles with his chalky smile and his bloodless courtesy. I can't stand the ineffable resignation with which he makes a fool of himself and of me.

(*Enter* MOYA.)

Well, have you seen him? Can't you speak?

MOYA: I will when I get my breath. Yes, I saw him, and oh, how good and –

CLAIRE: Stop that! We know all about that! Where is his answer? Quick!

MOYA: He is bringing it himself.

CLAIRE: Oh! (*Turns away.*) We don't want him here.

ARTE: Did you see the young master?

MOYA: No, Miss – nobody is let in to see him.

DOLAN: What kept you so long then?

MOYA: Conn came back wid me – and knowin' you did not want him round here, I was thryin' to get away from him, that's what kept me – but he was at my heels all the way, and Tatthers at his heels – a nice sthreel we made along the road.

DOLAN: Where is he?

MOYA: They are both outside.

DOLAN: The pair of vagabonds – why does he not go home?

MOYA: He says the ould woman is no consolation.

CONN: (*Sings outside.*)

If I was dead and in my grave,

---

sthreel: a word describing anything untidy or ungainly.

> No other tombstone I would have,
> But I'd dig a grave both wide and deep,
> Wid a jug of punch at my head and feet.
>   Ri-too-ral-loo.

DOLAN: Is that fellow so insensible to our sorrows that he sets it to the tune of a jug of punch?

CLAIRE: Don't blame poor Conn! the boy is so full of sport that I believe he would sing at his own funeral.

MOYA: Long life t'ye, Miss, for the good word.
                    (*Enter* CONN.)

CONN: (*speaking to his dog*) Lie down now, an' behave.

DOLAN: Where have you been all night?

CONN: Where would I be? I've been undher his prison windy, kapin' up his heart wid the songs and the divarshin.

ARTE: Diversion!

CONN: Sure, I had all the soldiers dancin' to my fiddle, and I put Tatthers through all his thricks, and I had 'em all in fits o' laffin' when I made him dance to my tunes; that's the way the masther knew I was waitin' on him. He guessed what I was at, for when I struck up 'Where's the slave?', he answered inside wid 'My lodging is on the cowld ground'. Then, when I made Tatthers dance to 'Tell me the sorrow in your heart' till I thought they'd a' died wid the fun, he sung back 'The girl I left behind me', manin' yourself, Miss Arte, God bless him! an' I pertended that the tears runnin' down my nose was wid the laffin'. (MOYA *wipes his eyes with apron.*)

DOLAN: (*crossing to* CONN) I did you great wrong. I ask your pardon.

ARTE: What is to be done?

CONN: I'd only have to whisper five words on the cross-roads, and I'd go bail I'd have him out o' that before night.

DOLAN: Yes. You would raise the country to attack the barracks and rescue him! I will not give countenance to violence.

CLAIRE: 'Tis the shortest way out.

ARTE: Oh, any way but that.

MOYA: (*aside to* CONN) Come into my kitchen; have you had nothing to ate since yesterda'?

CONN: Yes, my heart. I've had that in my mouth all night; I can't get it down at all; it stops my swally, but I find the dhrink slips by. (*Exit* MOYA. *He follows her.*)

CLAIRE: (*who is watching at window*) Here he comes. (*Stands with back to door as* MOLINEUX *passes window and knocks at door.*)

DOLAN: There's a knock at the door.

ARTE: 'Tis he.

CLAIRE: I know that.

DOLAN: Why did you not let him in? (*Crosses to door.*)

CLAIRE: (*aside*) Because I am trying to keep him out. (*Sits at fire, back to audience, as* FATHER DOLAN *admits* MOLINEUX.)

MOLINEUX: Good day, sir; I ventured to intrude in person, to bring you this order, necessary to obtain admission to see Mr. Ffolliott, and that I might entreat you to bear me no ill will for the painful duty I had to perform last night. (*Hands a paper to* ARTE.)

CLAIRE: Oh no, sir; you had to deprive us of a limb, and I suppose you performed the operation professionally well. Do you come for your fee in the form of our gratitude?

DOLAN: Forgive her, Sir. Claire, this is too bad!

MOLINEUX: (*awkward*) Oh not at all! Pray don't mention it, I assure you.

ARTE: This paper is signed by Mr. Kinchela! Are we indebted to him for this favour?

MOLINEUX: The prisoner is now in the custody of the civil power, and Mr. Kinchela is the magistrate of the district.

DOLAN: (*taking his hat from desk*) Come Arte. Come Claire.

ARTE: (*speaking pointedly to* CLAIRE) We are grateful, very grateful for your kindness in our affliction. (*aside to* MOLINEUX) Don't mind her. Heaven will reward you.

DOLAN: (*taking his hand*) A good action is its own reward. (*Exit with* ARTE.)

MOLINEUX: (*aside*) Don't mind her – I wish I did not. (*aloud*) May I be permitted to accompany you to –

CLAIRE: To the prison? Do you wish to make the people about here believe I am in custody? A fine figure I'd make hanging on the arm of the policeman who arrested my brother.

MOLINEUX: You cannot make me feel more acutely than I do the misery of my condition. I did not sleep a wink last night.

CLAIRE: And how many winks do you suppose I got?

MOLINEUX: I tried to act with as much tenderness as the nature of my duty would permit.

CLAIRE: That's the worst part of it.

MOLINEUX: Do you reproach me with my gentleness?

CLAIRE: I do! You have not left us even the luxury of complaint.

MOLINEUX: Really, I don't understand you.

CLAIRE: No wonder – I don't understand myself.

MOLINEUX: Well, if you don't understand yourself you shall understand me, Miss Ffolliott. You oblige me to take refuge from your cruelty, and to place myself under the protection of your generosity. You extort from me a confession that I feel is premature, for our acquaintance has been short.

CLAIRE: And not sweet.

MOLINEUX: I ask your pity for my position last night, when I found myself obliged to arrest the brother of the woman I love.

CLAIRE: Captain Molineux! do you mean to insult me? Oh sir, you know I am a friendless girl, alone in this house, my brother in jail. I have no protection.

MOLINEUX: Miss Ffolliott – Claire!

(*Enter* CONN, *followed by* MOYA.)

CONN: Did you call, Miss?

CLAIRE: (*after a pause*) No.

CONN: I thought I heard a screech. (*Music.*)

CLAIRE: Go away; I don't want you.

MOYA: (*aside to* CONN) Don't ye see what's the matther?

CONN: No.

MOYA: (*still aside*) You're an omadhaun. Come out of that an' I'll tell you. (*Exit CONN and MOYA.*)

CLAIRE: There! what will those pair think of us? Do you see what you have exposed me to? Is it not enough to play the character of the executioner of my brother, but you must add to your part this scene of outrage to me? (*Sits down and weeps passionately.*)

MOLINEUX: Forgive me. I ask it most humbly. If I said I would give my heart's blood to the last drop to spare you one of those tears, you might feel that avowal was an offence. What can I say? Miss Ffolliott, for mercy's sake don't cry so bitterly. Forget what I've done!

CLAIRE: I – I can't.

MOLINEUX: On my knees I implore your pardon. I'll go away; I'll never see you again. (*She suddenly and mechanically arrests his movement by catching his arm; he kisses her hand.*) Heaven bless you. (*She covers her face. He goes to the door, dejected.*)

CLAIRE: (*without removing her hands from her face*) Don't go.

MOLINEUX: Did I hear right? you bid me stay?

CLAIRE: Am I mad?

MOLINEUX: Miss Ffolliott, I am here.

CLAIRE: (*rising and going to fireplace*) I forgive you on one condition.

MOLINEUX: I accept it, whatever it may be.

CLAIRE: Save my brother.

MOLINEUX: I'll do my best! Anything else?

CLAIRE: Never speak a word of love to me again.

MOLINEUX: Never, never; on my honour, I will never breathe a –

CLAIRE: Until he is free.

MOLINEUX: And then, may I, may I? (*Stands beside her at the fireplace; her head is bent down. Steals his arm round her waist.*)

CLAIRE: Not a word until then. (*Buries her head on his shoulder.*)

MOLINEUX: Not a word.
          (*Scene closes in slowly.*)

SCENE 3. *A room in the barracks. Enter* SERGEANT *followed by* KINCHELA.

KINCHELA: I am Mr. Kinchela, the magistrate. I wish to see the prisoner. He must be removed to the police quarters.

SERGEANT: We shall be glad to get rid of him. It is police business. Our men don't half like it. (*Exit.*)

KINCHELA: Now I'll know at once by his greeting if those girls have been speaking about me.
          (*Enter ROBERT, followed by SERGEANT.*)

ROBERT: Kinchela! my dear friend. I knew you would not fail me.

KINCHELA: (*aside*) 'Tis all right. (*Turns coldly, and with stiff manner.*) Pardon me, Mr. Ffolliott, you forget your position and mine. I bear Her Majesty's commission as justice of the peace – and whatever friendship once united us, it ceased when you became a rebel.

ROBERT: Do I hear aright? Your letters to me breathed the most devoted –

KINCHELA: (*to the* SERGEANT) You can leave us. (*Exit* SERGEANT. KIN-
CHELA *suddenly changes his manner.*) My dear young master, forgive me. In
the presence of that fellow, I was obliged to play the magistrate.

ROBERT: Egad – you took my breath away!

KINCHELA: Didn't I do it well? My devotion to you and to the precious charge
you left in my care exposes me to suspicion. I'm watched – and to preserve
my character for loyalty, I'm obliged to put on airs. Oh! I'm your mortal
enemy – mind that.

ROBERT: You!

KINCHELA: Every man, woman and child in the County Sligo believes it and hates
me. I've played my part so well that your sister and Miss O'Neal took offence
at my performance.

ROBERT: No. Ha! ha!

KINCHELA: Yes. Ho! ho! They actually believe I am what I am obliged to appear,
and they hate me cordially. I'm the biggest blackguard –

ROBERT: You! my best friend!

KINCHELA: Oh, I don't mind it. The truth is, I was afeard if I had betrayed my
game to them – you know the wakeness of the sex! – they could not have
kept my sacret.

ROBERT: But surely Father Dolan –

KINCHELA: He is just as bad.

ROBERT: Forgive them.

KINCHELA: I do.

ROBERT: The time will come when they will repent their usage of you.

KINCHELA: Ay, by my soul, it will!

ROBERT: They will have no friend, no protector but you! For now my chains will
be riveted more firmly than ever.

KINCHELA: Whisht, you must escape!

ROBERT: It is impossible! How? When?

KINCHELA: To-night! To-morrow when you are removed to Sligo jail it might not
be so easy, but to-night I can help you.

ROBERT: To regain my freedom?

KINCHELA: Is the ship that landed you within reach?

ROBERT: Every night at eight o'clock she runs inshore and lies to off the coast. A
bonfire lighted on Rathgarron Head is to be the signal for her to send her
skiff under the ruins of St. Bridget's Abbey to take me on board.

KINCHELA: That signal will be fired to-night, and you shall be there to meet the boat.

ROBERT: Do you indeed mean this, Kinchela? Will you risk this for my sake?

KINCHELA: I will lay down my life, if you want it. (*They embrace.*)

ROBERT: What am I to do?

KINCHELA: Give me your promise that you will not breathe a word to mortal
about the plan I'm going to propose; neither to your sister, nor to Miss
O'Neal, nor, above all, to Father Dolan.

ROBERT: Must I play a part to deceive them?

KINCHELA: Recollect, my life and liberty are staked on the attempt, as well as
yours.

ROBERT: I give you the promise.

KINCHELA: To-night your quarters will be changed to the Old Gate Tower; wait
    until dark, and then use this chisel to pick out the stones that form the back
    of the fireplace in your room; the wall there is only one course thick. (*Gives
    him chisel.*)
ROBERT: You are sure?
KINCHELA: Conn, the Shaughraun, was shut up in that cell last spring, and he
    picked his way through the wall with a two-pronged fork; he was creeping out
    of the hole he had made when they caught him. The wall has been rebuilt,
    but the place has not served as a prison since.
ROBERT: Where shall I find myself when I am outside?
KINCHELA: In a yard enclosed by four low walls. There's a door in one of them
    that's bolted on the inside. Open that and you are free.
ROBERT: Are there no sentinels posted there?
KINCHELA: No; but if there is, here's a double-barrelled pistol – that will clear
    your road. (*Hands him a pistol.* ROBERT *examines it. Aside.*) I'll put Duff
    outside that door – there will be an end to him.
ROBERT: (*returning the pistol*) Take it back! I will not buy my liberty at the price
    of any man's life. I will take my chance. But stay! the signal on Rathgarron
    Head! Who will light the bonfire. (CONN *plays fiddle outside.*) Hark! 'tis
    Conn. Do you hear? Poor fellow, he is playing 'I'm under your window,
    darling'. Ha! I can employ him! He will do it. How will I send him word?
KINCHELA: You won't betray me?
ROBERT: No, no! (*Writes in his note-book – repeats as he writes.*) 'Be at Rath-
    garron Head to-night, beside the tar barrel.' What signal can I give him, that
    he will be able to hear or see across the bay?
KINCHELA: (*dictating*) 'When you hear two gun-shots in St. Bridget's Abbey, light
    the fire.' (*Offers the pistol.*)
ROBERT: For that purpose I accept it. (*Takes it, puts it into his pocket, and
    writes.*) 'When you hear two shots –
KINCHELA: (*aside*) No matther for what purpose – he will use it to serve mine.
    If they'd hang him for murdherin' Duff, I'd be afther killing two birds wid
    one stone.
ROBERT: Beg the sentry to come here.
KINCHELA: What are you going to do?
ROBERT: You will see. (*Takes out some coins.*)
KINCHELA: Here is the Sergeant.
                    (*Enter* SERGEANT.)
ROBERT: (*folding the money in the paper*) Will you give these few pence to that
    fiddler outside, and beg the fellow to move on? (*Hands the paper to* SER-
    GEANT.)
SERGEANT: The men encourage him about the place. (*going*) There's Father
    Dolan and Miss O'Neal outside; they have got a pass to see you.
ROBERT: Show them in. (*Exit* SERGEANT.)
KINCHELA: Now watch their manner towards me, but you won't mind a word
    they say against me.
ROBERT: Not I. I know you better. (CONN *plays fiddle outside.*) Hush! 'Tis Conn.
    Has he got the letter? Listen – 'I'll be faithful and true'. Ay, as the ragged dog

at your heels is faithful and true to you, so you have been to me, my dear, devoted, loving playfellow, my wild companion.

(*Enter* FATHER DOLAN *and* ARTE.)

ARTE: Robert! (*embracing him*) Mr. Kinchela!

DOLAN: I am surprised to find you here, sir!

KINCHELA: (*aside to* ROBERT) D'ye hear?

ROBERT: (*aside to him*) All right!

ARTE: You do not know that man.

KINCHELA: Oh, yes he does – I have made a clane breast of it.

ROBERT: Yes, he has told me all.

KINCHELA: How I brought him and all of you to ruin, betrayed my trust, and grew rich and fat on my plundher. I defy you to make me out a bigger black-guard than I've painted myself; so my sarvice to you. (*Exit.*)

DOLAN: When St. Patrick made a clean sweep of all the venomous reptiles in Ireland, some of the vermin must have found refuge in the bodies of such men as that.

ROBERT: That is the first uncharitable word I ever heard you utter.

DOLAN: Heaven forgive me for it, and him; you are right – my vocation is to redeem and pray for sinners, not to revile them.

ARTE: And mine is to comfort you, and not to bring our complaints to add to your misfortune.

ROBERT: Hold up your hearts; mine is full of hope.

DOLAN: Hope! where do you find it?

ROBERT: In her eyes! You might as well ask me where I find love. I was in prison when I stood liberated on American soil. The chains were on my soul when I stretched it, longing, across the ocean towards my home; and now I'm here, in prison. But this narrow cell is Ireland; I breathe my native air and I'm free.

DOLAN: They will send you back again.

ARTE: Ah! sure the future belongs to Heaven, but the present is our own.

DOLAN: I believe I was wrong to come here at all. I feel like a mourning band on a white hat. (*Music.*)

(*Enter* SERGEANT.)

SERGEANT: Sorry to disturb you, sir, but we are ordered to shift your quarters; you will occupy the room in the Old Gate Tower. The guard is waiting, sir, when you are ready.

ROBERT: I am prepared to accompany you.

ARTE: Must we leave you?

ROBERT: For the present: but we shall soon meet again! Now, will you indulge a strange humour of mine? You know the ruins of St. Bridget's Abbey, where we have so often sat together?

ARTE: Can I ever forget it? We go there often; the place is full of you.

ROBERT: Go there to-night at nine o'clock.

ARTE: I'll offer up a prayer at the old shrine.

ROBERT: Ay, with all your heart, for I may want it.

DOLAN: What do you mean? There's some mischief going on – I know it by his eye. He used to wear just the same look when he was going to give me the slip, and be off from his Latin grammar to play truant with Conn the Shaughraun.

ROBERT: Ask me nothing, for I can only answer you one word. Hope!

DOLAN: 'Tis the finest word in the Irish language.

ARTE: There's a finer – Faith! (*Embraces* ROBERT.)

DOLAN: And love is the mother of those heavenly twins. I declare my heart is
  lifted up between you, as if your young ones were its wings.

ROBERT: Good night, and not for the last time.

ARTE: Good night.

DOLAN: I leave my heart with you, Robert. God bless you.

ROBERT: Remember, to-night at the Abbey.

ARTE: At nine o'clock.

ROBERT: I shall be there. (*She utters an exclamation.*) Hush! (*Exit* FATHER
  DOLAN *and* ARTE.) You gave the money to the fiddler?

SERGEANT: Yes, sir.

ROBERT: (*aside*) Ah, I forgot! Conn can't read. What will he do to decipher my
  note? Bah! I must trust to his cunning to get at the contents. Now, sergeant,
  lead me to my new cell in the Gate Tower. (*Exeunt.*)

SCENE 4. *The exterior of* MRS. O'KELLY's *cabin. Evening. Enter* CONN, *with a
paper in his hand.*

CONN: There's writin' upon it. Himself has sent me a letther. Well, this is the first
  I ever got, and well, to be sure, (*Looks at it, turns it over.*) I'd know more
  about it if there was nothing in it; but it's the writin' bothers me.
          (*Enter* MRS. O'KELLY.)

MRS. O'K: Is that yourself, Conn?

CONN: (*aside*) I wish it was somebody else that had book larnin'.

MRS. O'K: What have ye there?

CONN: It's a letther, ma'am! the masther is after writin' to me.

MRS. O'K: What's in it?

CONN: Tuppence was in it for postage. (*aside*) And that's all I made out of it.

MRS. O'K: I mane what does he say in it?

CONN: Rade it!

MRS. O'K: You know I can't.

CONN: Ah, ye ignorant ould woman.

MRS. O'K: I am, Conn, but I tuk care to send you to school – though the sixpence
  a week you cost me was pinched out of my stomach and off my back.

CONN: The Lord be praised, mother, ye had it to spare anyway.

MRS. O'K: Go on now – is it making' fun of your ould mother you are? Tell me
  what the young masther says.

CONN: In the letter?

MRS. O'K: Yes.

CONN: (*aside*) Murdher, what'll I do? (*aloud*) Now mind, mother, it's a secret.
          (*Reads.*) 'Collee Costhoon garaya, caravat – Sillibubu lukli kastuck pig' –

MRS. O'K: What's that, it's not in English?

CONN: No, it's in writin' – now kape that to yourself, here comes the missus!
          (*Enter* CLAIRE.)

CLAIRE: Conn, there is some project on foot to-night to rescue my brother. Don't
  deny it! He has almost confessed as much to Father Dolan. Tell me the truth.

CONN: I would not deçave ye! Well, I promised not to say a word about it; but
    there it is, rade it for yureself!

CLAIRE: (*looking at the note*) Yes, 'tis his hand.

CONN: I knew it in a minute!

CLAIRE: It is in pencil.

CONN: (*turning to* MRS. O'KELLY) I tould ye it wasn't in English.

CLAIRE: (*Reads.*) 'Be at Rathgarron Head to-night beside the tar barrel. When you
    hear two gun-shots in St. Bridget's Abbey, light the fire.'

CONN: The signal fire that's to tell the ship out at sea beyant there to send a boat
    ashore to take him off.

MRS. O'K: Oh, blessed day, is it to escape from jail he'd be thrying?

CLAIRE: He has told my cousin Arte to be in the ruins to-night.

CONN: There's goin' to be a scrimmage, and I'm not to be in it. I'm to be sent
    away like this. It's too hard on me intirely. Oh, if I could find somebody to
    take my place, and fire the signal, I'd bring him out o' jail this night, if I had
    to tear a hole in the wall wid me five fingers.

CLAIRE: I'll take your place.

CONN: You will?

MRS. O'K: Oh Miss Claire, don't go – there's goin' to be gun-shots and bagginets.
    This is one of Conn's divilments – and you will all be murdhered. Oh! wieras-
    thru! what'll I do?

CONN: Will you hould yer whisht?

MRS. O'K: No! I won't. I'll go inform agin ye before you get into throuble, and then
    may be they will let you off asy.

CLAIRE: Here comes the Captain. For Heaven's sake, pacify her. She will betray us.

CONN: Well, come inside mother darlin'. There, I'll stop wid you. Will that aise
    your mind? Come you onsensible ould woman!

MRS. O'K: Ah, Conn, don't lave me alone in the world. Sure I've nobody left but
    yourself, and if you are taken from me, I'll be a widdy.

CONN: Don't ye hear? Miss Claire is goin' to take my place!

MRS. O'K: Heaven bless and purtect every hair of your head, Miss. And will ye
    indeed spend one night by the mother's fire-side?

CONN: An' I'll play all the tunes you love best on my fiddle, till I warm the cockles
    of your ould heart. (*Sings.*)

    Oh, then, Conn, my son, was a fine young man,
    And to every one cuish he had one shin;
    Till he went to the wars of a bloody day,
    When a big cannon-ball whipped his two shins away,
    An' my rickety a –
    (*Exeunt into cottage. Enter* MOLINEUX *and* ARTE.)

ARTE: I invited the Captain to pass the evening at Suil-a-beg, but he will not be
    persuaded.

MOLINEUX: I may not desert my post until the police arrive from Sligo to relieve
    me of my charge.

ARTE: But your soldiers are there.

---

bagginets: bayonets.   *cuish*: armoured thigh-piece.

MOLINEUX: Soldiers will not move without orders; besides, my men have such a distaste for this business that, I believe, if left to defend their prisoner against an attempt to rescue him, they would disgrace themselves.

ARTE: (*aside to* CLAIRE) Get him away! The attempt will be made to-night.

CLAIRE: (*aside to* ARTE) Leave us!

ARTE: Well, good day, Captain. Come, Claire. (*Exit.*)

CLAIRE: (*after a pause*) It is a lovely evening. (*going*)

MOLINEUX: You are going home?

CLAIRE: Not yet. I shall take a stroll along the shore to Rathgarron Head.

MOLINEUX: Alone?

CLAIRE: Yes – I suppose so.

MOLINEUX: Is it far?

CLAIRE: No.

MOLINEUX: Not far – ahem – would you allow me to go part of the way beside you? (*Looks at his watch. Music.*)

CLAIRE: Pray, do not neglect your duty on my account; and besides, I want to consult my feelings in solitude – uninfluenced by your presence.

MOLINEUX: Dear Claire! that sweet confession gives me hope and courage.

CLAIRE: Good night. Leave me; light a meditative cigar and go back to your duty. (*He takes out his cigar case.*) Leave me to wander by the light of the rising moon, and sit down on the rocks beside the sea. (*Takes his box of matches, and lights one for him.*)

MOLINEUX: How good you are – an angel!

CLAIRE: Of light. There now, good night. (*She keeps the box.*)

MOLINEUX: Good night! (*She goes off, very slowly. He moves away – turns.*) Oh, if I had some excuse to – to follow her a little way! She has taken away my box of matches! I envy those lucifers. (*He brushes the light away from the end of his cigar, and calls.*) Miss Ffolliott, pardon me, but my cigar is out, and you – ha! ha! so sorry to trouble you. Oh, don't come back, I beg. (*Follows her out.*)

    (CONN *leaps out of the window and fastens the shutters.*)

CONN: I've locked the dure and barred the shutters.

MRS. O'K: (*inside*) Conn, let me out.

CONN: Behave now, or I'll tell the neighbours you have been dhrinkin'. Good night, mother! (*He runs out.*)

SCENE 5. *The interior of prison. Large window. Old fire-place. Small window. Door. Through window is seen the exterior and courtyard. Night.* ROBERT *discovered listening at door.*

ROBERT: They are relieving guard. I shall not receive another visit for the night. Now to work. That must be the wall Kinchela spoke of. I see some new brick-work there, but where shall I land? Is there much of a drop into the yard below? (*Looks out at window.*) The wall hides the interior – can I reach this window? (*Climbs to small window as* CONN *is seen at large window.*)

CONN: Divil a sowl about this side of the tower. There's a light in his cell. I wondher, is he alone? No matther. Where's my iron pick? Now to make a hole in the wall. (*Disappears.*)

ROBERT: The yard seems to be on the level of this chamber. Where's my chisel? (*Begins to work.*) The mortar is as soft as butter. This was done by government contract. 'Tis an ill wind that blows nobody any – What's that? It sounds like something at work on the wall. Can it be a rat? (*Listens.*) No, it stops now. (*Works.*) There it goes again. (*Stops.*) Now it stops. It echoes me, as if there was someone on the other side. Oh, Lord! my heart sinks at the thought. I'll satisfy myself. (*Goes to small window.*)

CONN: (*appearing at large window*) There's a rat in the chimbley! Gorra! maybe I'm all wrong and himself is not in it at all. (*Looks in at large window as* ROBERT *looks out at small window.*)

ROBERT: I can't see round the corner, but there seems to be no one there.

CONN: Divil a sowl is in it! I wish I could see crooked. Here goes again. (*Disappears.*)

ROBERT: The noise has ceased – it was a rat. (*Works.*) This brick is nearly loose enough to pull out, but if that goes the rest seem shaky. They will fall together. (*A mass of brickwork falls and discovers* CONN.) Conn!

CONN: Whisht! Who the divil would it be? Asy for the love of Heaven now! Come asy! I've left Tatthers in the guard-room wid the men. Stop till I break another coorse of bricks away for ye.
> (*The scene moves, pivots on a point at the back. The prison moves off and shows the exterior of the tower, with* CONN *clinging to the walls and* ROBERT *creeping through the orifice. The walls of the yard appear to occupy three-fourths of the stage. Enter* KINCHELA, DUFF *and four* CONSTABULARY. CONN *and* ROBERT *disappear into the yard.*)

KINCHELA: Whisht! there's a noise in the yard! This door is boulted on the inside, but there's a pile of rubbish shot against the back wall there, we can see over. Harvey Duff, you will stand by there; the rest come wid me. (KINCHELA *and the four* CONSTABULARY *disappear behind wall.* DUFF, *holding a short carbine ready, stands by door with his back to wall.*)

DUFF: Now, my fine fellow; now, Mr. Robert Ffolliott, you said we'd meet once again on this side o' the grave, and so we will – ho! ha! (CONN's *head appears over the wall.*) I don't think you will like this meeting any more than you did the last. (CONN, *after signing to* ROBERT *inside, gets sitting on the wall with his legs dangling just above* DUFF's *head.*) You tould me to have me sowl ready; I wondher if yours is in good condition. Whisht! I hear the boults moving inside. He is coming, he is com – (CONN *drops onto* DUFF's *shoulders, who falls forward with a cry,* CONN *over him. Door opens:* ROBERT *appears.*)

CONN: Run, sir, run – I've got him safe.
> (ROBERT *leaps over* DUFF's *body and runs off. At the same moment, the* SERGEANT, *with a light, appears at the breach in the wall of the prison.*)

SERGEANT: Where is he?

CONN: I've got him – here he is, nivir fear! Hould him fast. Help! (CONSTABULARY *enter by door in the wall and seize* DUFF, *who is lying on his face.*) Don't let him go – hould him down. (*Runs off. They raise* DUFF.)

KINCHELA: (*coming around the corner*) Where is he? Harvey Duff! Bungling fools, he has escaped! (DUFF *gesticulates faintly and falls back. Scene closes in quickly.*)

SCENE 6. *The Coot's Nest. Night. Enter* ROBERT.
ROBERT: Escaped once more! and free. My disguise is secreted here in some nook of the rocks, in Conn's cupboard, as he calls it, but I cannot find it in this darkness. I hope the poor fellow got clear away; I would not have him hurt for my sake. (*A whistle outside heard.*) Ah! there he is. (*Whistles.*) I thank you, kind providence, for protecting him! Here he comes, leaping from crag to rock like a goat.
CONN: (*entering*) Hurroo! Tare an' ages, masther jewel, but we did that well. But it goes agin my conscience I did not crack the skull of that thief when I had him fair and asy under my fut. I'll never get absolution for that!
ROBERT: We must not remain in this place; it is the first they will search. I must make my way at once to St. Bridget's Abbey; there, Arte is waiting for me. Where is my great coat, my hat and beard?
CONN: I have the bundle snug inside; but sure, the Captain knows you in that skin! Didn't he meet yourself here? It will be no cover for you now. Whisht! (*Music.*)
ROBERT: What! do you hear anything?
CONN: No, but Tatthers does. I left the baste to watch on the cliff above. There again! d'ye hear him? He's givin' tongue; lie close, I'll go see what it is. (*Exit.*)
ROBERT: Yonder is the schooner, creeping in with the tide! I can reach the ruins by the seashore; the rocks will conceal me; then one brief moment with my darling girl.
                    (*Re-enter* CONN *with coat, hat and beard.*)
CONN: Spake low – they are close by.
ROBERT: The Constabulary?
CONN: Yes; and wid them those smugglin' thieves, Mangan, Sullivan and Reilly. They are guidin' the polis – the mongrel curs to go do that. They know every hole in these rocks.
ROBERT: But the signal! Who will set the match to the tar-barrel on Rathgarron Head?
CONN: Never fear, sir! Miss Claire is there by this time and waitin' beside it, lookin' and listenin' for the two gunshots your honour will fire in the ruins beyant.
ROBERT: Where is my pistol? (*Feels in his pockets.*) I cannot find it! Gone? No, it cannot be lost! By Heaven! it must have fallen from my pocket as I climbed the wall.
CONN: Murther alive! what will we do now?
ROBERT: I must swim out to the schooner.
CONN: It is a mile, and agin the tide! Stop, will ye lave it to me? and I'll go bail I'll find a way of gettin' them two shots fired for you! Ah, do sir! Only this once give me head and let me go.
ROBERT: What do you propose to do?
CONN: Don't you recollect one time when the Ballyragget hounds couldn't find a

fox. Afther dhrawin' every cover in the counthry, damn the hair o' one could they smell, and the whole field lookin' blue blazes. You were masther o' the hunt. What'll we do at all? ses you. Ye shall have a fox, ses I, and I whipt a red herrin' into the tail o' me coat, and away I wint across the hills.

ROBERT: Ha! ha! I remember it well.

CONN: You hunted me, and divil a one on the whole field but yourself knew there was a two legg'd fox to the fore. Now I'll give them vagabones above another taste of the red herrin'. I will cut in and cross your scent; I'll lade them off, never fear, and be japers I'll show them the finest run of the hunting sayson.

ROBERT: How, Conn, how?

CONN: Asy. Look! they are comin' down the cliff! Slip out this way. Quick! before they catch sight of us. When we get round the Coot's Corner, we divide up. You go by the shore below! I'll take the cliff above. (*Exit* ROBERT.) Oh, begorra! it isn't the first time I've played fox. Oh! this is elegant! (*Exit.*)

SCENE 7. *Rathgarron Head. Enter* CLAIRE *and* MOLINEUX.

CLAIRE: Here we are at Rathgarron Head – are you not tired?

MOLINEUX: I don't know; if you asked me if I was dying, I should say I could not tell. I feel as if it was all a dream, in which I am not myself.

CLAIRE: Who are you then?

MOLINEUX: Somebody much happier than I can ever be! I wish I could describe the change that has taken place in me since we met.

CLAIRE: Oh, I can understand it, for I feel the very – (*stopping suddenly.*)

MOLINEUX: Eh! what do you feel?

CLAIRE: Do you see those ruins on yonder headland? That is St. Bridget's Abbey. A lovely ruin! How effective is that picture with the moon shining upon it.

MOLINEUX: Splendid, no doubt – but when I am beside you, I cannot admire ruins or moonshine. The most effective picture is on this headland, and I cannot detach my eyes from the loveliness before me.

CLAIRE: (*aside*) I cannot stand this! I never played so contemptible a part!

MOLINEUX: What is the matter?

CLAIRE: Go home! Go away! Why did you come here?

MOLINEUX: My dear Miss Ffolliott, I – I hope I have not been intruding on you. If I have, I pray you to forgive me. I will retrace my steps. (*going*)

CLAIRE: No – stop!

MOLINEUX: (*returning*) Yes.

CLAIRE: I encouraged you to follow me.

MOLINEUX: I fear I pressed myself upon you.

CLAIRE: (*aside*) Oh, why is he so willingly deceived? His gentleness and truth make me ashamed of the part I play.

MOLINEUX: I have said or done something to offend you? Tell me what it is! It will afford me much pleasure to plead for pardon.

CLAIRE: You want to know what ails me?

MOLINEUX: Yes.

CLAIRE: Do you see that tar barrel?

MOLINEUX: Good gracious! what has that tar barrel to do with my offence?

CLAIRE: Nothing, but it has everything to do with mine!

MOLINEUX: (*after a pause, aside*) I wonder if there is madness in the family.

CLAIRE: Do you see that tar barrel?

MOLINEUX: I see something like a tar barrel in a pile of brushwood.

CLAIRE: Will you oblige me with a match?

MOLINEUX: Certainly. (*aside*) Poor thing! there's no doubt about it; so lovely, and yet so afflicted! Oh, I feel even more tenderly towards her than I did.

CLAIRE: If I were to ask you to light that bonfire, would you do it?

MOLINEUX: With pleasure. (*aside*) It is the moon that affects her; I wish I had an umbrella.

CLAIRE: Captain Molineux, my brother has escaped from the prison guarded by your soldiers; he is now in yonder ruins. This pile of fuel, when lighted, will be the signal for the schooner you see yonder to send a boat ashore to take off the fugitive. I have been a decoy to entice you away from your duty, so that I might deprive your men of the orders they await to pursue my brother, who has broken jail. Now do you understand my conduct?

MOLINEUX: Miss Ffolliott –

CLAIRE: Now do you understand why every tender word you have spoken has tortured me like poison? why every throb of your honest heart has been a knife in mine?

MOLINEUX: I thought you were mad; I fear 'tis I have been so.

CLAIRE: You can redeem your professional honour. You can repair the past. I have no means here of lighting that beacon; if the signal is not fired, my brother will be recaptured. But the blood that now revolts in my heart against what I am doing is the same that beats in his. He would disdain to owe his liberty to my duplicity and to your infatuation. There's your road! Good night. (*Exit hastily. Music.*)

MOLINEUX: So I have been her dupe – no, she was not laughing at me! (*Looks off.*) She is not laughing as one who – see where she has thrown herself on the ground. I hear her sobs. I cannot leave her alone, and in this wild place; and yet what can I do to – to – poor thing! I – I don't know how to act. There again – oh! what a moan that was! I cannot let her lie there. (*Exit hastily.*)

SCENE 8. *The ruins of St. Bridget's Abbey.* ARTE *discovered kneeling before the broken shrine.* MOYA *is looking off, down the cliff.*

MOYA: There's not a sound to be heard barrin' the sheam o' the waves, as they lick the shore below.

ARTE: I was afraid to come here alone. Even with you beside me I tremble.

MOYA: There's something movin' in the strand below. Look, Miss! Is it a goat? There it is, creeping along undher the shadow of the rocks.

ARTE: I see nothing.

MOYA: Whisht! I'll give him the offis. (*She sings.*)
(*Enter* DUFF, SULLIVAN, REILLY *and* MANGAN, SULLIVAN *and* MANGAN *carrying carbines.*)

DUFF: There they are. There's a pair o' them – 'tis Moya wid her. The Constabulary are givin' him chase. But here is where he will run to airth. Here's the thrap, and there's the bait.

VI The shooting of Conn in the ruins of St. Bridget's Abbey in Act II, scene 8 of *The Shaughraun*

ARTE: There! There he is! And see! Those men pursue him. Fly, Robert, fly!

MOYA: They will catch him, Miss.

ARTE: No, he gains upon them. He has turned the point. He will scale the cliff on this side. (*Crosses as if to meet him.*)

DUFF: (*seizing* MOYA) Reilly, take hould of her, quick!
            (REILLY *seizes* ARTE, *and drags her to front of shrine.*)

ARTE: Who are you, who dare to lay hands on me? Do you know who I am?

DUFF: Yes I do, well enough. You are the sweetheart of the man we want to catch.

ARTE: (*shouting*) Robert! Robert! Beware!

DUFF: Stop her screeching! She'll scare him off!

MOYA: Help! Murther! Thieves! Fire!

DUFF: Hould yur yelp, or I'll choke you! Gorra, she's bitin' me!

MOYA: Don't come here! Don't come! (DUFF *stifles her cries with her cloak.*)

KINCHELA: (*leaping over the parapet*) We have lost his track!

DUFF: Ay, but we have found it. Here he comes! Stand close, now, and head him off! (KINCHELA *disappears. The figure of* ROBERT *is seen emerging from one side of the ruins. He advances.* SULLIVAN *and* MANGAN *start out.* ROBERT *looks from side to side.*) Stand and surrender! (ROBERT *rushes up the ruins to window at back.*) Fire, Sullivan! Give it to him! Why don't you fire? (SULLIVAN *fires. The shot takes effect.* ROBERT *falls and rolls down to a lower platform.*) Ha! ha! that stopped him – he's got it! (ROBERT *raises himself and faintly tries to escape by a breach in the wall.*) Give it to him agin! (MANGAN *fires. Light Rathgarron fire instantly on second shot.* ROBERT *falls, and tumbling from one platform to another, rolls over on his face on the stage.* REILLY *releases* ARTE, *who falls fainting at the shrine.*)

KINCHELA: (*appearing*) What are you about? Those two shots are the signal; and see! the fire is lighted on Rathgarron Head.

DUFF: 'Tis lighted too late.

KINCHELA: No – for there comes the boat from the schooner; and see that man in the water, swimming towards her! 'Tis Robert Ffolliott escaped!

DUFF: Oho! if that's Robert Ffolliott, I'd like to know who's this?

CONN: (*raising himself slowly, and allowing his hat and beard to fall back; and facing* DUFF *with a smile on his bloodstained face*) The Shaughraun! (*He falls back.*)
            (MOYA, *who has been released by* DUFF *in his astonishment, utters a faint cry, and throws herself upon the body. A ray of moonlight, striking through the ruined window, falls on the figure of the Saint on the shrine, whose extended arms seem to invoke protection over the prostrate group.*)

ALL: The Shaughraun!

          ACT III

SCENE 1. MRS. O'KELLY'*s Cottage. Music. Enter* FATHER DOLAN *and* CLAIRE.

DOLAN: Be patient, Claire.

CLAIRE: Patient! My cousin has disappeared – no trace of Arte can be found.

Moya also has been spirited away – perhaps murdered, as they murdered Conn!

DOLAN: (*knocking at door*) Mrs. O'Kelly. 'Tis I, Father Dolan.

        (*Enter* MRS. O'KELLY.)

MRS. O'K: Blessings on your path – it always leads to the poor and to the sore-hearted.

DOLAN: This is a sad business. Did you hear why they killed your poor boy?

MRS' O'K: (*sobbing*) Because he'd got a fine shuite o' clothes on him. They shot at the man that wasn't in it – and they killed my poor boy.

CLAIRE: Did they bring him home insensible?

MRS. O'K: No, Miss, they brought him home on a shutter, and there now he lies, wid Tatthers beside him. The crature won't let a hand go near the body.

CLAIRE: Poor fellow. He met his death while aiding my brother to escape. (*Enter* MOLINEUX.) You see what your men have done!

MRS. O'K: It was the polis, not the sodgers, murdhered him. Don't blame the Captain, Miss. God bless him, sure, he was in my cabin before daylight. He never spoke a word, but he put five goolden pounds in my hand; and thanks to himself my Conn will have the finest wake this day! wid Nancy Malone and Biddy Madigan for keeners. And there will be atin' and dhrinkin', and six of the O'Kellys to carry him out as grand as a Mimber o' Parliament. Och–hone, my darlin' boy, it will be a proud day for you; but your poor ould mother will be left all alone in her cabin buried alive, while yourself is going to Glory. Och–o–o–hone! (*Exit crying.*)

MOLINEUX: In the name of Bedlam, does she propose to give a dance and a supper-party in honour of the melancholy occasion?

CLAIRE: They are only going to wake poor Conn.

DOLAN: And your five pounds will be spent in whisky and cakes and consolation and fiddlers and grief, with meat and drink for the poor.

MOLINEUX: What a compound! You Irish do mix up your –

CLAIRE: (*interrupting him*) Never mind what we mix. Have you discovered any traces of Arte and Moya? What have you done?

MOLINEUX: I have been thinking.

CLAIRE: Thinking! What's the good of thinking? My cousin has been stolen – where is she? The county is full of police and soldiers, yet two girls have been carried off under your noses – perhaps murdered for all you know or care! And there you stand like a goose – thinking!

MOLINEUX: Pray don't be so impetuous. You Irish –

CLAIRE: And I won't be called, 'you Irish'!

MOLINEUX: I beg pardon. You do make me so nervous.

CLAIRE: Oh, do I? My impetuosity didn't make you nervous last night, did it? No matter! Go on! A penny for your thoughts.

MOLINEUX: If Miss O'Neal and Moya were present in the ruins when Conn was shot, they must have been witnesses to the deed. Since then, they have disappeared. It struck me that those who killed the boy must have some reason for removing all evidence of the transaction.

DOLAN: He is right.

CLAIRE: Well?

MOLINEUX: I questioned the Constabulary, and find they had no hand in it. The deed was done by a posse of fellows assembled to assist in the pursuit by a police agent named Harvey Duff.

DOLAN and CLAIRE: Harvey Duff!

MOLINEUX: You know him?

CLAIRE: He has thought it out while we have been blundering. Blinded by our tears, we could not see. Deafened by our own complaints, we could not hear. (*Seizes both his hands.*) Forgive me!

MOLINEUX: There she goes again! I've done nothing to deserve all this.

CLAIRE: Nothing! You have unearthed the fox; you have drawn the badger. Now the rogue is in sight, our course is clear.

MOLINEUX: Is it? I confess I don't see it.

DOLAN: These two girls were the only witnesses of the deed!

CLAIRE: And that is why they have been carried off.

DOLAN: No one else was present to prove how Conn was killed.

CONN: (*looking out at the window*) Yes, I was there.

ALL: Conn! Alive!

CONN: Whisht! no, I'm dead!

DOLAN: Why, you provoking vagabond! Is this the way you play on our feelings? Are you hurt?

CONN: I've a crack over the lug an' a scratch across the small o' me back. Sure, Miss, unless I dhrawed them to shoot, you would never have had the signal.

MOLINEUX: Brave fellow! How did you escape?

CONN: I'll tell you sir; but whoo! gorra! they say dead men tell no tales, and here I am takin' away the caracther of the corporation. When the Masther got out o' the jail, there was Kinchela and his gang outside waitin' to murdher us. We ga' them the slip, and while the Masther got off, I led them away afther me to St. Bridget's. There, afther I got them two shots out o' them, I rouled down and lay as quiet as a sack o' pitates.

CLAIRE: Arte and Moya were in the ruins?

CONN: They were standin' by, and thryin' to screech blue murdher. Stop their mouths, ses a voice I knew was Kinchela. Reilly and Sullivan whipt them up and put them on a car that was waitin' outside. Afther that, sorra a thing I remember till I found myself laid out on a table wid candles all round me, and whisky bottles an' cakes an' sugar an' tobacco an' lemon an' bacon an' snuff and the devil an' all! I thought I was in Heaven!

DOLAN: And that's his idea of Heaven! And you let your poor old mother believe you dead? You did not relieve her sorrow?

CONN: Would you have me spile a wake? Afther invitin' all the neighbours!

MOLINEUX: Will you allow me, on this occasion, to say 'You Irish'?

CLAIRE: Yes, and you need not say any more.

CONN: Then I remembered the polis would be wantin' me for the share I had in helpin' the Masther to break jail. Ah, sir! don't let on to the mother; she'd never hould her whisht, and I want to be dead if yez plaze, to folly up the blackguards that have hoult of Moya and Miss O'Neal.

MOLINEUX: Do you know the place where these ruffians resort?

CONN: I'm concaited I do.

DOLAN: I'll answer for him; he knows every disreputable den in the county.

CONN: What would you do now if I didn't?

CLAIRE: Here comes your mother with the mourners.

CONN: Hoo! she'll find some of the whisky gone! (*Disappears at window.*)

CLAIRE: Now what is to be done?

MOLINEUX: I will proceed to Ballyragget House and see Mr. Kinchela. I'll confront him with this evidence!

CLAIRE: You don't know him.

MOLINEUX: I think I do, but he does not know me.

CLAIRE: You will fight him?

MOLINEUX: Oh no! I looked in his eye – there's no fight there! Men who bully women have the courage of the cur; there's no pluck in them. I shall take a guard and arrest him for aiding your brother to escape that he might murder him safely during his flight.

CLAIRE: Who can prove it?

> (*Enter* ROBERT.)

ROBERT: I can!

CLAIRE: Robert! (*They embrace.*)

DOLAN: Good gracious – what brings you back?

ROBERT: The news I heard on board the schooner. A pardon has been granted to the Fenian prisoners.

CLAIRE: A pardon!

MOLINEUX: I congratulate you, sir. Oh, by Jove! Excuse my swearing, but a light breaks in upon me. Kinchela knew of this pardon. I'll go to Ballyragget House at once.

ROBERT: I have just come from there. I went there to tax him with his villainy. He has fled.

MOLINEUX: I thought there was no fight in him.

CLAIRE: But Arte is in his power.

ROBERT: Arte in his power! What do you mean?

CLAIRE: He loves her; he has carried her off!

ROBERT: My wife and my fortune! ha! he played for a high game.

MOLINEUX: And, on finding he could not win, he stole half the stakes.

DOLAN: This man is in league with a desperate crew, half ruffians, half smugglers; their dens, known only to themselves, are in the bogs and caves of the seashore.

ROBERT: I'll unearth him wherever he is. (*Music.*) I'll hunt him with every honest lad in the County Sligo in the pack, and then kill him like a rat!

MOLINEUX: I'll send over to Sligo and get a warrant to arrest this fellow. I like to have the law on my side. If we are to hunt, let us have a licence. Where shall I find you?

DOLAN: At my house.

CLAIRE: (*to* ROBERT, *who offers his arm to her*) No; give your arm to Father Dolan.

DOLAN: Free, and at home. Heaven be praised!

ROBERT: Not free till Arte is so. (*Exit with* FATHER DOLAN.)

CLAIRE: (*After watching them off, turns and advances rapidly to* MOLINEUX.)
What's your Christian name, or have you English such things amongst you?
MOLINEUX: Yes; my Christian name is Harry.
CLAIRE: Harry! (*They embrace. She runs off. He pulls down his tunic, puts his
cap on one side, and goes off whistling 'The British Grenadiers'.*)
VOICES: (*outside*) Oh, ohone! Oh, hould up! Don't give way!
            (*Enter several* MEN *and* WOMEN. *They enter cabin at once. Then*
            MRS. O'KELLY, NANCY MALONE *and* BIDDY MADIGAN,
            smoking pipe.)
MRS. O'K: You are kindly welcome. The dark cloud is over the house, but –
NANCY: We come to share the sorrow that's in it this hour.
BIDDY: It will be a fine berryin', Mrs. O'Kelly! There will be a grand waste of
victuals.
MRS. O'K: Step inside, ma'am.
            (*They all enter the cabin. A woman enters and goes into the cabin.
            Then* REILLY – *very red and sandy* – *and* SULLIVAN – *very pale
            and dark. Music. The voices of the Keeners are heard inside, singing
            an Irish lament. Scene changes.*)

SCENE 2. *Interior of* MRS. O'KELLY's *cabin.* CONN *is lying on a shutter, supported on two ricketty chairs, a three-legged stool and a keg. Tables covered with
food and drinking cups.*

TABLEAU OF AN IRISH WAKE.

A group of women near CONN. MRS. O'KELLY *seated,* NANCY MALONE *and*
REILLY *near her. The women seated are rocking to and fro during the wail.*

CHORUS: 'The Oolaghaun'.

MALE VOICES:	Och! Oolaghaun! Och! Oolaghaun!
	Make his bed both wide and deep;
	Och! Oolaghaun! Och! Oolaghaun!
	He's only gone to sleep.
FEMALE VOICES:	Why did ye die? Oh, why did ye die?
	And lave us all alone to cry?
TOGETHER:	Why did ye die? Why did ye die?
	Laving us to sigh och hone?
	Why did ye die? Why did ye die?
	Oolaghaun! oh, Oolaghaun!

            (*During the following rhapsody, the music of the wail and the
            Chorus, subdued, recurs, as if to animate the keeners.*)
BIDDY: Oh, ho! oho! (*rocking herself*) Oh-oo, Oolaghaun! The widdy had a son –
an only son – wail for the widdy!
ALL: Why did ye die? Why did ye die?

Oolaghaun: an act of lamentation – also a traditional keening refrain.

BIDDY: I seen her when she was a fair young girl – a fair girl wid a child at her breast.

ALL: Laving us to sigh och hone.

BIDDY: Then I see a proud woman wid a boy by her side – he was bould as a bull-calf that runs by the side of a cow.

ALL: Why did ye die? Why did ye die?

BIDDY: For the girl grew ould as the child grew big, and the woman grew wake as the boy grew strong. (*rising and flinging back her hair*) The boy grew strong, for she fed him wid her heart's blood. Ah, hogoola! Where is he now? Could in his bed. Oh, why did ye die? (*Sits.*)

ALL: Oolaghaun!

BIDDY: None was like him – none could compare – and (*aside*) good luck t'ye, gi' me a dhrop of somethin' to put the sperret in one, for the fire is gettin' low. (SULLIVAN *hands her his jug of punch.*)

MRS. O'K: Oh! oh! 'tis mighty consolin' to hear this. Mrs. Malone, you are not atin'?

NANCY: No, ma'am, I'm dhrinkin'. I dhrink now and agin by way of variety. Biddy is not up to herself.

REILLY: Oh, wait till she'll rise on the top of a noggin.

BIDDY: (*placing the jug beside her after drinking*) He was brave. He was open-handed. He had the heart of a lion and the legs of a fox. (CONN *takes the jug and empties it quietly, unobserved by the rest, then replaces it.*) His voice was softer than the cuckoo of an evenin', and sweeter than the blackbird afther a summer shower. Wail, ye colleens! you will never hear the voice of Conn again. (*Blows her nose.*)

CONN: (*aside*) It's a mighty pleasant thing to die like this, once in a way, and hear all the good things said about you afther you are dead and gone.

BIDDY: His name will be the pride of the O'Kellys for evermore.

CONN: (*aside*) I was a big blackguard when I was alive.

BIDDY: Noble and beautiful.

CONN: (*aside*) Ah, go on out o' that!

BIDDY: (*taking up her jug*) Oh, he was sweet and sthrong – who the divil's been at my jug of punch?

> (*Knock at door. Enter* MOLINEUX. *They all rise.* MRS. O'KELLY *wipes down chair for him.*)

MOLINEUX: I do not come to disturb this – a – melancholy – a – entertainment. I mean – a – this festive solemnity.

MRS. O'K: Heaven bless your honour for comin' to admire the last of him. (*leading him to* CONN) Here he is – ain't he beautiful?

MOLINEUX: (*aside*) The vagabond is winking at me!

MRS. O'K: Look at him! How often I put him to bed as a child and sung him to sleep. Now he will be put to bed wid a shovel, and oh! the song was never sung that will awaken him.

MOLINEUX: If any words could put life into him, I have come here to speak them. (*Music.*) Robert Ffolliott has been pardoned, and has returned home a free man.

ALL: Hurroo! Hurroo!

MOLINEUX: But his home is desolate, for the girl he loved has been stolen away. The man who robbed him of his liberty first, then his estate, now has stolen his betrothed.

ALL: Who has done it? Who –

MOLINEUX: Mr. Corry Kinchela! The ruffians who shot the brave fellow who lies there were led by Kinchela's agent, Harvey Duff.

ALL: Harvey Duff!

> (BIDDY *seizes axe.* MRS. O'KELLY *crosses to fire for poker.* DONOVAN *gets scythe and file.* PEASANTS *rush for various implements that are about the stage.* MOLINEUX *comes on* BIDDY *with axe, backs to* MRS. O'KELLY *with poker, turns to* DONOVAN *with scythe, whom he eyes with his glass.*)

BIDDY: Harvey Duff sent my only boy across the say!

DONOVAN: I've a long reckoning agin him; but I've kept it warm in my heart. (*whetting scythe*)

MRS. O'K: I've a short one, and there it lies!

ALL: Where is he?

MOLINEUX: Kinchela and this man are hiding in some den where they hold Miss O'Neal and Moya prisoners.

ALL: Moya Dolan?

MOLINEUX: The niece of your minister; the sweetheart of poor Conn. My men shall aid you in the search, but you are familiar with every hole and corner in the county – you must direct it. Robert Ffolliott awaits you all at Suil-a-beg to lead the hunt – that is, after you have paid your melancholy respects to the Shaughraun.

MRS. O'K: No! You could not plaze him betther than to go now. Bring back the news that you have revenged his murdher, then he will go under the sod wid a light heart.

ALL: Hurroo! To Suil-a-beg! To Suil-a-beg!

> (*Exeunt. When the crowd is off* REILLY *watches at door,* SULLIVAN *at window.* MOLINEUX *gives* CONN *snuff; he sneezes. Seeing* MOLINEUX, REILLY *seizes pitcher and pretends to drink;* SULLIVAN *plays with his whiskers. They watch* MOLINEUX *off, then rush downstage.*)

REILLY: Sullivan, you must warn Kinchela. Quick! there's not an hour to lose.

SULLIVAN: Where will I find him?

> (CONN *rises and listens.*)

REILLY: At the Coot's Nest. The lugger came in last night. Tell him to get aboard, take the two women with him, for he will have to run for his life.

SULLIVAN: Ay, bedad, and for ours too! If he's caught we're in for it.

> (CONN *creeps to the door and locks it – very quietly.*)

REILLY: I feel the rope around my beck.

SULLIVAN: The other end of it is chokin' me.

REILLY: Away wid ye then, while I go warn Harvey Duff.

> (*As they turn to go, they face* CONN. *They stagger back and look at the shutter.*)

BOTH: Murdher alive!

CONN: That's it – murdher alive is what I am! Murdher that'll live to see you both hung for it. I'll be at your wake, and begorra I'll give ye both a fine characther. (*They rush for door.*) Asy boys, asy. The dure is fast, and here's the key. You are in a fine thrap – ho, ho! Yez made a mistake last night. (SULLIVAN *whispers to* REILLY.) Take it asy now. (*They rush to table, and each seizes a knife.*)

REILLY: Did ye forget, ma bouchal, that you are dead?

SULLIVAN: (*advancing slowly*) Sure, if we made a mistake last night, we can repair it now.

CONN: Oh! Tare an' ages – what'll I do? (*Retreats behind table.*)

REILLY: We'll just lay you out comfortable agin where you wor. Divil a sowl will be any the wiser.

CONN: Help! help!

(REILLY *advances and receives the contents of a jug; then* SULLIVAN, *who gets the snuff in his eyes.*)

REILLY: They are all miles away by this time. Schreechin' won't save you.

CONN: (*running to the window and dashing it open*) Help!

(REILLY *and* SULLIVAN *drag him back and throw him down.*)

SULLIVAN: Shut the windy – I'll quiet him.

(*As* REILLY *rushes up,* MOLINEUX *appears at window.*)

MOLINEUX: Drop those knives. (*a pause*) Do you hear what I said? Drop those knives. (*They let the knives fall.*) Now open this door.

CONN: There's the key. (*Hands it to* REILLY, *who doggedly unlocks door.*)

MOLINEUX: Now. (REILLY *makes a start as if he would escape.* MOLINEUX *presents pistol.*) If you put your head outside the cabin, I'll put a bullet in it. (*Appears at the door.*)

CONN: (*to* SULLIVAN) Help me up – the hangman will do as much for you one o' these days. (SULLIVAN *helps* CONN *to rise.*)

MOLINEUX: What men are these?

CONN: Two of Kinchela's chickens. They know the road we want to thravel.

MOLINEUX: Take that. (*Hands* CONN *the revolver.*) Do you know how to use it?

CONN: I'll thry – (*Turns to* SULLIVAN *and points pistol.*)

MOLINEUX: (*drawing his sword and turning to* REILLY.) Attention, my friend. Now put your hands in your pockets. (*Repeats.* REILLY *obeys him doggedly.*) That's right. Now take me direct to where your employer, Mr. Kinchela, has imprisoned Miss O'Neal; and if, on our road, you take your hands out of your pockets and attempt to move beyond the reach of my sword, upon my honour as an officer and a gentleman, I shall cut you down. Forward! (*Exeunt.*)

CONN: Attention – put your hand in my pocket. (SULLIVAN *obeys him.*) Now take me straight to where Moya Dolan is shut up; and if you stir a peg out o' that on the road, by the piper that played before Julius Caesar, I'll save the county six feet of rope. (*As they go out, the scene changes.*)

---

bouchal: boy.

SCENE 3. *Hogan's Shanty. Enter* ARTE *and* MOYA.

ARTE: 'Tis getting dark. Will they keep us another night in this fearful place?

MOYA: I don't care what becomes of me. I wish they would kill me as they killed Conn. I've nothin' to live for.

ARTE: I have. I'll live to bring Kinchela to the dock where he brought my Robert. I'll live to tear the mask from his face.

MOYA: I'd like to put my ten commandments on the face of Harvey Duff, the murderin' villain! If I could only live to see him go up a ladder and spoil a market.

> (*Enter* KINCHELA.)

KINCHELA: You look pale, but I see you kape a proud lip still, Miss O'Neal. Oh, you despise me now, but afther a month or two, never fear we'll get on finely together.

ARTE: Do you dream you can keep us here for a month? Why, before a week has passed there's not a sod in the County Sligo but will be turned over to search for us – and then we'll see who will look the paler, you or I.

KINCHELA: Before midnight, you will be safe on board a lugger that lies snug beside this shanty; and before daylight, we will be on our way to a delightful retirement, where you and I will pass our honeymoon together.

MOYA: And what's to become of me?

> (*Music. Enter* DUFF *with* MANGAN *and* DOYLE.)

DUFF: I'll take care of you. The wind is fair, and the tide will serve in an hour. Come ladies, all aboard is the word if you plaze.

> (MANGAN *and* DOYLE *seize* ARTE *and* MOYA.)

ARTE: Kinchela, I implore you not to add this cowardly act to your list of crimes. Release me and this girl, and on my honour I will bear no witness against you or against any concerned in last night's work.

DUFF: It is too late.

ARTE: (*struggling with* DOYLE) Kinchela, if you have any respect, any love for me, will you see me outraged thus?

DUFF: (*aside to* KINCHELA) Ffolliott has returned!

KINCHELA: Ha! Away with them.

> (DOYLE *takes out* ARTE.)

MOYA: (*to* MANGAN) Lave your hould! I'll go asy. (*Drops her cloak struggling with* MANGAN, *tears herself free, boxes his ears, and runs off, chased by* MANGAN.)

DUFF: Robert Ffolliott is pardoned, and he is hunting the bogs this minute with half the County Sligo at his back.

KINCHELA: Never fear; they can't discover this place until we are gone. No one ever knew of it but our own fellows.

DUFF: And Conn the Shaughraun.

KINCHELA: He is wiped out.

DUFF: We are safe.

KINCHELA: Go, keep watch on the cliff above, while I get these girls aboard.

DUFF: I'll be onaisy in my mind till we are clear out o' this. (*Exit.*)

KINCHELA: Robert Ffolliott pardoned, afther all the trouble I took to get him convicted! and this is the way a loyal man is thrated! I'm betrayed. No matther. If he can recover his estate, he can't recover his wife. She will be mine – mine! She hates me now – but I concait she will get over that. (*Exit.*)

    (*After a pause,* CONN *and* SULLIVAN *enter.*)

CONN: Not a sowl in it. You deceived me.

SULLIVAN: No! They are here. (*Points to cloak.*) What's that?

CONN: Moya's cloak! (*Runs to pick it up, releasing* SULLIVAN, *who creeps off while* CONN *examines cloak.*) 'Tis hers – she's here! He's off – gone to rouse up the whole pack! What will I do? Where can I hide until the Captain and the masther come up? They can't be far behind. If I could get behind one of them big hogsheads, or inside one o' them. Whisht! There was a cry. 'Twas Miss O'Neal's voice. I'm only one agin twenty, but I'll make it lively for them while it lasts. (*Wait scene-change till* CONN *is in barrel.*)

SCENE 4. *A shed looking out upon a rocky cove. The top masts of a ship are seen over the edge of the precipice. Bales, kegs, hogsheads, naval gear lie about. Music. Enter* DUFF *rapidly. He looks round – he is very pale.*

DUFF: Kinchela, hurry – quick!

    (*Enter* KINCHELA.)

KINCHELA: What's the matter?

DUFF: I was watching on the cliff above, where I could hear the shouts of the people in the glen as they hunted every hole in the rocks. I could see Robert Ffolliott and Miss Claire houndin' them on; when I turned my eyes down here, and on this very place where we are standing I saw –

KINCHELA: Who?

DUFF: Conn the Shaughraun!

KINCHELA: You are mad with fright!

DUFF: So would you be if you'd seen a dead man as plain as I saw him! (*Distant cries and shouts are heard.*) D'ye hear them? They are getting close to us.

KINCHELA: Go back to your post on the cliff, and keep watch while I get these women on board. We have no time to lose. Mangan! Doyle!

DUFF: (*looking round*) I'll be on my oath I saw him here.

    (*Enter* MOYA *and* MANGAN.)

MOYA: Where do you want me to go?

KINCHELA: On board that ship below there.

MOYA: D'ye think I'm a fly or a saygull?

KINCHELLA: You see this ladder? By that road you can gain the ledge below. There we'll find a basket will send you down like a bucket in a well.

MOYA: And if I don't choose to go down?

KINCHELA: Then you'll be carried, my beauty!

MOYA: Stand off!

KINCHELA: Tie her hands! Mangan, go get me a taste of a rope. (*Seizes her as* MANGAN *exits.*)

MOYA: Help! Oh, is there never a man widin reach of my voice?

KINCHELA: Mangan, bring the rope, curse you!

MOYA: Help! Murdher! Fire!

(*A shot is fired from the bunghole of a hogshead.* KINCHELA *throws up his hands, staggers back, and falls.* MOYA *utters a cry, and falls on her knees, covering her face with her hands. The hogshead rises a little, advances to* MOYA, *and covers her like an extinguisher. The legs of* CONN *have been seen under the barrel as it moves. Enter* MANGAN *with the rope,* DOYLE *with* ARTE, *and* SULLIVAN, *who kneels over* KINCHELA.)

MANGAN: Who fired that shot? Where's Moya?

DOYLE: She has killed him and escaped.

ARTE: Brave girl! She has avenged me.

SULLIVAN: He's not dead. See, he moves – there's life in him still.
    (*Shouts outside heard.*)

DOYLE: They are coming! Away wid ye to the lugger – quick!

SULLIVAN: Must we lave him here?

DOYLE: We can't carry him down the ladder.

SULLIVAN: Every one for himself – the divil take the hindmost!
    (*All three rush towards ladder.*)

ARTE: (*who has crept up unseen during the foregoing and who is now lifting the ladder*) Stop where you are! (*Throws the ladder over.*) I have been your prisoner; now you are mine.
    (*Shouts outside nearer. The men look bewildered from side to side, and then rush off.* CONN *knocks off top of hogshead and looks out.*)

CONN: Is that you, Miss?

ARTE: Conn, where's Moya?

CONN: She's inside. (*Raises hogshead, and they emerge from it.*)

DUFF: (*outside*) Kinchela, away with you! Quick!

CONN: Stand aside! Here comes the flower of the flock. (*They hide.*)

DUFF: (*rushing on, very pale*) The crowd are upon us! We are betrayed! What's the matter, man? Up, I tell you! Are you drunk? or mad? Stop, then! I'm off! (*Runs to ladder.*) The ladder gone! Gone! (*Runs to* KINCHELA.) Shpake, man! What will we do? What does it mean?
    (ARTE *appears from behind shed,* MOYA *from behind hogshead.*)

MOYA: It means that the wind has changed, and the tide doesn't serve.

ARTE: It means that you are on your way to a delightful retirement, where you and he will pass your honeymoon together.
    (CONN *appears.*)

DUFF: Conn! The murdher's out!

CONN: And you are in for it! (*shouts outside*) D'ye hear them cries? The hounds are on your track, Harvey Duff.

DUFF: Oh, what will I do? What will I do?

CONN: Say your prayers – if you ever knew any – for your time is come. Look! There they come, down the cliff-side! Ha! They've caught sight of you.
    (DUFF *rushes up to the edge of the precipice, looks over, wrings his hands in*

---

extinguisher: candle-snuffer.

terror.) D'ye see that wild ould woman wid the knife – that's Bridget Madigan whose son's life you swore away.

DUFF: Save me! You can! They will tear me to pieces. (*on his knees to* ARTE)

CONN: D'ye know Andy Donovan? That's him wid the scythe. You sent his young brother across the say. (*shouts outside*) Egorra, he knows you! Look at him!

DUFF: (*on his knees to* CONN) Spare me! Pity me!

CONN: Ay, as you spared me! As you spared them at whose side you knelt before the altar! As you pitied them whose salt you ate, but whose blood you dhrank! There's death coming down on you from above – there's death waiting for you below. Mr. Harvey Duff, take your choice.

> (DUFF, *bewildered with fright, and running alternately to the edge of the cliff and back to look at the approaching crowd, staggers like a drunken man, uttering inarticulate cries of fear. The crowd, headed by* BIDDY MADIGAN *and* NANCY MALONE *rush in.Uttering a scream of terror,* DUFF *leaps over the cliff. The crowd pursue him to the edge and lean over. Enter* CLAIRE, FATHER DOLAN *and* ROBERT.)

ROBERT: (*embracing* ARTE) Arte!

CLAIRE: Has the villain escaped?

> (*Enter* MOLINEUX, *followed by the* SERGEANT *and six* SOLDIERS, *with* MANGAN, SULLIVAN, REILLY *and* DOYLE *in custody.*)

MOLINEUX: I have bagged a few, but we missed the principal offender.

CONN: I didn't – there's my bird!

DOLAN: Is he dead?

MOLINEUX: (*approaching* KINCHELA *and examining him*) I fear not. The bullet has entered here, but it has struck something in his breast. (*Draws out a pocket-book.*) This pocket-book has saved his life. (*Hands it to* FATHER DOLAN, *who opens it, draws out a letter and reads.*)

KINCHELA: (*reviving and rising*) Where am I?

MOLINEUX: You are in custody.

KINCHELA: What for?

MOLINEUX: For an attempt to assassinate this gentleman.

KINCHELA: He was a felon escaping from justice.

DOLAN: He was a free man, and you knew it – as this letter proves!

> (*The crowd utter a cry of rage, and advance towards* KINCHELA. FATHER DOLAN *stands between them and him, while* KINCHELA *flies to the constabulary.*)

KINCHELA: Save me! Protect me!

DOLAN: (*facing crowd*) Stand back! D'ye hear me? Must I speak twice?

> (*The crowd retire, and lower their weapons.*)

MOLINEUX: Take him away!

KINCHELA: Yes, take me away! Quick! Don't you hear? or them divils won't give you the chance. (*Exit with* CONSTABULARY.)

MRS. O'K: (*outside*) Where's my boy? Where is he?

CONN: Och, murdher! Here's the ould mother. Hide me!

> (*Enter* MRS. O'KELLY.)

MRS. O'K: Where is he? Where is my vagabone? (FATHER DOLAN *brings him*
forward by the ear.) Oh, Conn, you thief o' the world! My boy, my darlin'.
(*Falls on his neck – then whacks him.*)

CONN: Whisht, mother, don't cry! And see this, I'll never be kilt agin.

MOYA: Sure, if he hadn't been murdhered, he couldn't have saved us.

MRS. O'K: And afther lettin' me throw all the money away over the wake!

MOLINEUX: Turn the ceremony into a wedding. I really don't see that you Irish
make much distinction.

CLAIRE: I believe that in England the wedding often turns out the more melancholy occasion of the two.

MOLINEUX: Will you try?

ROBERT: He has earned you, Claire. I give my consent.

ARTE: But what's to become of Conn? Father Dolan will never give his consent.

DOLAN: (*to* CONN) Come here, you vagabond. Will you reform?

CONN: I don't know what that is, but I will.

DOLAN: Will you mend your ways and your coat? No, you can't. How do I know
but you will go poaching of a night?

CONN: Moya will go bail I won't.

DOLAN: And the dhrink?

MOYA: I will take care there is no hole in the thimble.

DOLAN: I won't trust either of you – you have decaved me so often. Can you find
anyone to answer for you?

CONN: Oh murdher! What'll I do? Divil a friend I have in the world, barrin'
Tatthers! (MOYA *whispers in his ear.*) Oh, they won't.

MOYA: Thry!

CONN: (*to the audience*) She says you will go bail for me.

MOYA: I didn't.

CONN: You did.

MOYA: I didn't.

CONN: You are the only friend I have. Long life t'ye! Many a time you have
looked over my faults. Will you be blind to them now, and hould out your
hands once more to a poor Shaughraun?

ALL: Hurroo! Hurroo! (*till curtain*)

APPENDIX A A Source for *Jessie Brown*

Boucicault would have known no more than any intelligent newspaper reader about the events of 1857 in India. He cites, in particular, one press report:

The following account is taken from the letters of a lady, one of the rescued on the 26th of September, when Lucknow was relieved by the forces under Sir Colin Campbell.

'Death stared us in the face. We were fully persuaded that in twenty-four hours all would be over. The Engineers had said so, and all knew the worst. We women strove to encourage each other, and to perform the light duties which had been assigned to us, such as conveying orders to the batteries, and supplying men with provisions, especially cups of coffee, which we prepared day and night. I had gone to try and make myself useful, in company with Jessie Brown. Poor Jessie had been in a state of restless excitement all through the siege, and had fallen away visibly within the last few days. A constant fever consumed her, and her mind wandered occasionally, especially on that day, when the recollections of home seemed powerfully present to her. At last overcome with fatigue, she lay down on the ground, wrapped up in her plaid. I sat beside her, promising to awaken her when, as she said, "her father should return from ploughing". She at length fell into a profound slumber, motionless and apparently breathless, her head resting in my lap. I myself could no longer resist the temptation to sleep, in spite of the continual roar of the cannon. Suddenly I was aroused by a wild unearthly scream close to my ear; my companion stood upright beside me, her arms raised, and her head bent forward in the attitude of listening. A look of intense delight broke over her countenance; she grasped my hand, drew me towards her, and exclaimed, "Dinna ye hear it? dinna ye hear it? Aye, I'm no dreamin'; it's the slogan o' the Highlanders! We're saved, we're saved." Then flinging herself on her knees, she thanked God with passionate fervour. I felt utterly bewildered; my English ears heard only the roar of artillery, and I thought my poor Jessie was still raving, but she darted to the batteries, and I heard her cry incessantly to the men, "Courage, hark to the slogan of the Macgregor, the grandest of them a'. Here's help at last." To describe the effect of these words upon the soldiers would be impossible. For a moment they ceased firing, and every soul listened in intense anxiety. Gradually however there arose a murmur of bitter disappointment, and the wailing of the women who had flocked out began anew as the Colonel shook his head. Our dull lowland ears heard nothing but the rattle of musketry. A few minutes more of this deathlike suspense, of this agonizing hope, and Jessie who had again sunk on the ground, sprang to her feet, and cried in a voice so clear and piercing that it was heard along the whole line – "Will ye no believe it noo? The slogan has ceased indeed, but the Campbells are comin'. D'ye hear, d'ye hear?" At that moment indeed we seemed to hear the voice of God in the distance, when the bagpipes of the Highlanders brought us tidings of deliverance, for now there was no longer any doubt of the fact. That shrill, penetrating, ceaseless sound, which rose above all other sounds, would come neither from the advance of the enemy nor from the work of the Sappers. No, it was indeed the blast of the Scottish bagpipes, now shrill and harsh, as threatening vengeance on the foe, then in softer tones, seeming to promise succour to their friends in need. Never surely was there such a scene as that [in] which by one simultaneous impulse, [they] fell upon their knees, and nothing was heard but bursting sobs and the murmured voice of prayer. Then all arose, and there rang out from a thousand lips a great shout of joy which resounded far and wide, and lent new vigour to that blessed bagpipe. To our cheer of "God save the Queen!" they replied in the well-known strain that moves every Scot to tears, "SHOULD AULD ACQUAINTANCE BE FORGOT." &c. After that nothing else made any impression on me. I scarcely remember what followed.'

APPENDIX B   'The Pipes at Lucknow'

The American Quaker poet John Greenleaf Whittier (1808–1892) evidently read
the same news report. He was a noted humanitarian and a leading abolitionist, and
yet he was as ready as was Boucicault to present the Indians of Lucknow as savages.
In every age, after all, the enemy is wicked. Whittier's poem 'The Pipes at Lucknow'
is presented here as a fascinating parallel to Boucicault's play.

Pipes of the misty moorlands,
   Voice of the glens and hills;
The droning of the torrents,
   The treble of the rills!
Not the braes of broom and heather,
   Nor the mountains dark with rain,
Nor maiden bower, nor border tower,
   Have heard your sweetest strain!

Dear to the Lowland reaper,
   And plaided mountaineer, –
To the cottage and the castle
   The Scottish pipes are dear; –
Sweet sounds the ancient pibroch
   O'er mountain, loch, and glade;
But the sweetest of all music
   The pipes at Lucknow played.

Day by day the Indian tiger
   Louder yelled, and nearer crept;
Round and round the jungle-serpent
   Near and nearer circles swept.
'Pray for rescue, wives and mothers, –
   Pray to-day!' the soldier said;
'To-morrow, death's between us
   And the wrong and shame we dread.'

Oh, they listened, looked, and waited,
   Till their hope became despair;
And the sobs of low bewailing
   Filled the pauses of their prayer.
Then up spoke a Scottish maiden,
   With her ear unto the ground:

'Dinna ye hear it? – dinna ye hear it?
    The pipes of Havelock sound!'

Hushed the wounded man his groaning;
    Hushed the wife her little ones;
Alone they heard the drum-roll
    And the roar of Sepoy guns.
But to sounds of home and childhood
    The Highland ear was true; –
As her mother's cradle-crooning
    The mountain pipes she knew.

Like the march of soundless music
    Through the vision of the seer,
More of feeling than of hearing,
    Of the heart than of the ear,
She knew the droning pibroch,
    She knew the Campbell's call:
'Hark! hear ye no' MacGregor's, –
    The grandest o' them all!'

Oh, they listened, dumb and breathless,
    And they caught the sound at last;
Faint and far beyond the Goomtee
    Rose and fell the piper's blast!
Then a burst of wild thanksgiving
    Mingled woman's voice and man's;
'God be praised! – the march of Havelock!
    The piping of the clans!'

Louder, nearer, fierce as vengeance,
    Sharp and shrill as swords at strife,
Came the wild MacGregor's clan-call,
    Stinging all the air to life.
But when the far-off dust-cloud
    To plaided legions grew,
Full tenderly and blithesomely
    The pipes of rescue blew!

Round the silver domes of Lucknow,
    Moslem mosque and Pagan shrine,
Breathed the air to Britons dearest,
    The air of Auld Lang Syne.
O'er the cruel roll of war-drums
    Rose that sweet and homelike strain;

And the tartan clove the turban,
    As the Goomtee cleaves the plain.

Dear to the corn-land reaper
    And plaided mountaineer, –
To the cottage and the castle
    The piper's song is dear.
Sweet sounds the Gaelic pibroch
    O'er mountain, glen, and glade;
But the sweetest of all music
    The pipes at Lucknow played!

APPENDIX C   The ending of *The Octoroon*

The story of the ending of *The Octoroon* is tangled. It has been too readily believed that the 'unhappy' ending was liked at the Winter Garden in New York in 1859, and disliked – and, therefore, promptly replaced – at the Adelphi in London, when Boucicault brought the play there in 1861. The evidence is, rather, that the New York audience thought the fifth act a little weak, but that Boucicault retained his confidence in it, despite the disapprobation of the Adelphi audience, for the first three weeks of the London run. It was only after a strenuous press campaign had failed to change the hearts of London theatregoers that Boucicault rewrote his final act – 'composed by the Public, and edited by the Author', as he angrily observed – to suit the taste for melodramatic reprieves. The rewritten conclusion has been lost, though an *Illustrated London News* review of 14 December 1861 describes it clearly. From it, we learn that the fourth act ended with Zoe's escape in a canoe, into which M'Closky leaps to escape his executioners. For the fifth act:

> The curtain rises, discovering the ruffian and his unfortunate slave in the canebrake, with the sun dawning over the Attakapas – a beautiful scene. The ruffian is asleep, but he has secured his captive by tying her with a rope to a post, and when he awakes proceeds barbarously to compel her sharing with him all the dangers of his flight. Ultimately he is chased through the Red Cedar Swamp to the Painted Rocks, where he maintains his position from a rocky ledge against his assailants, having possessed himself of a gun with six charges, until he is brought down by a shot from George Peyton; Salem Scudder, by an act of self-sacrifice, having occasioned him to expose his body to Peyton's aim. The fair Octoroon is thus set at liberty; and the piece concludes with a declaration that in another land Zoe and Peyton will solemnise a lawful union, and live for the happiness of each other.

The wounded Scudder survives to marry Dora Sunnyside.

This is not the version we have in the two English acting editions (Lacy's 963 and Dicks' 391). The play is there reduced to four acts, perfunctorily concluded, from the point at which Wahnotee crosses to M'Closky just after sentence of death has been passed on M'Closky. It is unlikely that we will ever know the precise provenance of the copy from which these two acting editions were set up. For what it is worth, the conclusion of the four-act version is printed below, but printed in the full awareness that it was not what was acted at the Adelphi and is probably not by Boucicault at all. It represents the only printed text available to most English theatres during the early theatrical life of *The Octoroon*. At the very least, it says something about the constraints under which provincial and amateur theatres operated in nineteenth-century England.

The text continues from the point indicated on p. 164.

WAHNOTEE: (*crossing to* M'CLOSKY) Ugh!

SCUDDER: The Inginn, by thunder!

PETE: (*to* M'CLOSKY) You's a dead man, mas'r; you've got to b'lieve dat.

M'CLOSKY: No! If I must die, give me up to the laws, but save me from the tomahawk of the savage; you are a white man, you'll not leave one of your own
blood to be butchered by the scalping knife of the redskin.

SCUDDER: Hold on now, Jacob, we've got to figure that out; let us look straight
at the thing. Here we are on the confines of civilization; it ain't our sile, I
believe, rightly; Natur' has said that where the white man sets his foot the
red man and the black man shall up sticks and stan' round. Now, what do
we pay for that possession? In cash? No – in kind – that is, in protection and
forbearance, in gentleness, and in all them goods that show the critturs the
difference between the Christian and the Savage. Now what have you done to
show 'em the distinction? for darn me if I can find out.

M'CLOSKY: For what I've done let me be tried.

SCUDDER: Oh, you have been fairly and honestly tried, and convicted: Providence has chosen your executioner – I shan't interfere.

PETE: Oh! sar! hi, Mas'r Scudder, don't leave Mas'r Closky like dat – don't, sar –
'tain't what a good Christian would do.

SCUDDER: D'ye hear that, Jacob? – this old nigger, the grandfather of the boy you
murdered, speaks for you – don't that go through ye – d'ye feel it? Go on,
Pete, you've woke up the Christian here, and the old hoss responds.

WAHNOTEE: (*placing his hand on* M'CLOSKY's *head*) Wahnotee!

SCUDDER: No, Inginn, we deal justice here, not revenge; 'tain't you he has injured,
'tis the white man, whose laws he has offended.

RATTS: Away with him! put him down the hatch till we rig his funeral.

M'CLOSKY: Fifty against one! oh! if you were alone – if I had ye one by one in
the swamp, I'd rip ye all.

PETE: (*lighting him off*) Dis way, Mas'r Closky, take care, sar. (*Exit with*
M'CLOSKY *and* JACKSON *to steamer.*)

LAFOUCHE: Off with him quick – here come the ladies.

    (*Enter* MRS. CLAIBORNE.)

MRS. C: Shall we soon start, Captain?

RATTS: Yes, ma'am; we've only got a – Take my hand, ma'am, to steady you –
a little account to square, and we're off.

MRS. C: A fog is rising.

RATTS: Swamp mist; soon clear off. (*Hands her to steamer.*)

MRS. C: Good night.

RATTS: Good night, ma'am – good night.

SCUDDER: Now to business.

    (PETE *appears on deck.*)

PETE: Oh! law, sar. Dat debbel, Closky – he tore hisself from de gentleman – knock
me down – take away my light, and throwed it on de turpentine barrels – de
ship's on fire!

    (*All hurry off to ship – alarm bell rings – loud shouts; a hatch in the deck is opened – a glare of red – and* M'CLOSKY *emerges from the aperture; he is without his coat, and carries a bowie knife; he rushes down –* WAHNOTEE *alone is watching him.*)

M'CLOSKY: Ha, ha, ha! I've given them something to remember how they treated Jacob M'Closky. Made my way from one end of the vessel to the other, and now the road to escape is clear before me – and thus to secure it! (*He is met by* WAHNOTEE, *who silently confronts him.*)

WAHNOTEE: Paul.

M'CLOSKY: Devils! – you here! – stand clear!

WAHNOTEE: Paul.

M'CLOSKY: You won't – die, fool!

(*Thrusts at him –* WAHNOTEE, *with his tomahawk, strikes the knife out of his hand.* M'CLOSKY *starts back.* WAHNOTEE *throws off his blanket, and strikes at* M'CLOSKY *several times, who avoids him; at last he catches his arm, and struggles for the tomahawk, which falls; a violent struggle and fight takes place, ending with the triumph of* WAHNOTEE, *who drags* M'CLOSKY *along the ground, takes up the knife and stabs him repeatedly;* GEORGE *enters, bearing* ZOE *in his arms – all the characters rush on – noise increasing – The steam vessel blows up – grand Tableau, and*
CURTAIN.)

THE PLAYS OF DION BOUCICAULT

It is not possible to compile a wholly authoritative list of Boucicault's plays. His own evidence is unreliable, not least because his shifts of mood led him sometimes to overstate his prolific output and sometimes to disguise it. He thought nothing of producing the same play with a different title, if theatrical expediency invited it, and was not afraid to claim the authorship of work that he revised or adapted. The present list is based on that of Richard Fawkes, which is, in its turn, based on one compiled by Boucicault's great-grandson, Christopher Calthrop. I have attempted, where possible, to place the plays in chronological order of production.

1836.	*Napoleon's Old Guard*	Brentford Collegiate School
1838.	*A Legend of the Devil's Dyke*	(?) Brighton
18.2.1839.	*Lodgings to Let*	Theatre Royal, Bristol
26.12.1839.	*Jack Sheppard*	Theatre Royal, Hull
	(based on Harrison Ainsworth's novel)	
30.1.1840.	*The Old Guard*	Theatre Royal, Brighton
	(probably a revision of his first play)	
4.3.1841.	*London Assurance*	Covent Garden, London
7.2.1842.	*The Irish Heiress*	Covent Garden, London
	(also performed under the title *West End*)	
21.4.1842.	*A Lover by Proxy*	Haymarket, London
19.9.1842.	*Alma Mater; or, A Cure for Coquettes*	Haymarket, London
24.9.1842.	*Curiosities of Literature*	Haymarket, London
19.12.1842.	*The Bastille*	Haymarket, London
	(perhaps in collaboration with Benjamin Webster)	
1843.	*Sharp's the Word*	London
	(unconfirmed listing by Townshend Walsh: Hogan suggests a Covent Garden performance)	
2.10.1843.	*Woman*	Haymarket, London
1.11.1843.	*Victor and Hortense; or False Pride*	Haymarket, London
	(cf. *Paul Lafarge*, 7.3.1870)	
15.11.1843.	*Laying a Ghost*	Haymarket, London
6.2.1844.	*Used Up*	Haymarket, London
	(in collaboration with Charles Mathews)	
25.3.1844.	*Lolah; or The Wreck-Light*	Haymarket, London
22.4.1844.	*Love in a Sack*	Haymarket, London
22.4.1844.	*Mother and Son*	Adelphi, London
2.10.1844.	*The Fox and the Goose; or, The Widow's Husband*	Adelphi, London
	(operetta, in collaboration with Benjamin Webster)	
14.10.1844.	*Don Caesar de Bazan; or, Love and Honour*	Adelphi, London

(from the French play by Dumanoir and Dennery, in collaboration with Benjamin Webster)

18.11.1844.   *Old Heads and Young Hearts*   Haymarket, London
('modelled', Krause suggests, on Congreve's *The Double Dealer*)

6.2.1845.   *A Soldier of Fortune; or, The Irish*   Adelphi, London
Settler
(perhaps in collaboration with Benjamin Webster)

23.6.1845.   *Peg Woffington*   Adelphi, London

25.8.1845.   *Enquire Within*   Lyceum, London

5.2.1846.   *The Old School*   Haymarket, London

11.5.1846.   *Who Did It? or, What's in the Wind?*   Adelphi, London
(in collaboration with Charles Kenney; at first called *Felo de Se*, and later also called *Up the Flue*)

16.5.1846.   *Mr. Peter Piper, or, Found Out at Last*   Haymarket, London

15.7.1846.   *The Wonderful Water Cure*   Haymarket, London
(operetta, in collaboration with Benjamin Webster)

1846.   *Shakespeare in Love*   London
(unconfirmed listing by Townshend Walsh)

4.2.1847.   *The School for Scheming*   Haymarket, London
(later revised and retitled *Love and Money*)

18.5.1847.   *La Salamandrine*   Covent Garden, London
(ballet with narrative by Boucicault)

2.5.1848.   *A Confidence*   Haymarket, London

22.11.1848.   *The Knight of Arva*   Haymarket, London

26.11.1849.   *The Willow Copse*   Adelphi, London
(from Soulié's *La Closerie des Genêts*, perhaps in collaboration with Charles Kenney)

9.1.1850.   *La Garde Nationale*   Queen's, London
(also performed under the title *The Garde Mobile*)

12.9.1850.   *Giralda; or, The Invisible Husband*   Olympic, London
(revised as *A Dark Night's Work* and performed in a Boucicault double-bill at the Princess's, 7.3.1870)

1850.   *A Radical Cure*   London
(unconfirmed listing by Townshend Walsh)

13.1.1851.   *Belphegor*   Adelphi, London
(from the French play by Dennery, in collaboration with Benjamin Webster)

17.2.1851.   *Sixtus the Fifth; or, The Broken Vow*   Olympic, London
(also known as *The Pope of Rome*; adapted from *L'Abbaye de Castro* by Dinaux and Lemoine, in collaboration with John Bridgeman)

6.3.1851.   *Love in a Maze*   Princess's, London

17.3.1851.   *Pauline*   Princess's, London
(from the play by Dumas *père*. Despite his claims, the ascription to Boucicault is dubious; the version played at the Princess's was probably John Oxenford's)

| 29.3.1851. | *The Queen of Spades; or, The Gambler's Secret* | Drury Lane, London |

(from a French play by Eugène Scribe)

| 21.4.1851. | *O'Flannigan and the Fairies* | Adelphi, London |
| 24.2.1852. | *The Corsican Brothers; or, The Vendetta* | Princess's, London |

(from a French play based on a story by Dumas *père*)

| 14.6.1852. | *The Vampire* | Princess's, London |

(from a French play; Boucicault later revised and shortened it, retitling it *The Phantom*)

| 18.9.1852. | *The Prima Donna* | Princess's, London |
| 10.1.1853. | *The Sentinel* | Strand, London |

(operetta with music by Robert Stoepel)

| 20.6.1853. | *Genevieve; or, The Reign of Terror* | Adelphi, London |

(from *Le Chevalier de la Maison Rouge* by Dumas and Maquet)

| 19.9.1853. | *The Young Actress* | Theatre Royal, Montreal |
| 23.11.1853. | *The Fox Hunt; or, Don Quixote the Second* | Burton's, New York |

(revised as *The Fox Chase* for performance at the St. James's, London, 11.5.1864)

| 1.3.1854. | *Andy Blake, or, The Irish Diamond* | Boston Museum |

(sometimes called *The Dublin Boy* and *The Irish Boy*; adapted from Alfred Bayard's *Le Gamin de Paris*)

| 19.4.1854. | *Faust and Margaret* | Princess's, London |

(from the play by Michel Carré; the adaptation is sometimes attributed to Tom Robertson)

| 21.4.1854. | *The Devil's In It* | Chestnut Street, Philadelphia |

(from Scribe's *La Part du Diable*)

11.8.1854.	*Janet Pride*	Metropolitan, Buffalo
6.11.1854.	*The Fairy Star*	Broadway, New York
27.11.1854.	*Apollo in New York*	Walnut Street, Philadelphia
11.12.1854.	*Pierre the Foundling*	Adelphi, London

(from Mme Dudevant's *François le Champ*)

| 1.1.1855. | *Eugénie; or, A Sister's Vow* | Drury Lane, London |
| 13.1.1855. | *Louis XI* | Princess's, London |

(from the French play by Casimir Delavigne)

23.1.1855.	*Agnes Robertson at Home*	Pelican, New Orleans
27.6.1855.	*There's Nothing In It*	Walnut Street, Philadelphia
24.9.1855.	*Grimaldi; or, Scenes in the Life of an Actress*	National, Cincinnati

(adaptation of a French play; also called *The Life of an Actress* and *Violet*)

| 26.10.1855. | *The Cat Changed into a Woman* | National, Washington |

(based on a play by Eugène Scribe)

| 8.11.1855. | *Rachel Is Coming* | St Louis Theatre |
| 29.12.1855. | *The Chameleon* | Gaiety, New Orleans |

19.1.1856.	*Azael; or, The Prodigal Son*	Gaiety, New Orleans
10.2.1856.	*Una*	Gaiety, New Orleans
27.11.1856.	*Blue Belle*	Burton's, New York
	(adaptation of *Le Diable à Quatre*, by De Leuven, Mazilier and Adam)	
9.3.1857.	*George Darville*	Boston Theatre
9.11.1857.	*Wanted a Widow, with Immediate Possession*	Wallack's, New York
	(in collaboration with Charles Seymour)	
8.12.1857.	*The Poor of New York*	Wallack's, New York
	(adapted from *Les Pauvres de Paris* by Brisebarre and Nus; Boucicault was the chief of three or four collaborators on the adaptation)	
22.2.1858.	*Jessie Brown; or, The Relief of Lucknow*	Wallack's, New York
25.5.1858.	*Brigham Young; or, The Revolt of the Harem*	Wallack's, New York
4.10.1858.	*Pauvrette*	Niblo's Garden, New York
	(also called *The Snow Flower* and *The Maid of the Alps*; adapted from *La Bergère des Alpes* by Desnoyer and Dennery)	
14.9.1859.	*Dot*	Winter Garden, New York
	(from Dickens's *The Cricket on the Hearth*)	
19.10.1859.	*Chamooni III*	Winter Garden, New York
	(adaptation of Eugène Scribe's *L'Houri et la Pacha*)	
1.11.1859.	*Smike; or, Scenes from Nicholas Nickleby*	Winter Garden, New York
6.12.1859.	*The Octoroon; or, Life in Louisiana*	Winter Garden, New York
9.1.1860.	*Jeanie Deans; or, The Heart of Midlothian*	Keene's, New York
	(from Scott's novel; also called *The Trial of Effie Deans*)	
12.3.1860.	*Vanity Fair*	Keene's, New York
	(from a French play; not from Thackeray's novel)	
29.3.1860.	*The Colleen Bawn; or, The Brides of Garryowen*	Keene's, New York
10.2.1862.	*The Lily of Killarney*	Covent Garden, London
	(operatic version of *The Colleen Bawn*; words by Boucicault and John Oxenford, music by Benedict)	
26.12.1862.	*Lady Bird; or, Harlequin Lord Dundreary*	Astley's, London, and Wallack's, New York
	(a pantomime, staged by Boucicault at Astley's under that theatre's new name, Theatre Royal, Westminster)	
7.12.1863.	*How She Loves Him*	Prince of Wales's, Liverpool
10.2.1864.	*The Poor of Liverpool*	Royal Amphitheatre, Liverpool

(*The Poor of New York* slightly altered, as, for touring purposes, it would continue to be. Among its many metamorphoses are *The Poor of Leeds, The Poor of Manchester, The Streets of Islington, The Streets of London, The Poor of the London Streets, The Streets of Dublin, The Streets of Philadelphia* and *The Money Panic of '57*)

24.10.1864.   *Omoo; or, The Sea of Ice*   Royal Amphitheatre,
                                                                              Liverpool
                (adapted from *La Prière des Naufrages* by Dennery and Dugue)
7.11.1864.   *Arrah-na-Pogue; or, The Wicklow*   Old Theatre Royal,
                Wedding   Dublin
22.3.1864.   revised version of *Arrah-na-Pogue* presented at Princess's, London
4.9.1865.   *Rip Van Winkle*   Adelphi, London
                (a playhouse text, polished by Boucicault for Joseph Jefferson)
30.4.1866.   *The Parish Clerk*   Prince's, Manchester
30.7.1866.   *The Two Lives of Mary Leigh*   Prince's, Manchester
                (later retitled *Hunted Down*)
15.9.1866.   *The Long Strike*   Lyceum, London
                (also performed as *The Strike*; based on episodes from Mrs. Gaskell's
                Mary Barton and *Lizzie Leigh*)
6.10.1866.   *The Flying Scud; or, A Four Legged*   Holborn, London
                Fortune
29.4.1867.   *A Wild Goose Chase* (or *Wild Goose*)   Haymarket, London
                (revision of Lester Wallack's *Rosedale*)
28.5.1868.   *Foul Play*   Holborn, London
                (Boucicault's dramatisation of the novel he had written with Charles
                Reade; Reade also dramatised the novel)
12.8.1868.   *After Dark; a Tale of London Life*   Princess's, London
                (from *Les Bohémiens de Paris* by Dennery and Grangé)
1.5.1869.   *Seraphine; or, A Devotee*   Queen's, London
                (an adaptation of Victorien Sardou's play)
10.5.1869.   *Presumptive Evidence*   Princess's, London
                (one of the many nineteenth-century English versions of *Le Courrier
                de Lyon*; also performed as *Mercy Dodd*)
5.8.1869.   *Formosa; or, The Railroad to Ruin*   Drury Lane, London
2.10.1869.   *Lost at Sea; or, A London Story*   Adelphi, London
                (in collaboration with H. J. Byron)
7.3.1870.   *Paul Lafarge; or, Self Made*   Princess's, London
                (revision of *Victor and Hortense*, 1.11.1843)
28.4.1870.   *The Mad Boy*   Academy of Music, New
                (the ascription to Boucicault is uncertain)   York
2.9.1870.   *The Rapparee; or, The Treaty of*   Princess's, London
                Limerick
5.12.1870.   *Jezebel; or, The Dead Reckoning*   Holborn, London
                (based on *Le Pendu* by Anicet-Bourgeois and Masson)
24.12.1870.   *A Christmas Story*   Gaiety, London
                (this may be *Dot* – see 14.9.1859 – under a different title)
10.3.1871.   *Elfie; or, The Cherry Tree Inn*   Theatre Royal, Glasgow
7.9.1871.   *Night and Morning*   Prince's, Manchester
                (also called *Kerry*; an adaptation of *La Joie Fait Peur* by Emile de
                Girardin)
29.8.1872.   *Babil and Bijou; or, The Lost Regalia*   Covent Garden, London
17.3.1873.   *Daddy O'Dowd*   Booth's, New York

(revised as *The O'Dowd; or, Life in Galway*, and again as *Suil-a-Mor*; based on *Les Crochets du Père Martin* by Cormon and Grangé)

3.6.1873.	*Mora; or, The Golden Fetters*	Wallack's, New York
1.7.1873.	*Mimi*	Wallack's, New York

(an adaptation of *La Vie de Bohème* by Barrière and Murger)

6.12.1873.	*Led Astray*	Union Square, New York

(an adaptation of Feuillet's *La Tentation*)

22.12.1873.	*A Man of Honor*	Wallack's, New York

(an adaptation of *Le Fils Naturel* by Dumas *fils*)

1873.	*A Struggle for Life*	

(no record of performance for this play, copyrighted by Boucicault in 1873)

19.1.1874.	*Boucicault in California*	San Francisco Theatre
10.8.1874.	*Belle Lamar*	Booth's, New York

(revised as *Fin MacCool of Skibbereen* and *Fin Maccoul*)

14.11.1874.	*The Shaughraun*	Wallack's, New York
1874.	*Drink*	

(copyrighted in 1874; no record of performance)

1874.	*Free Cuba*	

(copyrighted by Boucicault and J. J. O'Kelly in 1874; no record of performance)

10.4.1875.	*Rafael*	Wallack's, New York

(the ascription to Boucicault is uncertain; the play is an adaptation from the French)

3.10.1876.	*Forbidden Fruit*	Wallack's, New York
1.10.1877.	*Marriage*	Wallack's, New York

(also known as *A Bridal Tour*: probably based on Labiche's *Un Chapeau de Paille d'Italie*)

28.1.1878.	*The Dead Secret*	5th Avenue, New York

(from the novel by Wilkie Collins)

10.9.1878.	*Clarissa Harlowe; or, The History of a Young Lady*	Wallack's, New York

(from Richardson's novel)

24.2.1879.	*Spell-Bound*	Wallack's, New York
4.9.1879.	*Rescued; or, A Girl's Romance*	Booth's, New York

(given a copyright performance at King's Cross Theatre, London on 27.8.1879)

4.10.1879.	*Contempt of Court*	Wallack's, New York

(given a copyright performance at Marylebone Theatre, London on 1.10.1879)

19.8.1880.	*Therese; or, The Maid of Croissey*	Adelphi, London
5.2.1883.	*The Amadan*	Boston Museum

(the performance at the Theatre Royal, Richmond on 29.1.1883 was probably for copyright purposes)

21.3.1883.	*Vice Versa*	Wallack's, Springfield,
	(based on *Le Truc d'Arthur* by Duru and Chivot)	Massachusetts
5.11.1884.	*Robert Emmet*	McVicker's, Chicago

(given a copyright performance at Prince of Wales's, Greenwich on 4.11.1884; revision of a play written by Frank Marshall for Henry Irving)

18.5.1885.	*The Jilt*	California, San Francisco

(given a copyright performance at Elephant and Castle, London on 13.5.1885)

30.3.1886.	*The Spae Wife*	Elephant and Castle, London

(copyright performance of this adaptation of Scott's novel, *Guy Mannering*)

12.9.1887.	*Phryne; or The Romance of a Young Wife*	Baldwin, San Francisco
20.2.1888.	*Cuishla-ma-Chree*	Hollis Street, Boston

(a revised version of *The Spae Wife*)

c. 1888.	*Ourselves*	

(no record of performance)

14.8.1890.	*A Tale of a Coat*	Daly's, New York

(as *Jimmy Watt*, given a copyright performance at Elephant and Castle, London on 1.8.1890)

25.8.1890.	*Lend Me Your Wife*	Boston Museum

(an adaptation of *Prête-moi Ta Femme* by Desvallières)

1890.	*The Luck of Roaring Camp*	

(version of Bret Harte's story; Boucicault was working on it shortly before his death)

5.10.1891.	*99*	Standard, London

(the ascription to Boucicault is uncertain)

In addition to the 141 plays listed above, Boucicault may well have completed all or some of the plays mentioned or signed by him at various times during his theatrical career:

False Colours (*c.* 1848)

The Letter of Introduction (*c.*1848)

Jack Weatherby (an undated, signed copy of this play is in the National Library of Ireland, Dublin)

Gabrielle (manuscript in the University of South Florida)

Excelsior (ditto)

Marie Antoinette (ditto)

The Grass Widow (ditto)

Bleak House (ditto)

Joy in the House (ditto)

Nectarine (ditto)

A White Crow (ditto)

Stella (*c.* 1852)

Edwin Drood (Dickens had arranged to collaborate with Boucicault on the dramatisation of this novel, a collaboration that was forestalled by Dickens's death in 1870 – with the novel still incomplete)

Among the plays by other authors of which Boucicault produced versions for the stage are:

Vanbrugh, *The Confederacy* (Haymarket, London, 1844)
Tom Taylor, *To Parents and Guardians* (Burton's, New York, 1853)
Tom Robertson, *Dreams* (5th Avenue Theatre, New York, 1869)
George Colman the Younger, *John Bull* (Prince's, Manchester, 1871)
Otway, *Venice Preserved* (Booth's, New York, 1874)
Sheridan, *The School for Scandal* (Wallack's, New York, 1878)
Haddon Chambers, *Captain Swift* (Madison Square, New York, 1888)

SELECT BIBLIOGRAPHY

The following modern anthologies include plays by Boucicault.

America's Lost Plays, Vol. 1: Forbidden Fruit and other plays by Dion Boucicault, ed. Allardyce Nicoll and Theodore Cloak, Princeton, 1940.
> *Forbidden Fruit*
> *Louis XI*
> *Dot*
> *The Flying Scud*
> *Mercy Dodd*
> *Robert Emmet*

British Plays of the Nineteenth Century, ed. J. O. Bailey, New York, 1966.
> *London Assurance*
> *After Dark*

The Dolmen Boucicault, ed. David Krause, Dublin, 1964.
> *The Colleen Bawn*
> *Arrah-na-Pogue*
> *The Shaughraun*

English Plays of the Nineteenth Century, Vol. 2, ed. Michael R. Booth, Oxford, 1969.
> *The Corsican Brothers*
> *The Shaughraun*

Representative American Plays from 1767 to the Present Day, ed. Arthur Hobson Quinn, New York, 1953.
> *Rip Van Winkle*
> *The Octoroon*

Plays for the College Theatre, ed. Garret H. Leverton, New York, 1937.
> *Belle Lamar*

Favorite American Plays of the Nineteenth Century, ed. Barrett H. Clark, Princeton, 1943.
> *The Flying Scud*

Nineteenth Century Plays, ed. George Rowell, London, 1953.
> *The Colleen Bawn*

Best Plays of the Early American Theatre, ed. John Gassner, New York, 1967.
> *The Octoroon*

Laurel British Drama: The Nineteenth Century, ed. R. W. Corrigan, New York, 1967.
> *London Assurance*

The Signet Classic Book of Eighteenth and Nineteenth Century English Drama, ed. Katharine Rogers, New York, 1979.
  The Octoroon

In addition, *London Assurance*, edited by Ronald Eyre after the Royal Shakespeare Company production of 1970, was published in a single volume by Methuen, London, 1971.

The largest single collection of Boucicault's plays readily available in Britain is in the Drama on Microfilm series of the University of Kent at Canterbury. It contains thirty-five plays from the Frank Pettingell Collection:

After Dark	*Louis XI*
Andy Blake	*The Octoroon*
Arrah-na-Pogue	*The O'Dowd*
Babil and Bijou	*The Old Guard*
The Colleen Bawn	*Old Heads and Young Hearts*
The Corsican Brothers	*Pauvrette*
Curiosities of Literature	*The Phantom*
Elfie	*The Poor of New York*
Formosa	*The Pope of Rome*
Foul Play	*The Prima Donna*
Grimaldi	*The Queen of Spades*
Jessie Brown	*The Rapparee*
Jezebel	*The School for Scheming*
The Jilt	*The Shaughraun*
Led Astray	*Used Up*
A Legend of the Devil's Dyke	*West End* (i.e. *The Irish Heiress*)
London Assurance	*The Willow Copse*
The Long Strike	

The microfilm is available from The Library, the University, Canterbury, Kent CT2 7NU.

BOUCICAULT'S NON-DRAMATIC WRITING

With Charles Reade: *Foul Play*, 1868.
The Story of Ireland, Boston, 1881.
The Art of Acting and *Actors and Acting*, reprinted in *Papers on Acting*, ed. Brander Matthews, New York, 1958.
'The Art of Dramatic Composition', *North American Review*, 126 (Jan.–Feb. 1878).
'The Decline of the Drama', *North American Review*, 125 (Sept. 1877).

BOOKS ABOUT BOUCICAULT

Townshend Walsh, *The Career of Dion Boucicault*, New York, 1915.
Robert Hogan, *Dion Boucicault*, New York, 1969.
John Broderick Lynaugh, *The Forgotten Contributions and Comedies of Dion Boucicault*, unpublished Ph.D. thesis, University of Wisconsin, 1974 (available in University Microfilms 74–24, 734, 1980).

Richard Fawkes, *Dion Boucicault*, London, 1979.
Sven Eric Molin and Robin Goodfellow, eds., *Dion Boucicault: A Documentary Life*, Newark, N.J., 1979.

ARTICLES ABOUT BOUCICAULT

John A. Degen, 'How to End *The Octoroon*', *Educational Theatre Journal*, 27 (1975).
Sheldon Faulkner, 'The *Octoroon* War', *Educational Theatre Journal*, 15 (1963).
Sheldon Faulkner, 'The Great Train Scene Robbery', *Quarterly Journal of Speech*, February 1964.
Harold F. Folland, 'Lee Moreton: The Debut of a Theatre Man', *Theatre Notebook*, 23 no. 4 (1969).
Sidney Kaplan, 'The Octoroon: Early History of the Drama of Miscegenation', *Journal of Negro Education*, 20 (1951).
Sean McMahon, 'The Wearing of the Green: The Irish Plays of Dion Boucicault', *Eire-Ireland*, 2 (1957).
Gary A. Richardson, 'Boucicault's *The Octoroon* and American Law', *Educational Theatre Journal*, 34 (1982).

G. C. D. Odell's *Annals of the New York Stage*, 15 vols. (1927) is an essential guide to Boucicault's American career.